THE
ART OF
DYING

THE ART OF DYING

EXPLORING THE MYSTERIES OF LIFE AND DEATH

OSHO

JAICO PUBLISHING HOUSE

Ahmedabad Bangalore Bhopal Bhubaneswar Chennai
Delhi Hyderabad Kolkata Lucknow Mumbai

Published by Jaico Publishing House
A-2 Jash Chambers, 7-A Sir Phirozshah Mehta Road
Fort, Mumbai - 400 001
jaicopub@jaicobooks.com
www.jaicobooks.com

To be sold only in India, Bangladesh, Bhutan,
Pakistan, Nepal, Sri Lanka and the Maldives.

THE ART OF DYING
ISBN 978-81-8495-966-6

First Jaico Impression: 2017
Second Jaico Impression: 2018

The material in this book is a transcript of a series of original OSHO
Talks, *The Art of Dying*, given to a live audience. All of Osho's talks
have been published in full as books, and are also available as original
audio recordings. Audio recordings and the complete text archive can
be found via the online OSHO Library at www.osho.com/library

Photos of Osho: Courtesy OSHO International Foundation

OSHO is a registered trademark of OSHO International
Foundation, used under license. www.osho.com/trademarks

Page design and layout: Yogesh Typesetting, Pune

Printed by
Snehesh Printers
320-A, Shah & Nahar Ind. Est. A-1
Lower Parel, Mumbai - 400 013

Preface

Death is an illusion. It is always somebody else who dies; you never die. It means death has always been seen from the outside, it is the outsider's view. Those who have seen their inner world are unanimous in saying that there is no death.

You don't know what constitutes your consciousness; it is not constituted of breathing, it is not constituted of heartbeats, it is not constituted of blood circulation. So when the doctor says that a man is dead, it is an outsider's conclusion; all that he is saying is, "This man is no longer breathing, his pulse has stopped, his heart is not beating." Are these three things equivalent to death? They are not.

Consciousness is not your body, nor your mind, nor your heart.

So when a person dies, he dies for you, not for himself. For himself he simply changes the house, perhaps moves into a better apartment. But because the old apartment is left, and you are searching for him in the old apartment and you don't find him there, you think the poor guy is dead. All that you should say is, "The poor guy escaped. Now where he has gone, we don't know."

In fact, medical science is going beyond its limits when it says that some person is dead. Medical science has no right yet, because it has no definition yet of what constitutes death. It can simply say, "This man is no longer breathing. His heart has stopped. His pulse is no longer functioning." To conclude that he is dead is going beyond what you are seeing. But because science does not have any idea of consciousness, the death of the body becomes the death of the being.

Those who have known the being... And it is not necessary that you should die and then you know; you can just go inside. That's what I call meditation – just go inside and find out what is your center, and at your center there is no breathing, there is no heartbeat, there is no thought, no mind, no heart, no body, and *still you are*.

Once a person has experienced himself – that he is not the body, *not* the mind, *not* the heart, but pure awareness – he knows there is no death for him, because he does not depend on the body.

Osho
Beyond Enlightenment

Introduction

Every few thousand years an individual appears who irrevocably changes the world around him in ways that are never immediately apparent, except to the most perceptive.

Osho is one such individual: his spoken words will resonate for centuries to come.

All those words have been recorded and transcribed into books like this one; written words that can carry a transforming message to the reader.

For Osho, all change is individual. There is no 'society' to change – it can only happen to each one of us, one at a time. So, no matter what the subject matter of the book, the thread that runs through all Osho's words is like a love song that we can suddenly, mysteriously, hear at just the right moment. And strangely, no matter what the words seem to be referring to, they are really only referring to us.

And this is no ordinary love song; it is more an invitation to open our hearts to hear something beyond the words, beyond the heart...a silence beyond all understanding. Where we all belong.

Contents

Know How to Live

When Rabbi Birnham lay dying,
his wife burst into tears.
He said, "What are you crying for?
My whole life was only that I might learn how to die."

Life is in living. It is not a thing, it is a process. There is no
way to attain to life except by living it, except by being alive,
flowing, streaming with it. If you are seeking the meaning of
life in some dogma, in some philosophy, in some theology, that
is the sure way to miss life and meaning both.

Life is not somewhere waiting for you, it is happening
in you. It is not in the future as a goal to be arrived at, it is
herenow, this very moment – in your breathing, circulating in
your blood, beating in your heart. Whatsoever you are is your
life, and if you start seeking meaning somewhere else you will
miss it. Man has done that for centuries.

Concepts have become very important, explanations have
become very important – and the real has been completely forgotten. We don't look to that which is already here; we want
rationalizations.

I have heard a very beautiful story:

Some years ago a successful American had a serious identity crisis. He sought help from psychiatrists but nothing came of it, for there were none who could tell him the meaning of life – which is what he wanted to know. By and by he learned of a venerable and incredibly wise guru who lived in a mysterious and most inaccessible region of the Himalayas. Only that guru, he came to believe, would tell him what life means and what his role in it ought to be. So he sold all his worldly possessions and began his search for the all-knowing guru. He spent eight years wandering from village to village throughout the Himalayas in an effort to find him. And then one day he chanced upon a shepherd who told him where the guru lived and how to reach the place.

It took him almost a year to find him, but he eventually did. There he came upon his guru, who was indeed venerable, in fact well over one hundred years old. The guru consented to help him, especially when he learned of all the sacrifices the man had made toward this end.

"What can I do for you, my son?" asked the guru.

"I need to know the meaning of life," said the man.

To this the guru replied, without hesitation, "Life," he said, "is a river without end."

"A river without end?" said the man in a startled surprise. "After coming all this way to find you, all you have to tell me is that life is a river without end?"

The guru was shaken, shocked. He became very angry and he said, "You mean it is not?"

Nobody can give you the meaning of your life. It is your life; the meaning has also to be yours. Himalayas won't help. Nobody except you can come upon it. It is your life and it is only accessible to you. Only in living will the mystery be revealed to you.

The first thing I would like to tell you is: don't seek it anywhere else. Don't seek it in me, don't seek it in scriptures, don't seek it in clever explanations – they all explain away; they do not explain. They simply stuff your empty mind; they don't make you aware of what is. And the more the mind is stuffed with dead knowledge, the more dull and stupid you become. Knowledge makes people stupid; it dulls their sensitivity. It stuffs them, it becomes a weight on them, it strengthens their ego but it does not give light and it does not show them the way. That is not possible.

Life is already there bubbling within you. It can be contacted only there. The temple is not outside; you are the shrine of it. So the first thing to remember if you want to know what life is, is: never seek it without, never try to find out from somebody else. The meaning cannot be transferred that way. The greatest masters have never said anything about life – they have always thrown you back upon yourself.

The second thing to remember is: once you know what life is you will know what death is because death is also part of the same process. Ordinarily we think death comes at the end, ordinarily we think death is against life, ordinarily we think death is the enemy. Death is not the enemy. And if you think of death as the enemy it simply shows that you have not been able to know what life is.

Death and life are two polarities of the same energy, of the same phenomenon – the tide and the ebb, the day and the night, the summer and the winter. They are not separate and not opposites, not contraries; they are complementary. Death is not the end of life; in fact, it is a completion of one life, the crescendo of one life, the climax, the finale. And once you know your life and its process, then you understand what death is.

Death is an organic, integral part of life, and it is very friendly to life. Without it life cannot exist. Life exists because of death; death gives the background. Death is, in fact, a process of renewal. And death also happens each moment, as life happens, because the renewal is needed each moment. The moment you breathe in and the moment you breathe out, both happen. Breathing in, life happens; breathing out, death happens. That's why when a child is born the first thing he does is breathe in; then life starts. And when an old man is dying, the last thing he does is breathe out; then life departs. Breathing out is death, breathing in is life – and both are like two wheels of a bullock cart.

You live by breathing in as much as you live by breathing out. The breathing out is part of breathing in. You cannot breathe in if you stop breathing out. You cannot live if you stop dying. The man who has understood what his life is allows death to happen; he welcomes it. He dies each moment and each moment he is resurrected. His cross and his resurrection are continuously happening as a process. He dies to the past each moment and he is born again and again into the future.

If you look into life you will be able to know what death is. If you understand what death is, only then are you able to understand what life is. They are organic. Ordinarily, out of fear, we have created a division. We think that life is good and death is bad. We think that life has to be desired and death is to be avoided. We think somehow we have to protect ourselves against death. This absurd idea creates endless miseries in our lives, because a person who protects himself against death becomes incapable of living. He is the person who is afraid of exhaling, then he cannot inhale; then he is stuck. Then he simply drags; his life is no longer a flow, his life is no more a river.

If you really want to live, you have to be ready to die. Who is afraid of death in you? Is life afraid of death? It is not possible. How can life be afraid of its own integral process? Something else is afraid in you. The ego is afraid in you. Life and death are not opposites; ego and death are opposites. Life and death are not opposites; ego and life are opposites. Ego is against both life and death. The ego is afraid to live and the ego is afraid to die. It is afraid to live because each effort, each step toward life, brings death closer.

If you live you are coming closer to dying. The ego is afraid to die, hence it is afraid to live also. The ego simply drags.

There are many people who are neither alive nor dead. This is worse than anything. A man who is fully alive is full of death also. That is the meaning of Jesus on the cross. Jesus carrying his own cross has not really been understood. And he says to his disciples, "You will have to carry your own cross." The meaning of Jesus carrying his own cross is very simple, nothing but this: everybody has to carry his death continuously, everybody has to die each moment, everybody has to be on the cross because that is the only way to live fully, totally.

Whenever you come to a total moment of aliveness, suddenly you will see death there also. In love it happens. In love, life comes to a climax – hence people are afraid of love.

I have been continually surprised by people who come to me and say they are afraid of love. What is the fear of love? – because when you really love somebody your ego starts slipping and melting. You cannot love with the ego; the ego becomes a barrier. And when you would like to drop the barrier the ego says, "This is going to be a death. Beware!"

The death of the ego is not your death. The death of the ego is really your possibility of life. The ego is just a dead crust around you, it has to be broken and thrown away. It comes into being naturally – just as when a traveler passes the dust collects on his clothes, on his body, and he has to take a bath to get rid of the dust.

As we move in time the dust of experiences, of knowledge, of lived life, of the past, collects. That dust becomes our ego. Accumulated, it becomes a crust around you which has to be broken and thrown away. One has to take a bath continuously – every day, in fact every moment – so that this crust never becomes a prison. The ego is afraid to love because in love, life comes to a peak. But whenever there is a peak of life there is also a peak of death – they go together.

In love you die and you are reborn. The same happens when

you come to meditate or to pray, or when you come to a master to surrender. The ego creates all sorts of difficulties, rationalizations not to surrender: "Think about it, brood about it, be clever about it." When you come to a master, again the ego becomes suspicious, doubtful, creates anxiety. Again you are coming to life, to a flame where death will also be as much alive as life.

Let it be remembered that death and life both become aflame together; they are never separate. If you are very, very minimally alive, at the minimum, then you can see death and life as being separate. The closer you come to the peak, the closer they start coming. At the very apex they meet and become one. In love, in meditation, in trust, in prayerfulness, wherever life becomes total, death is there. Without death, life cannot become total.

But the ego always thinks in divisions, in dualities; it divides everything. Existence is indivisible; it cannot be divided. You were a child, then you became young. Can you demark the line when you became young? Can you demark the point in time where suddenly you were no longer a child and you had become young? One day you became old. Can you demark the line when you became old?

Processes cannot be demarked. Exactly the same happens when you are born. Can you demark when you are born? When life really starts? Does it start when the child starts breathing – the doctor spanks the child and the child starts breathing? Then life is born? – or is it when the child got into the womb, the mother became pregnant, the child was conceived? Did life start then? – or even before that? When does life exactly start?

It is a process of no ending and no beginning. It never starts. When is a person dead? When the breathing stops? Many yogis have now proved it on scientific grounds that they can stop breathing and they are still alive and they can come back. So the stopping of the breathing cannot be the end. Where does life end?

It never ends anywhere, it never begins anywhere. We are

involved in eternity. We have been here since the very beginning – if there was any beginning – and we are going to be here to the very end, if there is going to be any end. In fact, there cannot be any beginning and there cannot be any end. We are life – forms change, bodies change, minds change. What we call life is just an identification with a certain body, with a certain mind, with a certain attitude, and what we call death is nothing but getting out of that form, out of that body, out of that concept.

You change houses. If you get too identified with one house, then changing the house will be very painful. You will think that you are dying because the old house was what you were – that was your identity. But this doesn't happen, because you know that you are only changing the house, you remain the same. Those who have looked within themselves, those who have found who they are, come to know an eternal, non-ending process. Life is a process, timeless, beyond time. Death is part of it.

Death is a continuous revival, a help to life to resurrect again and again, a help to life to get rid of old forms, to get rid of dilapidated buildings, to get rid of old confining structures so that again you can flow and you can again become fresh and young, and you can again become virgin.

I have heard:

A man was browsing through an antique shop near Mount Vernon and ran across a rather ancient-looking axe.

"That's a mighty old axe you have there," he said to the shop owner.

"Yes," said the man, "it once belonged to George Washington."

"Really?" said the customer. "It certainly stood up well."

"Of course," said the antique dealer, "it has had three new handles and two new heads."

But that's how life is – it goes on changing handles and heads. In fact it seems everything goes on changing and yet something remains eternally the same. Just watch. You were a child – what has remained of that now? Just a memory. Your body has changed, your mind has changed, your identity has changed. What has remained of your childhood? Nothing has remained, just a memory. You cannot even make a distinction between whether it really happened or you had seen a dream, or you had read it in a book, or somebody has told you about it – whether the childhood was yours or somebody else's? Sometimes have a look at an album of old photographs. Just see, this was you. You will not be able to believe it, you have changed so much. In fact everything has changed – handles and heads and everything has changed. And still, deep down, somewhere, something remains a continuity; a witnessing remains continuous.

There is a thread, howsoever invisible. Everything goes on changing. That invisible thread remains the same. That thread is beyond life and death. Life and death are two wings for that which is beyond life and death. That which is beyond goes on using life and death as two wheels of a cart, complementaries. It lives through life; it lives through death. Death and life are its processes, like inhalation, exhalation.

But something in you is transcendental. *That art thou...* That is transcendental.

But we are too identified with the form – that creates the ego. That's what we call "I". Of course the "I" has to die many times. It is constantly in fear, trembling, shaking, always afraid, protecting, securing.

A Sufi mystic knocked at the door of a very rich man. He was a beggar and he wanted just enough so that he could have his meal.

The rich man shouted at him and said, "Nobody knows you here!"

"But I know myself," said the dervish. "How sad it would be if the reverse were true. If everybody knew me and I was not aware of who I am, how sad it would be. Yes, you are right, nobody knows me here. But I know myself."

These are the only two situations possible. And you are in the sad situation – everybody may be knowing about you, who you are, but you yourself are completely oblivious of your transcendence, of your real nature, of your authentic being. This is the only sadness in life. You can find many excuses, but the real sadness is this: you don't know who you are.

How can a person be happy not knowing who he is, not knowing from where he is coming, not knowing where he is going? Then a thousand and one problems arise because of this basic self-ignorance.

A bunch of ants came out of the darkness of their underground nest in search of food. It was early in the morning. The ants happened to pass by a plant whose leaves were covered with morning dew.

"What are these?" asked one of the ants, pointing to the dewdrops. "Where do they come from?"

Some said, "They come from the earth."

Others said, "They come from the sea."

Soon a quarrel broke out – there was a group who adhered to the sea theory, and a group who attached themselves to the earth theory.

Only one, a wise and intelligent ant, stood alone. He said, "Let us pause a moment and look around for signs, for everything has an attraction toward its source. Or, as it is said, everything returns to its origin. No matter how far into the air you throw a brick it comes down to the earth. Whatever leans toward the light, must originally be of the light."

The ants were not totally convinced yet and were about to resume their dispute, but the sun had come up and the dewdrops were leaving the leaves, rising, rising toward the sun and disappearing into the sun.

Everything returns to its original source, has to return to its original source. If you understand life then you understand death also. Life is a forgetfulness of the original source, and death is again a remembrance. Life is going away from the original source, death is coming back home. Death is not ugly, death is beautiful. But death is beautiful only for those who have lived their life unhindered, uninhibited, unsuppressed. Death is beautiful only for those who have lived their life beautifully, who have not been afraid to live, who have been courageous to live – who loved, who danced, who celebrated.

Death becomes the ultimate celebration if your life is a celebration. Let me tell you in this way: whatsoever your life is, death reveals only that. If you have been miserable in life, death reveals misery. Death is a great revealer. If you have been happy in your life, death reveals happiness. If you have lived only a life of physical comfort and physical pleasure, then of course death is going to be very uncomfortable and unpleasant because the body has to be left. The body is just a temporary abode, a *serai* in which we stay for the night and have to leave in the morning. It is not your permanent abode, it is not your home.

So if you have lived just a bodily life and you have never known anything beyond the body, death is going to be very, very ugly, unpleasant, painful. Death is going to be an anguish. But if you have lived a little higher than the body – if you have loved music and poetry, and you have loved, and you have looked at the flowers and the stars, and something of the non-physical has entered into your consciousness – death will not be so bad, death will not be so painful. You can take it with equanimity, but still it cannot be a celebration.

If you have lived something of the transcendental in yourself, if you have entered your own nothingness at the center, the center of your being – where you are no longer a body and no longer a mind; where physical pleasures are completely left far away and mental pleasures also: the pleasures of music and poetry and literature and painting – then death is going to be a great celebration, a great understanding, a great revelation. Everything is left far away; you are simply just pure awareness, consciousness.

If you have known anything of the transcendental in you, death will reveal to you the transcendental in the universe – then death is no more a death but a meeting with existence, a date with existence.

So you can find three expressions about death in the history of human mind. One expression is of the ordinary man who lives attached to his body, who has never known anything greater than the pleasure of food or sex, whose whole life has been nothing but food and sex, who has enjoyed food, has enjoyed sex, whose life has been very primitive, whose life has been very gross, who has lived in the porch of his palace, never entered it, and who had been thinking that this is all life is. Then at the moment of death he will try to cling. He will resist death, he will fight death. Death will come as the enemy.

Hence, all over the world, in all societies, death is depicted as dark, as devilish. In India they say the messenger of death is very ugly – dark, black – and comes sitting on a very big, ugly buffalo. This is the ordinary attitude. These people missed, they have not been able to know all the dimensions of life. They have not been able to touch the depth of life and they have not been able to fly to the height of life. They missed the plenitude, they missed the benediction.

Then there is a second type of expression. Poets, philosophers, have sometimes said that death is nothing bad, death is nothing evil, it is just restful – a great rest, like sleep. This is better than the first. At least these people have known something beyond the body, they have known something of the mind. They have not had only food and sex, their whole life has not been only in eating and reproducing. They have a little sophistication of the soul, they are a little more aristocratic, more cultured. They say death is like great rest; one is tired and one goes into death and rests. It is restful. But they too are far away from the truth.

Those who have known life in its deepest core say that death is godliness; not only a rest, but a resurrection, a new life, a new beginning; a new door opens.

When a Sufi mystic, Bayazid, was dying, people who had gathered around him – his disciples – were suddenly surprised, because when the last moment came his face became radiant, so powerfully radiant. It had such a beautiful aura. Bayazid was a beautiful man, and his disciples had always felt an aura around him, but they had not known anything like this; so radiant.

They asked, "Bayazid, tell us what has happened to you. What is happening to you? Before you leave us, give us your last message."

He opened his eyes and he said, "Existence is welcoming me. I am going into its embrace. Good-bye."

He closed his eyes, his breathing stopped. But at the moment his breathing stopped there was an explosion of light, the room became full of light, and then the light disappeared.

When a person has known the transcendental in himself, death is nothing but a face of existence. Then death has a dance to it. And unless you become capable of celebrating death itself, remember, you have missed life. The whole life is a preparation for this ultimate.

This is the meaning of this beautiful story:

When Rabbi Birnham lay dying,
his wife burst into tears.
He said, "What are you crying for?
My whole life was only that I might learn how to die."

"My whole life has been just a preparation, a preparation to learn the secrets of dying."

All religions are nothing but a science – or an art – to teach you how to die. And the only way to teach you how to die is to teach you how to live. They are not separate. If you know what right living is, you will know what right dying is.

So the first thing, or the most fundamental thing, is: how to live.

Let me tell you a few things. First: your life is your life, it is nobody else's. So don't allow yourself to be dominated by others, don't allow yourself to be dictated to by others; it is a betrayal of life. If you allow yourself to be dictated to by others – maybe your parents, your society, your education system, your politicians, your priests, whosoever they are – if you allow yourself to be dominated by others you will miss your life. Because the domination comes from outside and life is within you. They never meet.

I am not saying that you should become a no-sayer to each and everything. That too is not of much help. There are two types of people. One is a very obedient type, ready to surrender to any and everybody. They don't have any independent soul in them; they are immature, childish, always searching for a father-figure, for somebody to tell them what to do and what not to do. They are not able to trust their own being. These people are the greater part of the world, the masses.

Then there are, against these people, a small minority who reject society, who reject the values of the society. They think they are rebellious. They are not, they are only reactionaries. Because whether you listen to society or you reject society, if society remains in either way the determining factor, then you are dominated by the society.

Let me tell you an anecdote:

Once Mulla Nasruddin had been away for a while and arrived back in town wearing a long beard. His friends naturally kidded him about the beard and asked him how he happened to acquire the fur-piece. The Mulla with the beard began to complain and curse the thing in no uncertain terms. His friends were amazed at the way he talked and asked him why he continued to wear the beard if he did not like it.

"I hate the blasted thing!" the Mulla told them.

"If you hate it, then why don't you shave it off and get rid of it?" one of his friends asked.

A devilish gleam shone in the eyes of the Mulla as he answered, "Because my wife hates it too!"

But that does not make you free. The hippies, the yippies and others, they are not really rebellious people, they are reactionaries. They have reacted against the society. A few are obedient, a few are disobedient, but the center of domination is the same. A few obey, a few disobey, but nobody looks at his own soul.

A really rebellious person is one who is neither for society nor against society, who simply lives his life according to his own understanding. Whether it goes against society or it goes with society is not a consideration, it is irrelevant. Sometimes it may go with the society, sometimes it may not go with the society, but that is not the point to be considered. He lives according to his understanding, according to his small light. And I am not saying that he becomes very egoistic about it. No, he is very humble. He knows that his light is very small, but that is all the light that there is. He knows that he may be wrong. He is not adamant, he's very humble. He says, "I may be wrong, but please allow me to be wrong according to myself."

That is the only way to learn. To commit mistakes is the only way to learn. To move according to one's own understanding is the only way to grow and become mature. If you are always looking at somebody to dictate, whether you obey or disobey makes no difference. If you are looking at somebody else to dictate and then you will decide for or against, you will never be able to know what your life is. It has to be lived, and you have to follow your own small light.

It is not always certain what to do. You are very confused. Let it be so. But find a way out of your confusion. It is very cheap and easy to listen to others because they can hand over dead dogmas to you, they can give you commandments – do this, don't do that. And they are very certain about their commandments. Certainty should not be sought; understanding should be sought. If you are seeking certainty you will become a victim of some trap or other. Don't seek certainty, seek understanding. Certainty can be given to you cheap, anybody can give it to you. But in the final analysis you will be a loser. You lost your life just to remain secure and certain, and life is not certain, life is not secure.

Life is insecurity. Each moment is a move into more and more insecurity. It is a gamble. One never knows what is going to happen. And it is beautiful that one never knows. If it was predictable life would not be worth living. If everything was as you would like it and everything was certain you would not be a man at all, you would be a machine. Only for machines everything is secure and certain.

Man lives in freedom. Freedom needs insecurity and uncertainty. A real man of intelligence is always hesitant because he has no dogma to rely upon, to lean upon. He has to look and respond.

Lao Tzu says, "I am hesitant, and I move alertly in life because I don't know what is going to happen. And I don't have any principle to follow. I have to decide every moment. I never decide beforehand. I have to decide when the moment has come!"

Then one has to be very responsive. That's what responsibility is. Responsibility is not an obligation, responsibility is not a duty – it is a capacity to respond. A man who wants to know what life is has to be responsive. That is missing. Centuries of conditioning have made you more like machines. You have lost your manhood, you have bargained for security. You are secure and comfortable and everything has been planned by others. And they have put everything on the map, they have measured everything. This is all absolutely foolish because life cannot be measured, it is immeasurable. And no map is possible because life is in constant flux, everything goes on changing. Nothing except change is permanent. Says Heraclitus, "You cannot step in the same river twice."

And the ways of life are very zigzag. The ways of life are not like the tracks of a railway train. No, it does not run on tracks. And that's the beauty of it, the glory of it, the poetry of it, the music of it – that it is always a surprise.

If you are seeking for security, certainty, your eyes will become closed and you will be less and less surprised, and you will lose the capacity to wonder. Once you lose the capacity to wonder, you have lost religion. Religion is the opening of your wondering heart. Religion is a receptivity for the mysterious that surrounds us.

Don't seek security; don't seek advice on how to live your life. People come to me and they say, "Osho, tell us how we should live our lives." You are not interested in knowing what life is, you are more interested in making a fixed pattern. You are more interested in killing life than in living it. You want a discipline to be imposed on you.

There are, of course, priests and politicians all over the world who are ready, just sitting waiting for you. Come to them and they are ready to impose their disciplines on you. They enjoy the power that comes through imposing their own ideas upon others.

I'm not here for that. I am here to help you to become free. And when I say that I am here to help you to become free, I am included. I am to help you to become free of me also. My sannyas is a very paradoxical thing. You surrender to me in order to become free. I accept you and initiate you into sannyas to help you to become absolutely free of every dogma, of every scripture, of every philosophy – and I am included in it. Sannyas is as paradoxical as life itself is – it should be. Then it is alive.

So the first thing is: don't ask anybody how you should live your life. Life is so precious – live it! I am not saying that you will not make mistakes; you will. Remember only one thing: don't make the same mistake again and again. That's enough.

If you can find a new mistake every day, make it. But don't repeat mistakes; that is foolish. A man who can find new mistakes to make will be growing continuously – that is the only way to learn, that is the only way to come to your own inner light.

I have heard:

One night the poet, Awhadi of Kerman, a very great Muslim poet, was sitting on his porch bent over a vessel. Shams e-Tabrizi, a great Sufi mystic, happened to pass by.

Shams e-Tabrizi looked at the poet, at what he was doing. He asked the poet, "What are you doing?"

The poet said, "Contemplating the moon in a bowl of water."

Shams e-Tabrizi started laughing, with an uproarious laughter, a mad laughter. The poet started feeling uncomfortable; a crowd gathered. And the poet said, "What is the matter? Why are you laughing so much? Why are you ridiculing me?"

Shams e-Tabrizi said, "Unless you have broken your neck, why don't you look directly at the moon in the sky?"

The moon is there, the full moon is there, and this poet was sitting with a bowl of water and looking into the bowl of water at the reflection of the moon!

Seeking truth in scriptures, seeking truth in philosophies, is looking at the reflection. If you ask somebody else how you should live your life you are asking for misguidance, because that man can only talk about his own life. And never, never, are two lives the same. Whatsoever he can say or impart to you will be about his own life – and that too only if he has lived. He may have asked somebody else, he may have followed somebody else, he may have been an imitator himself; then it is a reflection of a reflection. And centuries pass and people go on reflecting the reflection of the reflection of the reflection – and the real moon is always there in the sky waiting for you.

It is your moon, it is your sky, look directly. Be immediate about it. Why borrow my eyes or anybody else's eyes? You have been given eyes, beautiful eyes to see, and to see directly. Why borrow understanding from anybody? Remember, it may be an understanding to me, but the moment you borrow it, it becomes knowledge to you – it is no longer understanding.

Understanding is only that which has been experienced by the person himself. It may be understanding for me, if I have looked at the moon, but the moment I say it to you it becomes knowledge, it is no longer understanding. Then it is just verbal, then it is just linguistic. And language is a lie.

Let me tell you an anecdote:

A chicken farmer, dissatisfied with the productivity of his flock, decided to use a bit of psychology on his hens. Accordingly he purchased a gay-colored, talking parrot and placed him in the barnyard. Sure enough, the hens took to the handsome stranger immediately, pointed out the best tidbits for him to eat with joyous clucks, and generally followed him around like a bevy of teenage girls following a new singing star sensation. To the delight of the farmer, even their egg-laying capacities improved.

The barnyard rooster, naturally jealous of being ignored by his harem, set upon the attractive interloper, assailed him with beak and claws, pulling out one green or red feather after the other. Whereupon the intimidated parrot cried out in trepidation, "Desist sir! I beg of you, desist! After all, I am only here in the capacity of a language professor!"

Many people live their life as language professors. That is the falsest kind of life. Reality needs no language; it is available to you on a non-verbal level. The moon is there; it needs no bowl and no water, it needs no other medium. You have just to look at it; it is a non-verbal communication. The whole of life is available – you just have to learn how to communicate with it non-verbally.

That's what meditation is all about – to be in such a space where language does not interfere, where learned concepts don't come in between you and the real.

When you love a woman, don't be bothered about what others have said about love because that is going to be an interference. You love the woman, the love is there, forget all that you have learned about love. Forget all Kinseys, forget all Masters and Johnsons, forget all Freuds and Jungs. Please don't become a language professor. Just love the woman and let love be there, and let love lead you and guide you into its innermost secrets, into its mysteries. Then you will be able to know what love is.

What others say about meditation is meaningless. Once I came upon a book about meditation written by a Jaina saint. It was really beautiful, but there were a few places by which I could see that the man had never meditated himself – otherwise those places could not be there. But they were very few and far between. The book on the whole, almost ninety-nine per cent, was perfect. I loved the book. Then I forgot about it.

For ten years I was wandering around the country. Once in a village of Rajasthan, that saint came to meet me. His name looked familiar, and suddenly I remembered the book. And I asked the saint why he had come to me. He said, "I have come to you to know what meditation is."

I said, "I remember your book. I remember it very well, because it really impressed me. Except for a few defects which showed that you have never meditated, the book was perfectly right – ninety-nine percent right. And now you come here to learn about meditation. Have you never meditated?"

He looked a little embarrassed because his disciples were also there. I said, "Be frank. Because if you say you know meditation, then I am not going to talk about it. Then finished! You know; there is no need. If you say to me frankly – at least be true once – if you say you have never meditated, only then can I help you toward meditation."

It was a bargain, so he had to confess. He said, "Yes, I have never said it to anybody. I have read many books about meditation, all the old scriptures. And I have been teaching people, that's why I feel embarrassed before my disciples. I have been teaching meditation to thousands, and I have written books about it, but I have never meditated."

You can write books about meditation and never come across the space that meditation is. You can become so efficient in verbalizing, you can become so clever in abstraction, in intellectual argumentativeness, and you can forget completely that all the time that you have been involved in these intellectual activities has been a sheer wastage.

I asked the old man, "How long have you been interested in meditation?"

He said, "My whole life." He was almost seventy. He said, "When I was twenty I took sannyas, I became a Jaina monk, and those fifty years since then I have been reading and reading and thinking about meditation."

Fifty years of thinking and reading and writing about meditation, even guiding people into meditation, and he has not even tasted once what meditation is!

And this is the case with millions of people. They talk about love, they know all the poetries about love, but they have never loved. Or even if they thought they were in love, they were never in love. That too was a "heady" thing, it was not of the heart. People live and go on missing life. It needs courage. It needs courage to be realistic; it needs courage to move with life wherever it leads. The paths are uncharted, there exists no map. One has to go into the unknown.

Life can be understood only if you are ready to go into the unknown. If you cling to the known you cling to the mind, and the mind is not life. Life is non-mental, non-intellectual, because life is total. Your totality has to be involved in it, you cannot just think about it. Thinking *about* life is not life; beware of this "about-ism." One goes on thinking about and about: there are people who think about God, there are people who think about life, there are people who think about love. There are people who think about this and that.

Mulla Nasruddin became very old and he went to his doctor. He was looking very weak so the doctor said, "I can say only one thing. You will have to cut your love life to half." The Mulla said, "Okay. Which half? Talking about it or thinking about it?"

That's all. Don't become a language professor, don't become a parrot. Parrots are language professors. They live in words, concepts, theories, theologies, and life goes on passing, slipping out of their hands. Then one day suddenly they become afraid of death. When a person is afraid of death, know well that that person has missed life. If he has not missed life there cannot be any fear of death. If a person has lived life, he will be ready to live death also. He will be almost enchanted by the phenomenon of death.

When Socrates was dying he was so enchanted that his disciples could not understand what he was feeling so happy about. One disciple, Credo, asked, "Why are you looking so happy? We are crying and weeping."

Socrates said, "Why should I not be happy? I have known what life is, now I would like to know what death is. I am at the door of a great mystery, and I am thrilled! I am going on a great journey into the unknown. I am simply full of wonder! I cannot wait!" And remember, Socrates was not a religious man; Socrates was not in any way a believer.

Somebody asked, "Are you so certain that the soul will survive after death?"

Socrates said, "I don't know."

To say "I don't know" is the greatest courage in the world. It is very difficult for the language professors to say "I don't

21

know." It is difficult for the parrots. Socrates was a very sincere and honest man. He said, "I don't know."

Then the disciple asked, "Then why are you feeling so happy? If the soul does not survive, then...?"

Socrates said, "I have to see. If I survive there can be no fear about it. If I don't survive, how can there be fear? If I don't survive, I don't survive. Then where is the fear? There is nobody there, so fear cannot exist. If I survive, I survive. There is no point in getting afraid about it. But I don't know exactly what is going to happen. That's why I am so full of wonder and ready to go into it. I don't know."

To me, this is what a religious man should be. A religious man is not a Christian, or a Hindu, or a Buddhist, or a Mohammedan. All these are ways of knowledge. A Christian says, "I know." And his knowledge comes from the Christian dogmas. The Hindu says, "I also know." And his knowledge comes from the Vedas and the Gitas and his dogmas. And a Hindu is against the Christian, because he says, "If I am right, you cannot be right. If you are right, then I cannot be right." So there is great argument and there is much dispute and much debate and unnecessary conflict.

A religious man, a really religious man – not the so-called religious people – is one who says "I don't know." When you say "I don't know," you are open, you are ready to learn. When you say "I don't know," you don't have any prejudice this way or that, you don't have any belief, you don't have any knowledge. You have only awareness. You say, "I am aware and I will see whatsoever happens. I will not carry any dogma from the past."

This is the attitude of a disciple, the attitude of one who wants to learn. And *discipline* simply means learning. A disciple means a learner, one who is ready to learn, and discipline means learning.

I am not here to teach you any dogmas; I am not imparting any knowledge to you. I am simply helping you to see that which is. Live your life whatsoever the cost. Be ready to gamble with it.

I have heard about a business man. He was walking from his office to a restaurant for lunch when he was stopped by a stranger who said to him, "I don't think that you remember me, but ten years ago I came to this city broke. I asked you for a loan and you gave me twenty dollars because you said you were willing to take a chance to start a man on the road to success."

The business man thought for a while and then he said. "Yes, I remember the incident. Go on with your story."

"Well," remarked the stranger, "are you still willing to gamble?"

Life asks you the same question again and again and again: "Are you still willing to gamble?" It is never certain. Life has no insurance in it; it is simply an opening, a wild opening, a chaotic opening. You can make a small house around you, secure, but then that will prove to be your grave. Live with life.

And we have been doing that in many ways. Marriage is man-created; love is part of life. When you create marriage around love you are creating security. You are making something which cannot be made – love cannot be made legal. You are trying to do the impossible, and if in that effort love dies, it is no wonder. You become a husband, your beloved becomes a wife. You are no longer two alive persons; you are two functionaries. The husband has a certain function, the wife has a certain function; they have certain duties to fulfill. Then life has ceased to flow. They are frozen.

Watch a husband and wife. You will always see two persons frozen, sitting side by side, not knowing what they are doing here, why they are sitting here. Maybe they have nowhere to go.

When you see love between two persons something is flowing, moving, changing. When there is love between two persons they live in an aura, there is a constant sharing. Their vibrations are reaching to each other; they are broadcasting their being to each other. There is no wall between them, they are two and yet not two – they are one also.

The husband and wife are as far away as it is possible to be, even though they may be sitting by the side of each other. The husband never listens to what the wife is saying; he has become deaf long ago. The wife never sees what is happening to the husband; she has become blind to him. They take each other absolutely for granted; they have become things. They are no longer persons because persons are always open, persons are always uncertain, persons are always changing. Now they have a fixed role to fulfill. They died the day they got married. Since that day they have not lived.

I'm not saying not to get married, but remember that love is the real thing. And if it dies then marriage is worthless.

And the same is true about everything in life, about everything. Either you can live it – but then you have to live with this hesitation, not knowing what is going to happen the next moment – or you can make everything certain about it. There are people who have become so certain about everything that they are never surprised. There are people whom you cannot surprise. And I am here to deliver to you a message which is very surprising – you will not believe it, I know. You cannot believe it, I know. I am here to tell you something which is absolutely unbelievable – that you are gods and goddesses. You have forgotten.

Let me tell you an anecdote:

Harvey Firestone, Thomas A. Edison, John Burroughs and Henry Ford stopped at a rural service station on their way to Florida for the winter.

"We want some bulbs for our headlights," said Ford. "And by the way, that is Thomas Edison sitting there in the car, and I am Henry Ford."

The fellow at the service station did not even look up, just spat out some tobacco juice with obvious contempt.

"And," said Ford, "we would like to buy a new tire if you have any Firestone tires. And that other fellow in the car is Harvey Firestone himself."

Still the old fellow said nothing. While he was placing the tire on the wheel, John Burroughs, with his long white beard, stuck his head out the window and said, "How do you do, stranger?"

Finally the old man at the service station came alive. He glared at Burroughs and said, "If you tell me you are Santa Claus I will be damned if I don't crush your skull with this lug wrench."

He could not believe that Harvey Firestone, Thomas A. Edison, John Burroughs and Henry Ford were all traveling in one car. They were all friends and they used to travel together.

When I say to you, you are gods and goddesses, you will not believe me because you have completely forgotten who is traveling within you, who is sitting within you, who is listening to me, who is looking at me. You have completely forgotten. You have been given some labels from the outside and you have trusted those labels – your name, your religion, your country – all bogus! It does not make any sense if you are a Hindu or a Christian or a Mohammedan if you don't know yourself. These labels make no sense at all. Maybe they are of a certain utility. What sense does it make whether you are a Hindu, or a Christian, or a Moham-medan, or an Indian, or an American, or Chinese? How does it make sense, how does it help you to know your being? All are irrel-evant – because the being is neither Indian, nor Chinese, nor American; and the being is neither Hindu, nor Mohammedan, nor Christian. The being is simply a pure "is-ness."

The pure "is-ness" is what I call godliness. If you can under-stand your inner divinity you have understood what life is. Otherwise you have not been able yet to decode life. This is the message. The whole life is pointing at one thing, continuously – that you are gods. Once you have understood it, then there is no death. Then you have learned the lesson. Then in death gods will be returning back to their homes.

When Rabbi Birnham lay dying,

his wife burst into tears.
He said, "What are you crying for?
My whole life was only that I might learn how to die."

The whole life – just a training: how to go back home, how to die, how to disappear. Because the moment you disappear, godliness appears in you. Your presence is the absence of godliness; your absence is the presence of godliness.

Enough for today.

2

With Nothing to Lose

The first question:

Osho,
How can we prepare ourselves for death?

Don't accumulate anything whatever: power, money, prestige, virtue, knowledge, even the so-called spiritual experiences. Don't accumulate. If you don't accumulate you are ready to die any moment, because you have nothing to lose. The fear of death is not really fear of death; the fear of death comes out of the accumulations of life. Then you have too much to lose. You cling to it. That is the meaning of Jesus' saying: Blessed are the poor in spirit.

I don't mean become a beggar, and I don't mean renounce the world. I mean be in the world, but don't be of the world. Don't accumulate inside, be poor in spirit. Never possess anything – and then you are ready to die. Possessiveness is the problem, not life itself. The more you possess, the more you are afraid to lose. If you don't possess anything, if your purity, if your spirit is uncontaminated by anything, if you are simply

27

there alone, you can disappear any moment; whenever death knocks on the door it will find you ready. You are not losing anything. By going with death you are not a loser. You may be moving into a new experience.

And when I say don't accumulate, I mean it as an absolute imperative. I'm not saying don't accumulate things of this world and go on accumulating virtue, knowledge, and so-called spiritual experiences, visions – no. I am talking in absolute terms: don't accumulate. There are people, particularly in the East, who teach renunciation. They say, "Don't accumulate anything in this world because it will be taken away from you when death comes." These people seem to be basically greedier than the ordinary, worldly people. Their logic is: don't accumulate in this world because death will take it away, so accumulate something that death cannot take away from you – accumulate virtue, *punya;* accumulate character, morality, knowledge; accumulate experiences, spiritual experiences, experiences of kundalini, meditation, this and that; accumulate something that death cannot take away from you.

But if you accumulate, with that accumulation comes fear. Each accumulation brings fear in its own proportion; then you are afraid. Don't accumulate and fear disappears. I don't teach you renunciation in the old sense; my sannyas is an absolutely new concept. It teaches you to be in the world and yet to be not of it. Then you are always ready.

I have heard about a great Sufi mystic, Abraham Adam. Once he was the Emperor of Bokhara, then he left everything and became a Sufi beggar. When he was staying with another Sufi mystic he was puzzled because every day the man was continuously complaining of his poverty.

Abraham Adam said to him, "The way you abuse it, it may be that you have bought your poverty cheaply."

"How stupid you must be!" the man retorted, not knowing to whom he was talking, not knowing that Abraham was once the emperor. He said, "How stupid you must be to think that one buys poverty."

Abraham replied, "In my case, I paid my kingdom for it. I would even give away a hundred worlds for a single moment of it, for every day its value becomes more and more to me. No wonder then that I give thanks for it while you lament it."

The purity of the spirit is the real poverty. The word *sufi* comes from an Arabic word *safa. Safa* means purity. *Sufi* means one who is pure in the heart.

And what is purity? Don't misunderstand me, purity has nothing to do with morality. Don't interpret it in a moralistic way. Purity has nothing to do with puritans. Purity simply means an uncontaminated state of mind, where only your consciousness is and nothing else. Nothing else really enters into your consciousness, but if you hanker to possess, that hankering contaminates you. Gold cannot enter into your consciousness. There is no way. How can you take gold into your being? There is no way. Money cannot enter into your consciousness. But if you want to possess, that possessiveness can enter into your consciousness. Then you become impure. If you don't want to possess anything you become fearless. Then even death is a beautiful experience to pass through.

A man who is really spiritual has tremendous experiences, but he never accumulates them. Once they have happened he forgets about them. He never remembers, he never projects them into the future. He never says that they should be repeated or that they should happen again to him. He never prays for them. Once they have happened they have happened. Finished! He is finished with them and he moves away from them. He is always available for the new, he never carries the old.

And if you don't carry the old you will find life absolutely new – incredibly, unbelievably new at each step. Life is new, only the mind is old; and if you look through the old mind life also looks like a repetition, a boring thing. If you don't look through the mind... Mind means your past, mind means the accumulated experiences, knowledge and everything. Mind means that through which you have passed, but which you are still hanging onto. Mind is a hang-over, dust from the past covering your mirrorlike consciousness. Then when you look through it everything becomes distorted. Mind is the faculty of distortion. If you don't look through the mind you will be ready for death. In fact not looking through the mind you will know that life is eternal. Only mind dies – without mind you are deathless. Without mind nothing has ever died; life goes on and on and on forever. It has no beginning and no end.

Accumulate – then you have a beginning, and then you will have an end.

This is the way, how to prepare yourself for death. When I say "how to prepare for death," I don't mean preparing for the death that will come in the end – that is very far away. If you prepare for it you will be preparing for the future and again the mind will come in. No, when I say prepare for death, I don't mean the death that will come finally; I mean the death that visits you every moment with each exhalation. Accept this death each moment and you will be ready for the final death when it comes.

Start dying each moment to the past. Clean yourself of the past each moment. Die to the known so that you become available to the unknown. With dying and being reborn each moment you will be able to live life and you will be able to live death also.

And that's what spirituality is really all about: to live death intensely, to live life intensely; to live both so passionately that nothing is left behind unlived, not even death. If you live life and death totally, you transcend. In that tremendous passion and intensity of life and death, you transcend duality, you transcend the dichotomy, you come to the one. That one is really the truth. You can call it godliness, you can call it life, you can call it truth, *samadhi*, ecstasy, or whatsoever you choose.

The second question:

> Osho,
> At times you seem to intend to confuse us about love
> and meditation. Sometimes you stress the ultimate
> futility of love; on other occasions you pronounce
> meditation as being useless. And sometimes you say
> both love and meditation are fundamental paths of
> enlightenment.

The questioner says, "At times you seem to intend to confuse us." No, you have not listened to me well. I am always confusing, not only at times. Confusion is my method.

What I am trying to do by confusing you is to uproot you from your mind. I would not like you to have any roots in the mind in the name of love or in the name of meditation or in the name of God. Your mind is very cunning. It can thrive on anything; on meditation, on love, it can thrive. The moment I see that your mind is thriving on anything, I immediately have to uproot you from it. My whole effort is to create a no-mind state in you. I am not here to convince you about anything. I am not here to give you a dogma, a creed to live by. I am here to take all creeds away from you because only then will life happen to you. I am not giving you anything to live by, I am simply taking all props away from you, all crutches.

The mind is very clever. If you say, "Drop money," the mind says, "Okay. Can I cling to meditation?" If you say to the mind, "Renounce the world," the mind says, "Okay. Can I now possess spiritual experiences?" If you say, "Renounce the world," the mind says, "I can renounce the world, but now I will cling to the idea of God." And nothing is a greater barrier to godliness than the idea of God.

The word God has become a great barrier, the belief in God has become a great barrier. If you want to reach to godliness you will have to drop all ideas about God, all beliefs about God –

Hindu, Christian, Mohammedan. You will have to be absolutely silent, unclinging, not-knowing. In that profound ignorance godliness reveals itself to you – only in that profound ignorance.

My effort is totally different from your effort. What you are doing here is diametrically opposite to what I am doing here. My effort is to create a profound ignorance in you, so I will have to confuse you. Whenever I see that some knowledge is being gathered, I immediately jump on it and destroy it. By and by you will learn – being close to me you are bound to learn – that it is futile to accumulate because this man will not leave you in peace. If you cling to something he is going to take it away, so what is the point? One day you will simply listen to me, not clinging, not making any belief out of it, not creating a philosophy, a theology out of it; simply listening as you listen to the birds, as you listen to the wind passing through the pines, as you listen to the river rushing toward the ocean, as you listen to the wild roar of the ocean waves. Then you don't create a philosophy, you simply listen.

Let me be a wild ocean roaring in front of you, or a wind passing through the trees, or birds singing in the morning. I am not a philosopher, I am not imparting knowledge to you. I am trying to point to something which is beyond knowledge.

So the moment I see that you are nodding, the moment I see that you are saying, "Yes, this is true," the moment I see that you are accumulating something, immediately I have to jump upon it and contradict it to confuse you. Confusion is my method; I am doing it all the time. I will not leave you to rest unless you drop that whole effort of philosophizing, unless you start listening to me without any mind – out of the sheer joy of it, as you listen to music. When you start listening to me in that way then you will never feel confused. You feel confused because first you cling to something, then in the next step I destroy it. You feel confused. You were making a house and again I come there and destroy it.

Your confusion is in fact created by yourself. Don't create

that house, then I cannot destroy it. If you create, I am going to destroy. If you stop creating houses – card-houses, they are – if you stop creating houses, if you say, "This man will come and destroy," if you simply wait and listen and you don't bother to make any house to live in, then I cannot confuse you. And the day I cannot confuse you will be a great day of rejoicing for you because that very moment you will be able to understand me, not by your intellect but by your being. It will be a communion, not a communication. It will be a transfer of energy, not of words. You will have entered into my house.

I will not allow *you* to create any house because that will be a barrier. Then you will start living in that house and I am trying to bring you into my house. Jesus says to his disciples, "In my God's house there are many mansions." I also say to you, "I am taking you on a journey to where a great palace is waiting for you." But I see you making houses by the side of the road and I have to destroy them, otherwise your journey will be destroyed and you will never reach the goal. You start worshipping anything. You are in such a hurry, you are so impatient, that whatsoever I tell you, you simply grab it.

I am not going to allow it to happen. So, be alert. If you are alert there will be no need to confuse you. In fact, if you are alert, whatsoever I do I cannot confuse you. The day you can say, "Now, Osho, you cannot confuse me. Whatsoever you say I listen, I rejoice in it, but I don't make any conceptualization" is the day I cannot confuse you. Until that moment I am going to confuse you again and again and again.

The third question:

Osho,
As sex is closely related to death, what is the meaning of spontaneous celibacy?

Sex is more closely related to birth than to death. Birth is out of sex; birth is a sexual phenomenon. Naturally, sex is also closely related to death – but as a by-product. Because birth is out of sex, death is also going to be out of sex. Hence the non-sensical idea arose in the East that if you remain celibate, if you remain a *brahmachari*, if you go beyond sex, you will never die – you will become an immortal. That is foolish, because death is not something that is going to happen in the future, it has already happened with birth. You cannot avoid it. You can indulge in sex or you can indulge in celibacy, it is going to make no difference.

Mulla Nasruddin had completed his hundredth year, and a few journalists came to interview him. He was the first citizen of his town who had become a centenarian. They asked how he had attained to such great age.

He said, "I never touched wine, I was never interested in women. That must be the reason for it."

Immediately something in the next room fell very loudly and there was a racket. The journalists became very alert. They said, "What is going on?"

Mulla said, "It must be my dad. It seems he is again running after the maid, and he seems to be drunk."

The old man must be one hundred and twenty-five. Mulla had said, "I have attained to this age because of celibacy and because I never touched any wine, I have remained away from women," but here is his father still rushing, drunk, trying to catch hold of a woman.

Death has already happened the moment you became incarnated in the body. The moment you entered the womb, death has already happened. Your clock, the clock of your life, can run only so far – seventy years, eighty years – it depends on a thousand and one things. But your clock can only run so far. It makes no difference how you live your life, death is going to happen. Death cannot be avoided.

The questioner has asked: "As sex is closely related to death what is the meaning of spontaneous celibacy?"

The first thing is: birth and death are both related to sex, but just by becoming celibate you are not going to transcend death. Death has already happened in birth, there is no way to transcend it. It is going to happen because in fact it has already happened. It is only a question of time unfolding. You are rushing toward it each moment.

So don't try to be celibate just to avoid death, because that too again is fear. The people who try to become celibate are afraid of death, and one who is afraid of death can never know what death is, can never know what deathlessness is. So don't be afraid.

And celibacy can only be spontaneous. You ask: "What is the meaning of spontaneous celibacy?" Celibacy can only be spontaneous; there is no other type of celibacy. If it is not spontaneous, it is not celibacy. You can force it, you can control your sexuality, but that is not going to help. You will not be celibate, you will be only more and more sexual. Sex will spread all over your being. It will become part of your unconscious. It will move your dreams, it will become your motivation in dreams, it will become your fantasy. In fact, you will become more sexual than you were ever before. You will think more about it and you will have to repress it again and again. And whatsoever is repressed has to be repressed again because the victory is never complete.

There is no way to destroy sex by force, by violence. There is no way to control and discipline it. The people who have tried to control and discipline it have made the whole world very pornographic. Your so-called saints have a very pornographic mind. If a window can be created and a hole can be made in their heads, you will be able to see just sex, pornography. It is bound to be so. It is natural.

Never enforce any celibacy on yourself. Try to understand what sexuality is, go deep into it. It has a tremendous beauty of its own. It is one of the profoundest mysteries of life. Life comes out of it – it has to be a great mystery. Sex is not sin; repression is a sin. Sex is very natural, very spontaneous. You have not done anything to have it, it is inborn, it is part of your being. Don't condemn it, don't judge it, don't fear it, don't fight with it. Simply go into it more – more meditatively. Let it happen in such silence, in such deep acceptance, that you can know the very core of it. The moment you penetrate to the very core of sexual orgasm, by and by you will see sex is losing its appeal for you, your energy is moving in a higher plane, you are becoming more loving and less sexual. And this happens spontaneously.

I am not saying become more loving. I am saying that if you go deep into the mystery of sex, love arises out of it naturally. You become more loving and sexuality becomes less and less and less. And one day there is just a pure flame of love, all the smoke of sex has disappeared. The crude energy of sex has been transformed into a more subtle perfume – the perfume of love.

Then I will say go deep into love. If you go deep into love, again you will come to the very core of it. And in that moment prayerfulness will arise. That too happens spontaneously. In sex you are more concerned with the body; in love you are more concerned with the psyche; in prayerfulness you suddenly become concerned with the soul. These are the three possibilities hidden in the seed of sex. And when sex has disappeared into love and love has disappeared into prayerfulness, there is a spontaneous celibacy.

The Indian term for it is very beautiful. It is *brahmacharya*. The word literally means living like a god. *Brahmacharya* means living like a god. The whole energy is just prayerfulness, the whole energy is just a grace, a gratitude, a benediction. One becomes absolutely divine.

But I am not saying that sex is not divine; it is the seed. Love is the tree, prayer is the flowering. Prayer arises out of sex energy. You have to be grateful toward it, you have to respect it. Sex should be respected because everything is going to happen out of it. Life has happened out of it; death is going to happen out of it; love, prayer and godliness are going to happen out of it. Sex carries the whole blueprint of your destiny. To me, sex is not just sex, sex is all.

So if from the very beginning you take an "anti" attitude you will be missing the whole journey of life. And you will get involved in such a fight which leads nowhere, you will get involved in a fight in which your defeat is certain. You cannot defeat sexual energy because in sexual energy godliness is hidden, in sexual energy love and prayer are hidden. How can you defeat it? You are very tiny and sexual energy is very universal. This whole existence is full of sexual energy.

But the word *sex* has become so condemned. It has to be taken out of the mud. It has to be cleaned. A temple has to be made around it. And remember, celibacy can only be spontaneous, there is no other type of celibacy. It is not a control, it is not a discipline; it is a tremendous understanding of your own energies and their possibilities.

The fourth question:

Osho,
You said nobody should dictate what you should do
with your life. How does that fit with being available
and surrendering to you?

In the first place I am a nobody. Now listen to the question again. "You said nobody should dictate what you should do with your life." And the second thing: don't surrender to me because I dictate to you. But if you feel like surrendering, what can I do? If you feel like surrendering, it is your feeling. If I am dictating to you to surrender to me, don't listen to me. But if your heart is dictating, then what are you going to do? If I tell you to be available to me, don't listen at all. But if your own understanding says, "Be available to this man," then be.

And here there is nobody. If you look deeply into me you will not find anybody there. The house is empty, the whole space is yours, just for the asking. I am just a space. The man you see here sitting in the chair died long before. There is no entity who can dictate anything to you.

Just last night one woman seeker was saying, "I would like to do what other sannyasins are doing, but I cannot surrender. I cannot lose my freedom. I have lived in many confinements from my very childhood, in many disciplines. Now I am afraid to get involved in another imprisonment." I said, "Don't be worried. I confer freedom upon you, an absolute freedom."

Sannyas is freedom. If you understand rightly, it is absolute freedom. And the woman understood the point because I said, "Now you are afraid that you may get into another trap. But are you aware that your ego itself can become the trap, and the greatest of all?" You have lived within many other commitments and you found they all became imprisonments – but your own ego can become the imprisonment.

When you surrender to a nobody he cannot imprison you, and the very danger of your own ego becoming an imprisonment for you disappears. When you surrender to me you are not really surrendering to me, because I am not here. And I'm not enjoying your surrender at all – whether you surrender or not makes no difference to me. In fact, when you surrender to me, you surrender yourself. You don't surrender to me, you simply surrender your ego. I am just a device, an excuse. It will be difficult for you to go and surrender to the river, or to the sky, or to the stars – it will be very difficult and you will look a little ridiculous. So I pretend to be here just to help you so that you don't feel ridiculous. You can put your ego here. There is nobody to receive it and nobody to be happy about it, but it helps.

Buddha used to call such things devices – *upaya*. It is just an *upaya*, a device to help those who cannot put their egos down unless they find some feet. I make my feet available to you, but inside there is nobody.

The fifth question:

Osho,
Why do you give us these religious titles? They seem
absurd. Outside the ashram Indians seldom call me
swami with a straight face.

You must be hankering for it. I have not called you *swami*
to be swami for others. The word *swami* means lord. Don't
hanker for others to call you lord. I have called you swami just
to indicate your path – so that you become lord of yourself. It is
not to make others slaves to you; it is just to make a master of
you. The word *swami* is intended for self-mastery. So don't feel
frustrated if nobody calls you swami. In fact if somebody calls
you swami be alert, because there is danger. You may start
thinking that you are a swami, you may start thinking that you
are some holy man or something. Don't carry that type of nonsense. I am not here to make you holy or saintly or anything.

You ask why I give you these religious titles because they
seem absurd. They are! Really my whole intention is to make
you so ridiculous, so absurd, that others laugh at you and you
can also laugh at yourself. That is the whole trick in it.

And also for another purpose I call you swami. I give you
these religious titles because to me the profane and the sacred
are not two separate things; the profane is the sacred, the ordinary is the extraordinary, and the natural is the super-natural.

God is not somewhere away from the world. God is in the
world, immanent. That's my whole approach: that everything
is divine as it is. The old concept of a religious man is that he is
anti-life. He condemns this life, this ordinary life – he calls it
mundane, profane, illusion. He denounces it. I am so deeply in
love with life that I cannot denounce it. I am here to enhance
the feeling for it.

When I give you these religious titles I am not making you
in any way superior to others. Don't carry any idea of "holier

39

than you," don't carry any idea of that sort. That is stupid.

I give you these orange clothes. These clothes have been used for centuries down through the ages for a specific purpose – to make a demarcation between the ordinary life and the religious life. I want to dissolve all those differences. Hence I give you these robes and I don't take you away from life.

You will be sitting in ordinary life, working in ordinary life, walking in ordinary life. You will be in the marketplace, you will be in the shop or in the factory, you will be a laborer, a doctor, an engineer. I am not making you special in any way – because that very desire to become special is irreligious.

And I have given you these robes to destroy the whole concept completely. That's why the traditional sannyasins are very much against me. I am destroying their whole superiority. Now sooner or later there will be no distinction. My swamis are growing so fast that the old traditional swamis will be simply lost in the jungle of my swamis. And people will not know who is who. That's the purpose behind it. I want to make religious life ordinary life, because this is the only life there is. All else is just an ego trip. And this life is so beautiful, there is no need to create another life superior to it.

Go deeper into it, move deeper into it, and profounder depths will be revealed to you. This ordinary life is carrying tremendous possibilities. So I don't want you to become religious in the sense that others are not religious. I want to drop all distinctions between the profane and the sacred, between the holy and the unholy. It is a great revolution. You may not even be aware of what is happening.

And if the traditionalists are against me, I can understand. I am destroying their whole "holier than you" attitude. That's why I have chosen the orange particularly. That has been the traditional dress for sannyasins. But I have chosen only the dress; nothing else is there in you – nothing else of the traditional discipline. There is just awareness, a love for life, a respect for life, a reverence for life. I have given you the orange robe. The day

I see that now the traditional distinction has been destroyed, I will free you from the orange robe. There is no need then. But it will take time because they have been creating the distinction for centuries.

You cannot conceive of what is happening. When an orange-robed sannyasin walks with his girlfriend on the street, you cannot conceive what is happening. It has never happened in India, not for ten thousand years. People cannot believe it – and you are expecting that they should call you swami? It is enough that they are not killing you! You are destroying their whole tradition. A sannyasin was one who would never *look* at a woman. Touching was out of the question – and holding the hand, impossible! That was enough to throw him into hell.

I have made you a totally new kind of sannyasin. It is a neosannyas. And behind whatsoever I am doing there is a method. You may be aware of it or not. I want to destroy the whole traditional attitude. Life should be religious and religion should not have any other life. The distinction between the marketplace and the monastery should not be there. The monastery should be in the marketplace; the divine dimension should become part of everyday life.

Somebody asked Bokoju, "What do you do? What is your religious discipline?"

He said, "I live an ordinary life. That is my discipline. When I feel hungry I eat, and when I feel sleepy I sleep."

Yes, this is exactly how it should be.

The questioner was puzzled. He said, "But I don't see anything special in it."

Bokoju said, "That is the point. There is nothing special All hankering for the special is of the ego."

The questioner was still puzzled. He said, "But this is what everybody else is doing – when hungry they eat, when feeling sleepy they sleep."

Bokoju laughed. He said, "No, when you eat, you do a

sand and one things also. You think, you dream, you imagine, you remember. You are not there just eating. When I eat, I simply eat. Then there is only eating and nothing else. It is pure. When you sleep you do a thousand and one things – you dream, fight, have nightmares. When I sleep I simply sleep, there is nothing else. When sleep is there, there is only sleep. Not even Bokoju exists. When eating is there, there is only eating. Not even Bokoju exists. When there is walking, there is only walking – no Bokoju. There is walking, simply walking."

This is what I would like you to become. Be ordinary, but bring a quality of awareness to your ordinary life. Bring truth to your ordinary life, introduce godliness into your ordinary life. Sleep, eat, love, pray, meditate, but don't think that you are making or doing something special. And then you will be special. A man who is ready to live an ordinary life is an extraordinary man. Because to be extraordinary, to desire to be extraordinary, is a very ordinary desire. To relax and to be ordinary is really extraordinary.

The sixth question:

> Osho,
> Why is this life, which has no end and no beginning,
> so mysterious? Please explain.

Now, not only do I give you absurd answers, you have started asking absurd questions. Why is this life so mysterious? How am I supposed to know? It is so! It is simply a fact. I am not talking about theories. I'm not saying that it is my theory that life is mysterious – then you could ask why. It is simply so. The trees are green. You ask why. The trees are green because they are green. There is no question of why.

If you can ask why and the question can be answered, then life will not be a mystery. If the why can be answered, then life cannot be a mystery. Life is a mystery because no why is relevant.

"Why is this life, which has no end and no beginning, so mysterious?"

Now you make me feel guilty, as if I am responsible for life having no beginning and no end. It should have. I agree perfectly with you, but what to do? It has no beginning and no end.

I have heard:

Mulla Nasruddin was saying to one of his disciples that life is like a woman. I was surprised, so I listened attentively to what he was saying.

He was saying, "The man who says he understands women is bragging. The man who thinks he understands them is gullible. The man who pretends to understand them is ambiguous. The man who wants to understand them is wistful. On the other hand, the man who does not say he understands them, does not think he understands them, does not pretend to understand them, does not even want to understand them – he understands them!"

And that's how life is also. Life is a woman. Try to understand life and you will become a mess. Forget all about understanding. Just live it and you will understand it. The understanding is not going to be intellectual, theoretical; the understanding is going to be total. The understanding is not going to be verbal; it is going to be non-verbal. That is the meaning when we say life is a mystery. It can be lived but it cannot be solved.

You can know what it is, but you cannot say what it is. That is the meaning of mystery. When we say that life is a mystery, we are saying that life is not a problem. A problem can be solved. A mystery is that which cannot be solved; insolubility is inbuilt. And it is good that life cannot be solved, otherwise what would you do then? Just think of it. If life is not a mystery and somebody comes and explains it to you – then what will you do? There will be nothing left except to commit suicide. Even that will look meaningless.

Life is a mystery; the more you know it, the more beautiful it is. But the less you know – a moment comes when suddenly you start living it, you start flowing with it. An orgasmic relationship evolves between you and life, but you cannot figure out what it is. That's the beauty of it, that's its infinite depth.

And yes, there is no beginning and no end. How can there be any beginning to life and any end to life? Beginning will mean that something came out of nothing, and end will mean that something was there and went into nothing. That will be an even bigger mystery. When we say life has no beginning, we simply say it has always been there. How can there be a beginning? Can you mark a line and say that at this moment life started? – as Christian theologians used to say. Just four thousand years before Jesus Christ, they say, life started on a certain Monday. Of course, it must have been in the morning. But how can you call it Monday if there was no Sunday before it? And how can you call it morning if there was no night before it? Just think of it.

No, you cannot make a mark – that is foolish. It is not possible to mark a line because even to mark a line something is needed. Something is needed to precede it, otherwise demarcation is not possible. You can mark a line if there are two things, but if there is only one thing, how can you mark a line? The fence around your house is possible because there is a neighbor. If there is no neighbor, nothing beyond your fence, the fence cannot exist. Just think of it. If there is absolutely nothing beyond your fence, your fence will fall down into nothing. How can it exist? Something is needed beyond the fence to hold it.

If on a certain Monday life started, a Sunday is needed to precede it. Otherwise the Monday will fall, topple down and disappear. And in the same way there is no possibility of any end. Life is, life simply is. It has been, it will be. It is eternity.

And don't start thinking about it. Otherwise you will be missing it, because all the time that you waste in thinking about it, is simply waste. Use that time, use that space, use that energy to live it.

The seventh question:

Osho,
Why do you prefer to call meditation the art of dying
rather than calling it the art of growing?

Because I know your ego will like it very much if I called it
the art of growing. The art of dying comes like a shock.

Let me tell you an anecdote:

One day Mulla Nasruddin saw a crowd gathered around a
pond. A Muslim priest with a huge turban on his head had
fallen into the water, and was calling for help. People were
leaning over and saying, "Give me your hand, Reverend, give
me your hand!" But the priest didn't pay attention to their offer
to rescue him. He kept wrestling with the water and shouting
for help.

Finally Mulla Nasruddin stepped forward: "Let me handle
this!" He stretched out his hand toward the priest and shouted
at him, "Take my hand!" The priest grabbed Mulla's hand and
was hoisted out of the pond.

People were very surprised and asked Mulla for the secret of
his strategy. "It is very simple," he said. "I know this miser
would not give anything to anyone, not even his hand. So
instead of saying, 'Give me your hand' I said, 'Take my hand,
your Reverence.' And sure enough, he took it."

I know you would like it to be called the art of growing.
Then your ego would feel perfectly good: "So it is a question of
growth; so I am going to remain and grow." That's what the
ego always wants.

I have knowingly called it the art of dying. Meditation is the
art of dying. Then your ego will be shocked.

And it is also truer to call it the art of dying, because your
ego is not going to grow, your ego is going to die in meditation.

These are the only two possibilities: either your ego goes on growing more, it becomes stronger, or it disappears. If your ego goes on growing and becomes stronger and stronger, you are getting more and more into the mud. You are getting more and more into fetters, you are getting more and more into the imprisonment of it. You will be suffocated. Your whole life will become a hell.

The growth of the ego is a cancerous growth. It is like cancer, it kills you. Meditation is not growth of the ego, it is death of the ego.

The eighth question:

> Osho,
> The more you talk about death, the greater my desire for life. I have just realized that I have not really lived. While I can understand that life and death come together, there is a yearning inside me that cries out for life, love and passionate intensity. I have discovered I am anguished at the thought of surrendering my unfulfilled desires. Can one give up what one has never had? I feel I would only return to the body again. Illusion or not, to my great amazement I have to admit that I still desire, and I have never felt such hunger.

When I say "to die" I really mean to live intensely; I really mean to live passionately. How can you die unless you have lived totally? In total life there is death, and *that* death is beautiful. In a passionate, intense life, death comes spontaneously – as a silence, as a profound bliss. When I say "to die", I am not saying anything against life; in fact, if you are afraid of death you will be afraid of life also. That's what has happened to the questioner.

A man who is afraid of death will be afraid of life also, because life brings death. If you are afraid of the enemy and you close your door, the friend will also be prohibited. And you are so afraid of the enemy that you close the door; the enemy may enter so you close the door for the friend also. And you become so afraid that you cannot open for the friend, because who knows? The friend may turn out to be the enemy. Or, when the door is open, the enemy may enter.

People have become afraid of life because they are afraid of death. They don't live because at the highest points, peaks, death always penetrates into life. Have you watched this happening? Almost the majority of women have lived a frigid life – they are afraid of orgasm, they are afraid of that wild explosion of energy. For centuries women have been frigid; they have not known what orgasm is.

And almost the majority of men suffer because of that fear too – ninety-five percent of men suffer from premature ejaculation. They are so afraid of orgasm, there is so much fear, that somehow they want to finish it, somehow they want to get out of it.

Again and again they go into lovemaking and there is fear. The woman remains frigid and the man becomes so afraid that he cannot stay in that state any longer. The very fear makes him ejaculate sooner than is natural, and the woman remains rigid, closed, holding herself. Now orgasm has disappeared from the world because of the fear. In the deepest orgasm, death penetrates; you feel as if you are dying. If a woman goes into orgasm she starts moaning, she starts crying, screaming. She may even start saying, "I am dying. Don't kill me!" That actually happens. If a woman goes into orgasm she will start mumbling, she will start saying, "I am dying! Don't kill me! Stop!" A moment comes in deep orgasm where ego cannot exist, death penetrates. But that is the beauty of orgasm.

People have become afraid of love because in love also, death penetrates. If two lovers are sitting side by side in deep love and intimacy, not even talking… Talking is an escape, an escape from love. When two lovers are talking that simply shows they are avoiding the intimacy. Words in-between give distance; with no words distance disappears, death appears. In silence there is death just lurking around – a beautiful phenomenon. But people are so afraid that they go on talking whether it is needed or not. They go on talking about anything, everything – but they cannot keep silent.

If two lovers sit silently, death suddenly surrounds them. And when two lovers are silent you will see a certain happiness and also a certain sadness – happiness because life is at its peak, and sadness because at its peak death also comes in. Whenever you are silent you will feel a sort of sadness. Even looking at a roseflower, if you are sitting silently and not saying anything about the roseflower, just looking at it, in that silence you will suddenly feel it is there – death. You will see the flower withering, within moments it will be gone, lost forever. Such a beauty, and so fragile! Such a beauty, and so vulnerable! Such a beauty, such a miracle and soon it will be lost forever and it will not return again. Suddenly you will become sad.

Whenever you meditate you will find death moving around. In love, in orgasm, in any aesthetic experience – in music, in song, in poetry, in dance – wherever you suddenly lose your ego, death is there.

So let me tell you one thing. You are afraid of life because you are afraid of death. And I would like to teach you how to die so that you lose all fear of death. The moment you lose the fear of death you become capable of living.

I am not talking against life. How can I talk against life? I am madly in love with life! I am so madly in love with life that because of it I have fallen in love with death also. It is part of life. When you love life totally how can you avoid death? You have to love death also. When you love a flower deeply, you love its withering away also. When you love a woman deeply, you love her getting old also, you one day love her death also. That is part, part of the woman. The old age has not happened from the outside, it has come from the inside. The beautiful face has become wrinkled now – you love those wrinkles also. They are part of your woman. You love a man and his hair has grown white – you love those hairs also. They have not happened from the outside; they are not accidents. Life is unfolding. Now the black hair has disappeared and the grey hair has come. You don't reject them, you love them; they are a part. Then your man becomes old, becomes weak – you love that too. Then one day the man is gone – you love that too.

Love loves all. Love knows nothing else than love. Hence, I say, love death. If you can love death it will be very simple to love life. If you can love even death, there is no problem.

The problem arises because the questioner must have been repressing, must be afraid of life. And then repression can bring dangerous outcomes. If you go on repressing, repressing, one day you will lose all aesthetic sense. You lose all sense of beauty, sense of grace, sense of divinity. Then the very repression becomes such a feverish state that you can do anything which may be ugly.

Let me tell you a beautiful anecdote. Chinmaya has sent this. He sends beautiful jokes:

A marine is sent to a distant island outpost where there are no women, but there is a large monkey population. He is shocked to see that without exception his fellow marines all make love with the monkeys, and he swears to them that he will never get that horny. They tell him not to be closed-minded. But as the months passed by, the marine can hold out no longer. He grabs the first monkey he can and gets caught in the act by his buddies, who start laughing their heads off.

Surprised, he says to them, "What are you guys laughing at? You keep telling me to do it!"

They answer, "Yeah, but did you have to pick the ugliest one?"

If you repress, the possibility is that you may choose the ugliest life. If you go on repressing, then the very fever is so

49

much that you are not in your consciousness. Then you are almost in neurosis. Before the repression becomes too much, relax, move into life. It is your life! Don't feel guilty. It is your life to live and love and to know and be. And whatsoever instincts existence has given to you, they are just indications of where you have to move, where you have to seek, where you have to find your fulfillment.

I know that this life is not all – a greater life is hidden behind it. But it is hidden *behind* it. You cannot find that greater life against this life; you have to find that greater life only by indulging deeply in this life. There are waves on the oceans. The ocean is hidden just behind the waves. If, seeing the turmoil and the chaos and you escape from the waves, you will be escaping from the ocean and its depth also. Jump in; those waves are part of it. Dive deep and waves will disappear, and then there will be the depth, the absolute silence of the ocean.

So this is my suggestion for the questioner. You have waited long, now no more. Enough is enough.

Let me tell you an anecdote, an old Italian joke:

The Pope's personal waiter was delivering His Holiness' breakfast, when he slipped and threw the food all over the floor. "Godammit!" he screamed as he fell.

His Holiness came out of the door of his room and said, "No cursing in here, my son. Say instead, Ave Maria."

The following morning as he attempted to deliver His Holiness' breakfast, the waiter slipped again, throwing the food on the floor. "Godammit!" screamed the poor man.

"No, my son," said the Pope. "Ave Maria."

On the third day the waiter was trembling with fear, but this time he remembered. "Ave Maria!" he yelled out as soon as he started falling with the breakfast on the floor.

"No!" exclaimed the Pope. "Godammit! This is my third day of skipping breakfast! Enough is enough!"

It is your life. There is no need going on skipping breakfast every day. And twice Ave Maria is good, but when it comes finally, it is Godammit!

The last question:

> Osho,
> I am a piece of rock in the middle of the mountain.
> Even this I don't dare to realize. I dream instead.
> Osho, why did you tell me about rivers, the ocean and
> the sky? And how could you give me sannyas? I am a
> piece of rock in the middle of the mountain.

Everybody is a piece of rock. Unless you attain to your uttermost glory, you are bound to be a piece of rock. But nothing is wrong in being a piece of rock. Because the piece of rock is nothing but existence fast asleep, snoring. A piece of rock is godliness asleep. Nothing is wrong in the piece of rock, it has to be awakened. Hence, I have given you sannyas.

You say, "And how could you give me sannyas?"

Sannyas is nothing but an effort to wake you, an effort to shake you, an effort to shock you into awareness. Sannyas is nothing but an alarm.

"Even this I don't dare to realize" – that I am a piece of rock in the middle of the mountain – "I dream instead."

That's how the rock avoids its own growth, the rock avoids its own future – by dreaming. Dreaming is the barrier. By dreaming we are avoiding the reality, by dreaming we avoid the real. It is our escape. You don't have any other escape. This is the only escape route – dreaming.

When you are listening to me, you can dream also. Sitting here you can have a thousand and one thoughts roaming around in your mind. You can think of the future or of the past. You can be for and against what I am saying, you can argue, you can debate with me inside yourself, but then you are missing me. I am a fact here. You need not dream here, you can just be here with me. And tremendous will be the result of it.

But we go on dreaming. People are dreamers, and that is their way. When they are making love to a woman, then they are dreaming; when they are eating, they are dreaming. When they are walking on the road – they have gone for a walk in the morning, the sun is rising, the day is beautiful, the people are getting up, the life is coming back again – they are dreaming. They are not looking at anything. We go on dreaming. Dreaming functions as a blindfold, and we go on missing the reality.

"Osho, why did you tell me about rivers, the ocean and the sky?"

Because those are your possibilities. The rock can fly; the rock can grow wings. I myself was a rock once, then I started growing wings – so I know. I know your possibility, you may not know it. Hence I talk about the rivers, the ocean and the sky. The rock can become a flower, the rock can become a river, the rock can become the ocean, the rock can become the sky – infinite are your possibilities! Your possibilities are as many as the possibilities of existence. You are multi-dimensional.

That's why I go on talking about the rivers and the ocean and the sky. Some day or other a great thirst will possess you, a new passion will arise for the impossible and you will be able to fly into the sky. It is yours, claim it! You only look like a rock. Rocks also only look like rocks. If they make a little effort, if they shake themselves a little, they will find wings are hidden there. They will find infinite possibilities opening, doors upon doors.

But dreaming functions as the barrier. Being a rock is not the problem: being too much in dreams is the problem. Start dropping dreams. They are futile, meaningless, a wastage and nothing more. But people go on dreaming, go on dreaming... By and by people start thinking that dreaming is their only life. Life is not a dream and dreaming is not life. Dreaming is avoiding life.

Let me tell you an anecdote:

On his seventy-fifth birthday, Turtletaub rushed into a physician's office. "Doctor," he exclaimed, "I have got a date tonight with a twenty-two-year-old girl. You gotta give me something to pep me up."

The MD smiled sympathetically and supplied the old man with a prescription. Later that night, out of curiosity, the medical man phoned his elderly patient, "Did the medicine help?"

"It's wonderful," replied Turtletaub. "Seven times already."

"That's great," agreed the doctor. "And what about the girl?"

"The girl?" said Turtletaub. "She didn't get here yet!"

Don't go on dreaming, otherwise you will miss the girl. You will miss life. Stop dreaming, look at that which is. And it is already in front of you. It is already around you, it is within and without. Godliness is the only presence if you are not dreaming. If you are dreaming, then your dreams occupy your inner space. They become the hindrances for godliness to enter into you. This dreaming we call *maya*. *Maya* means a magic show, a dream show. When you are not dreaming, when you are in a state of no-dream, the reality is revealed.

The reality is already there, you are not to achieve it. You have only to do one thing: you have to put aside your dreams. And you will no more be a rock, you can fly with me to the very end of the sky.

Receive my invitation, receive my challenge. That's what sannyas is all about.

Enough for today.

3

Walking the Tightrope

Once, when the Hasidim were seated together
in all brotherliness,
pipe in hand, Rabbi Israel joined them.
Because he was so friendly they asked him,
"Tell us, dear Rabbi, how should we serve God?"
He was surprised at the question,
and replied, "How should I know?"
But then he went on to tell them this story...
There were two friends of the king,
and both were proved guilty of a crime.
Since he loved them the king wanted to show them mercy,
but he could not acquit them
because even a king's word cannot prevail over the law.
So he gave this verdict:
A rope was to be stretched over a deep chasm,
and, one after another, the two were to walk across it.
Whoever reached to the other side
was to be granted his life.
It was done as the king ordered,
and the first of the friends got safely across.
The other, still standing on the same spot, cried to him,

"Tell me, friend, how did you manage to cross?"
The first called back,
"I don't know anything but this:
Whenever I felt myself toppling over to one side,
I leaned to the other."

Existence is paradoxical; paradox is its very core. It exists through opposites, it is a balance in the opposites. And one who learns how to balance becomes capable of knowing what life is, what existence is, what truth is. The secret key is balance.

A few things before we enter into this story... First, we have been trained in Aristotelian logic – which is linear, one dimensional. Life is not Aristotelian at all, it is Hegelian. Logic is not linear, logic is dialectical. The very process of life is dialectic, a meeting of the opposites – a conflict between the opposites and yet a meeting of the opposites. And life goes through this dialectical process: from thesis to antithesis, from antithesis to synthesis – and then again the synthesis becomes a thesis. The whole process starts again.

If Aristotle is true then there will be only men and no women, or, only women and no men. If the world was made according to Aristotle then there will be only light and no darkness, or only darkness and no light. That would be logical. There would be either life or death but not both.

But life is not based on Aristotle's logic, life has both. And life is really possible only because of both, because of the opposites: man and woman, yin and yang, day and night, birth and death, love and hate. Life consists of both.

This is the first thing you have to allow to sink deep into your heart – because Aristotle is in everybody's head. The whole education system of the world believes in Aristotle – although for the very advanced scientific minds Aristotle is out of date. He no longer applies. Science has gone beyond Aristotle because science has come closer to existence. And now science understands that life is dialectical, not logical.

I have heard:

Do you know that on Noah's Ark, making love was forbidden while on board?

When the couples filed out of the ark after the flood, Noah watched them leave. Finally the tomcat and the she-cat left, followed by a number of very young kittens. Noah raised his eyebrows questioningly and the tomcat said to him, "You thought we were fighting!"

Noah must have been Aristotelian; the tomcat knew better. Love is a sort of fight, love *is* a fight. Without fight love cannot exist. They look opposite – because we think lovers should never fight. It is logical: if you love somebody how can you fight? It is absolutely clear, obvious to the intellect, that lovers should never fight – but they do in fact. They are intimate enemies; they are continuously fighting. In that very fight the energy that is called love is released. Love is not only fight, love is not only struggle, that's true – it is more than that. It is fight too, but love transcends; the fight cannot destroy it. Love survives fight, but it cannot exist without it.

Look into life: life is non-Aristotelian, non-Euclidean. If you don't force your concepts on life, if you simply look at things as they are, then you will be suddenly surprised to see that opposites are complementaries, and the tension between the opposites is the very basis on which life exists – otherwise it would disappear. Think of a world where death does not exist. Your mind may say, "Then life will be there eternally," but you are wrong. If death does not exist life will simply disappear. It cannot exist without death; death gives it the background, death gives it color and richness, death gives it passion and intensity.

So death is not against life – the first thing – death is involved in life. And if you want to live authentically you have to learn how to continuously die authentically. You have to keep a balance between birth and death and you have to remain just in the middle. That remaining in the middle cannot be a static thing: it is not that once you have attained to balance, finished, then there is nothing to be done. That is nonsense. One never achieves balance forever; one has to achieve it again and again and again.

This is very difficult to understand because our minds have been cultivated in concepts which are not applicable to real life. You think that once you have attained meditation then there is no need of anything more, then you will be in meditation. You are wrong. Meditation is not a static thing. It is a balance. You will have to attain it again and again and again. You will become more and more capable of attaining it, but it is not going to remain forever, like a possession in your hands. It has to be claimed each moment – only then is it yours. You cannot rest, you cannot say, "I have meditated and I have realized that now there is no need for me to do anything more. I can rest." Life does not believe in rest; it is a constant movement from perfection to more perfection.

Listen to me: from perfection to more perfection. It is never imperfect, it is always perfect, but always more perfection is possible. Logically these statements are absurd.

I was reading an anecdote:

A man was charged with using counterfeit money to pay a bill. At his hearing, the defendant pleaded that he didn't know the money was phony. Pressed for proof, he admitted: "Because I stole it. Would I be stealing money that I knew was counterfeit?"

After thinking it over, the judge decided that made good sense, so he then tossed out the counterfeit charge. But he substituted a new charge – theft.

"Sure, I stole it," the defendant conceded amiably. "But counterfeit money has no legal value. Since when is it a crime to steal nothing?"

No one could find any flaw in his logic, so the man went free.

But logic won't do in life. You cannot go free so easily.

You can come out of a legal trap legally and logically because the trap consists of Aristotelian logic – you can use the same logic to come out of it. But in life you will not be able to come out only because of logic, only because of theology, only because of philosophy, only because you are very clever – clever in inventing theories. You can come out of life or you can go beyond life only through actual experience.

There are two types of people who are religious. The first type is childish, people who are searching for a father figure. The first type is immature; they cannot rely upon themselves, hence they need a god somewhere or other. The god may exist or not – that is not the point – but a god is needed. Even if the god is not there the immature mind will invent him, because the immature mind has a psychological need. It is not a question of truth whether God is there or not, it is a question of a psychological need.

In the Bible it is said God made man in his own image, but the reverse is truer: man made God in his own image. Whatsoever is your need you create that sort of god; that's why the concept of God goes on changing in every age. Every country has its own concept because every country has its own need. In fact, every single person has a different concept of God because his own needs are there and they have to be fulfilled.

So the first type of religious person – the so-called religious person – is simply immature. His religion is not religion but psychology. And when religion is psychology it is just a dream, a wish-fulfillment, a desire. It has nothing to do with reality.

I was reading:

A small boy was saying his prayers and concluded with this remark, "Dear God, take care of Mommy, take care of Daddy, take care of baby sister and Aunt Emma and Uncle John and Grandma and Grandpa – and, please God, take care of yourself, or else we're all sunk!"

59

This is the God of the majority. Ninety percent of the so-called religious people are immature people. They believe because they cannot live without belief; they believe because belief gives a sort of security; they believe because belief helps them to feel protected. It is *their* dream, but it helps. In the dark night of life, in the deep struggle of existence, without such a belief they will feel left alone. But their God is *their* God, not the God of reality. And once they get rid of their immaturity, their God will disappear.

That's what has happened to many people. In this century many people have become irreligious – not that they have come to know that God does not exist, but only because this age has made man a little more mature. Man has come of age; man has become a little more mature. So the God of the childhood, the God of the immature mind has simply become irrelevant.

That is the meaning when Friedrich Nietzsche declares that "God is dead." It is not God that is dead, it is the God of the immature mind that is dead. In fact to say that God is dead is not right because that God was never alive. The only right expression will be to say that "God is no longer relevant." Man can rely more upon himself – he does not need belief, he does not need the crutches of belief.

Hence people have become less and less interested in religion. They have become indifferent to what goes on in the church. They have become so indifferent to it that they will not even argue against it. If you ask, "Do you believe in God?" they will say, "It's okay whether he is or not, it doesn't make any difference, it doesn't matter." Just to be polite, if you believe, they will say, "Yes, he is." If you don't believe, they will say, "Yes, he is not." But it is no longer a passionate concern.

This is the first type of religion; it has existed for centuries, down the centuries, down the ages, and it is becoming more and more outmoded, out of date. Its time is finished. A new God is needed – who is not psychological. A new God is needed – who is existential, the God of reality or God as reality.

We can even drop the word *God* – "the real" will do, "the existential" will do.

Then there is a second type of religious people for whom religion is not out of fear. The first type of religion is out of fear, the second type – also bogus, also pseudo, also so-called – is not out of fear, it is only out of cleverness. There are very clever people who go on inventing theories, who are very trained in logic, in metaphysics, in philosophy. They create a religion which is just an abstraction: a beautiful piece of artwork, of intelligence, of intellectuality, of philosophizing. But it never penetrates life, it never touches life anywhere, it simply remains an abstract conceptualization.

Once Mulla Nasruddin was saying to me, "I have never been what I oughta been. I stole chickens and watermelons, got drunk and got in fights with my fists and my razor, but there is one thing I ain't never done: in spite of all my meanness I ain't never lost my religion."

Now what kind of religion is that? It has no impact on life. You believe, but that belief never penetrates your life, never transforms it. It never becomes an intrinsic part of you, it never circulates in your blood, you never breathe it in or breathe it out, it never beats in your heart – it is simply something useless. Ornamental maybe, at the most, but of no utility to you. Sunday you can go to the church; it is a formality, a social need. And you can pay lip service to God, to the Bible, to the Koran, to the Vedas, but you don't mean it, you are not sincere about it. Your life goes on without it, your life goes on in a totally different way – it has nothing to do with religion.

Watch: somebody says he is a Mohammedan, somebody says he is a Hindu, somebody says he is a Christian, somebody says he is a Jew – their beliefs are different, but watch their life and you will not find any difference. The Mohammedan, the Jew, the Christian, the Hindu – they all live the same life. Their life is not at all touched by their belief. In fact, beliefs cannot touch your life, beliefs are devices. Beliefs are cunning devices through which you say "I know what life is," and you can rest at ease, you are not troubled by life. You hold a concept and that concept helps you to rationalize. Then life does not bother you much. You have all the answers to all the questions.

But remember, unless religion is personal, unless religion is not abstract but real, deep in your roots, deep in your guts, unless it is like blood and bone and marrow, it is futile, it is of no use. It is the religion of the philosophers, not the religion of the sages.

When the third type comes in... And that is the real type; these other two are the falsifications of religion, pseudo dimensions, cheap, very easy, because they don't challenge you. The third is very difficult, arduous; it is a great challenge, it will create a turmoil in your life – because the third, the real religion, says existence has to be addressed in a personal way. You have to provoke it and you have to allow it to provoke you and you have to come to terms with it; in fact you have to struggle with it, you have to clash against it. You have to love it and you have to hate it; you have to be a friend and you have to be an enemy; you have to make your experience of existence a lived experience.

I have heard about a small child – and I would like you to be like this small child. He was really smart:

A little boy was lost at a Sunday school picnic. His mother began a frantic search for him, and soon she heard loud sounds in a childish voice calling, "Estelle, Estelle!"

She quickly spotted the youngster and rushed up to grab him in her arms. "Why did you keep calling me by my name, Estelle, instead of Mother?" she asked him, as he had never called her by her first name before.

"Well," the youngster answered, "it was no use calling out 'Mother' – the place is full of them."

If you call "mother," there are so many mothers – the place

is full of them. You have to call in a personal way, you have to call the first name.

Unless God is also called in a personal way, addressed with the first name, it will never become a reality in your life. You can go on calling "father" but whose father are you talking about? When Jesus called him "father" it was a personal address, when you call, it is absolutely impersonal. It is Christian but impersonal. When Jesus called him "father" it was meaningful; when you call "father" it is meaningless – you have made no contact, no real contact with him. Only experience of life – neither belief nor philosophy – only experience of life will make you able to address him in a personal way. Then you can encounter him.

And unless existence is encountered you are simply deceiving yourself with words – with words which are empty, hollow, with words which have no content.

There was a very famous Sufi mystic, Shaqiq was his name. He trusted existence so deeply, so tremendously, that he lived only out of that trust.

Just as Jesus says to his disciples, "Look at those lilies in the field – they labor not and yet they are so beautiful and so alive that not even Solomon was so beautiful in all his glory." Shaqiq lived the life of a lily. There have been very few people who have lived that way, but there have been mystics who have lived that way. The trust is so infinite, the trust is so absolute that there is no need to do anything – existence goes on doing things for you. In fact even when you are doing them it is doing them; it is only that you think you are doing them.

One day a man came to Shaqiq accusing him of idleness, laziness, and asked him to work for him. "I will pay you according to your services," the man added.

Shaqiq replied, "I would accept your offer if it weren't for five drawbacks. First, you might go broke. Second, thieves might steal your wealth. Third, whatever you give me you will do so grudgingly. Fourth, if you find faults with my work, you'll probably fire me. Fifth, should death come to you, I'll lose the source of my sustenance.

"Now," Shaqiq concluded, "it happens that I have a master who is totally devoid of such imperfections."

This is what trust is. Trust in life then you cannot lose anything. But that trust cannot come by indoctrination, that trust cannot come by education, preaching, studying, thinking; that trust can only come by experiencing life in all its opposites, in all its contradictions, in all its paradoxes. When within all the paradoxes you come to the point of balance, there is trust. Trust is a perfume of balance, the fragrance of balance.

If you really want to attain to trust, drop all your beliefs. They will not help. A believing mind is a stupid mind; a trusting mind has pure intelligence in it. A believing mind is a mediocre mind; a trusting mind becomes perfect. Trust makes perfect.

And the difference between belief and trust is simple. I am not talking about the dictionary meaning of the words – in the dictionary it may be so: belief means trust, trust means faith, faith means belief – I am talking about existence. In an existential way belief is borrowed; trust is yours. Belief you believe in, but doubt exists just underneath. Trust has no doubt element in it; it is simply devoid of doubt. Belief creates a division in you: a part of your mind believes, a part of your mind denies. Trust is a unity within your being, your totality.

But how can your totality trust unless you have experienced it? The God of Jesus won't do, the God of *my* experience won't do for you, the God of Buddha's experience won't do – it has to be your experience. And if you carry beliefs you will come again and again to experiences which don't fit the belief, and then there is the tendency of the mind not to see those experiences, not to take note of them because they are very disturbing. They destroy your belief and you want to cling to your belief. Then you become more and more blind to life – belief becomes a blindfold on the eyes.

Trust opens the eyes; trust has nothing to lose. Trust means whatsoever is real is real: "I can put my desires and wishes aside, they don't make any difference to reality. They can only distract my mind from reality."

If you have a belief and you come against an experience which the belief says is not possible, or the experience is such that you have to drop the belief, what are you going to choose – the belief or the experience? The tendency of the mind is to choose the belief, to forget about the experience. That's how you have been missing many opportunities when existence has knocked at your door.

Remember it is not only you who are seeking truth – truth is also seeking you. Many times the hand has come very close to you, it has almost touched you, but you shrugged yourself away. It was not fitting with your belief and you chose to choose your belief.

I have heard a very beautiful Jewish joke:

There is a joke about a vampire who flew into Patrick O'Rourke's bedroom one night for the purpose of drinking his blood. Remembering the stories his mother told him, O'Rourke grabbed a crucifix and brandished it frantically in the vampire's face. The vampire paused for a moment, shook his head condolingly, clucked his tongue, and commented genially in the purest Yiddish, "Oy vey, bubbula! Have you ever got the wrong vampire!"

Now, if the vampire is Christian, good! You can show the cross. But if the vampire is Jewish, then what? Then "Oy vey, bubbula! Have you ever got the wrong vampire!"

If you have a certain belief and life does not fit with it, what are you going to do? You can go on showing your crucifix – but the vampire is a Jew. Then he is not going to take any note of your cross. Then what are you going to do?

Life is so vast and beliefs are so small; life is so infinite and beliefs are so tiny. Life never fits with any belief and if you try to force life into your beliefs you are trying to do the impossible. It has never happened; it cannot happen in the nature of things. Drop all beliefs and start learning how to experience.

Now this story:

> *Once when the Hasidim were seated together*
> *in all brotherliness,*
> *pipe in hand, Rabbi Israel joined them.*
> *Because he was so friendly they asked him,*
> *"Tell us, dear Rabbi, how should we serve God?"*

A few things about Hasidism. First, the word *hasid* comes from a Hebrew word which means pious, pure. It is derived from the noun *hased*, which means grace.

This word *hasid* is very beautiful. The whole standpoint of Hasidism is based on grace. It is not that you *do* something, life is already happening – you just be silent, passive, alert, receiving. Godliness comes through grace, not through your effort. So Hasidism has no austerities prescribed for you. Hasidism believes in life, in joy. Hasidism is one of the religions in the world which is life-affirmative. It has no renunciation in it; you are not to renounce anything. Rather, you have to celebrate. The founder of Hasidism, Baal Shem, is reported to have said, "I have come to teach you a new way. It is not fasting and penance, and it is not indulgence, but joy in God."

The Hasid loves life, tries to experience life. That very experience starts giving you a balance. And in that state of balance, some day, when you are really balanced, neither leaning on this side nor leaning on that side, when you are exactly in the middle, you transcend. The middle is the beyond, the middle is the door from where one goes beyond.

If you really want to know what existence is, it is neither in life nor in death. Life is one extreme, death is another extreme. It is just exactly in the middle where neither death is nor life is, where one is simply unborn, deathless. In that moment of balance, equilibrium, grace descends.

I would like you all to become Hasids, receivers of grace. I would like you to learn this science, this art of balance.

The mind very easily chooses the extreme. There are people who indulge: they indulge in sensuality, sexuality, food, clothes, houses, this and that. There are people who indulge – they lean too much toward life, they fall down, they topple. Then there are people who, seeing people toppling down from the tightrope of existence into indulgence, falling into the abyss of indulgence, become afraid; they start leaning toward the other extreme. They renounce the world, they escape to the Himalayas. They escape from the wife, the children, the home, the world, the marketplace and they go and hide themselves in monasteries. They have chosen another extreme. Indulgence is extreme life; renunciation is extreme death.

So there is some truth in Friedrich Nietzsche's comment upon Hinduism – that Hinduism is a religion of death. There is some truth when Nietzsche says that Buddha seems to be suicidal. The truth is this: you can move from one extreme to another.

The whole Hasidic approach is not to choose any extreme, just to remain in the middle, available to both and yet beyond both, not getting identified with either, not getting obsessed and fixated with either: just remaining free and joyously enjoying both. If life comes, enjoy life; if death comes, enjoy death. If out of its grace existence gives love, life – good. If it sends death, it must be good – it is its gift.

Baal Shem is right when he says, "I have come to teach you joy in God." Hasidism is a celebrating religion. It is the purest flowering of the whole Judaic culture. Hasidism is the fragrance of the whole Jewish race. It is one of the most beautiful phenomena on the earth.

Once, when the Hasidim were seated together in all brotherliness... Hasidism teaches life in community. It is a very communal approach. It says that man is not an island, man is not an ego – should not be an ego, should not be an island. Man should live a life of community.

We are growing a Hasidic community here. To live in a community is to live in love; to live in a community is to live in commitment, caring for others.

There are many religions which are very, very self-oriented; they only think of the self, they never think of the community. They only think of how *I* am going to become liberated, how *I* am going to become free, how *I* should attain *moksha* – *my moksha, my* freedom, *my* liberation, *my* salvation. But everything is preceded by *my*, by the self. And these religions try hard to drop the ego, but their whole effort is based on the ego. Hasidism says if you want to drop the ego, the best way is to live in a community, live with people, be concerned with people – with their joy, with their sadness, with their happiness, with their life, with their death. Create a concern for the others, be involved, and then the ego will disappear on its own accord. And when the ego is not, one is free. There is no freedom of the ego, there is only freedom *from* the ego.

Hasidism uses community life as a device. Hasids have lived in small communities and they have created beautiful communities, very celebrating, dancing, enjoying the small things of life. They make the small things of life holy – eating, drinking. Everything takes the quality of prayer. The ordinariness of life is no longer ordinary, it is suffused with divine grace.

Once, when the Hasidim were seated together in all brotherliness... This is the difference. If you see Jaina monks sitting, you never see any brotherliness – it is not possible. The very approach is different. Each Jaina monk is an island. But the Hasids are not islands; they are a continent, a deep brotherliness.

Remember it. The community I would like to grow here should be more like the Hasidim, less like Jaina monks, because a man alone, confined to himself, is ugly. Life is in love, life is in flow, in give and take and sharing.

You can go to a Jaina monastery or a Jaina temple where

Jaina monks are sitting – you can just watch. You will see exactly how everybody is confined to himself; there is no relationship. That is the whole effort: how not to be related. The whole effort is how to disconnect all relationship.

But the more you are disconnected with community and life, the more dead you are. It is very difficult to find a Jaina monk who is still alive. And I know it very deeply because I was born a Jaina and I have watched them from my very childhood. I was simply surprised! What calamity has happened to these people? What has gone wrong? They are dead. They are corpses. If you don't go near them already prejudiced – thinking that they are great saints – if you simply go, observing without any prejudice, you will be simply puzzled, confused. What illness, what disease has happened to these people? They are neurotic. Their concern about themselves has become their neurosis.

Community has completely lost meaning for them – but all meaning is in community. Remember, when you love somebody, it is not only that you give love to them – in giving, *you* grow. When love starts flowing between you and the other you both are benefited, and in that exchange of love your potentialities start becoming actualities. That's how self-actualization happens. Love more and you will be more; love less and you will be less. You are always in proportion to your love. The proportion of your love is the proportion of your being.

Once, when the Hasidim were seated together in all brotherliness, pipe in hand... Can you think of any saint, pipe in hand? *...pipe in hand, Rabbi Israel joined them.* Ordinary life has to be hallowed, has to be made holy – even a pipe. You can smoke in a very prayerful way. Or, you can pray in a very unprayerful way. It is not a question of what you do. You can go into the temple, you can go into the mosque, but still you can pray in a very unprayerful way. It depends on you; it depends on the quality you bring to your prayer. You can eat, you can smoke, you can drink, and you can do all these small things, mundane things, in such gratitude that they become prayers.

Just the other night a man came. He bowed down and touched my feet. But the way he was doing it was, I could see, very unprayerful. He was an Indian, so he was doing it just out of duty, it seemed. Or he was not even conscious of what he was doing; he must have been taught. But I could feel, I could see his energy was absolutely unprayerful. And I was wondering why he had come. He wanted to become a sannyasin. I never refuse, but I wanted to refuse him. I thought for a moment what to do. If I refuse, it doesn't look good – and the man is absolutely wrong. Finally I said, "Okay, I will give you sannyas" – because I cannot refuse, I cannot say no. That word I feel very difficult to use.

So I gave him sannyas, and then everything became clear. Immediately after sannyas he said, "I have come to your feet, now help me. I am posted" – he was in the army – "I have been posted somewhere in Palanpur. Now, Osho, with your spiritual power, help me to be transferred to Ranchi."

My spiritual power has to be used for his transfer to Ranchi! Now what type of concept does he have of spiritual power? Now everything was clear. He was not interested in sannyas – that taking sannyas was just a bribery. He must have thought that if he asks for the transfer without sannyas it won't look good. So first become a sannyasin and then ask.

Just to *think* in these terms is unprayerful, unspiritual. And that man thinks he is very spiritual. He says he is a follower of Paramahansa Yogananda and the way he said it was so egoistic, he felt so good, so superior – "I am a follower of Paramahansa Yogananda; I am a disciple. And I have been working on myself for many years, and that's why I want to go to Ranchi." Ranchi is the center of Paramahansa Yogananda's disciples.

Now this man is absolutely unspiritual. His whole approach is unspiritual, unprayerful.

The point that I want to make clear to you is this: that it does not depend on what you *do*. You can touch my feet in a very unprayerful way – then it is meaningless; but you can smoke and you can do it in a prayerful way and your prayer will reach to existence.

It is very difficult for people who have very fixed concepts about religion, spirituality, but I would like you to become more liquid. Don't have fixed concepts. Watch.

...pipe in hand, Rabbi Israel joined them. Because he was so friendly they asked him, "Tell us dear Rabbi, how should we serve God?" Yes, only in deep friendliness can something be asked. And only in deep friendliness can something be answered. Between the master and the disciple there is a tremendous friendship. It is a love affair. And the disciple has to wait for the right moment and the master has also to wait for the right moment; when the friendship is flowing, when there is no hindrance, then things can be answered. Or even, sometimes, without answering them, they can be answered; even without using verbalization the message can be delivered.

*He was surprised at the question,
and replied, "How should I know?"*

In fact, that is the answer of all those who know: How should I know? "How to serve God? You are asking such a great question, I am not worthy to answer it," said the master. "How should I know?"

Nothing can be known about love; nothing can be known about how to serve God – it is very difficult.

But then he went on to tell them this story...

First he says, "How should I know?" First he says that knowledge is not possible about such things. First he says that he cannot give you any knowledge about such things. First he says that he cannot make you more knowledgeable about these things – there is no way. But then he tells his story.

A story is totally different from talking in terms of theories.

A story is more alive, more indicative. It does not say much, but it shows much. And all the great masters have used stories, parables, anecdotes. The reason is that if you say something directly, it kills much. A direct expression is too crude, primitive, gross, ugly. The parable is saying the thing in a very indirect way. It makes things very smooth; it makes things more poetic, less logical, closer to life, more paradoxical. You cannot use a syllogism for God, you cannot use any argument, but you can tell stories.

And the Jewish race is one of the richest races on the earth for parables. Jesus was a Jew, and he has told a few of the most beautiful parables ever uttered. Jews have learned how to tell stories. In fact Jews don't have much philosophy, but they have beautiful philosophical parables. They say much; without saying, without hinting anything directly, they create an atmosphere. In that atmosphere something can be understood. That is the whole device of a parable.

But then he went on to tell them this story... First he said, "How should I know?" First he simply denies any knowledge or any possibility to know about it. A philosopher says, "Yes, I know" and a philosopher proposes a theory in clear-cut statements – logical, mathematical, syllogistic, argumentative. He tries to convince. He may not convince, but he can force you into silence.

A parable never tries to convince you. It takes you unaware, it persuades you, it tickles you deep inside.

The moment the master says, "How should I know?" he is saying to them, "Relax, I am not going to give any argument for it, any theory for it. And you need not be worried that I am going to convince you about something. Just enjoy a little parable, a little story." When you start listening to a story, you relax; when you start listening to a theory, you become tense. And that which creates tension in you cannot be of much help. It is destructive.

But then he went on to tell them this story...

There were two friends of the king,
and both were proved guilty of a crime.
Since he loved them the king wanted to show them mercy,
but he could not acquit them
because even a king's word cannot prevail over the law.
So he gave this verdict:
A rope was to be stretched over a deep chasm,
and, one after another, the two were to walk across it.
Whoever reached to the other side
was to be granted his life.

A parable has an atmosphere, a very homely atmosphere –
as if your grandmother is telling you a story when you are
falling asleep. Children ask, "Tell us stories." It helps them relax
and go into sleep. A story is very relaxing and does not create
any pressure on your mind; rather, it starts playing with your
heart. When you listen to a story, you don't listen from the
head – you cannot listen to a story from the head. If you listen
from the head you will miss. If you listen from the head there is
no possibility of understanding a story; a story has to be understood from the heart. That's why races and countries which are
very "heady" cannot understand beautiful jokes. For example,
Germans! They cannot understand. They are one of the most
intelligent races of the world, but they don't have any good
stock of jokes.

A man was telling a German – I have just overheard this – a
man was telling a German that he had heard a very beautiful
German joke.
The German said, "But remember, I am a German."
So the man said, "Okay, then I will tell it very, very slowly."

It is very difficult. Germany is the country of the professors,
logicians – Kant, Hegel, and Feuerbach – and they have always
been thinking through the head. They have cultivated the head,

73

they have created great scientists, logicians, philosophers, but they have missed something.

In India we don't have many jokes; there is a great poverty of spirit. You cannot find a specifically Hindu joke, no. All the jokes that go on in India are borrowed from the West. No Indian joke exists. I have not come across any. And you can rely on me because I have come across all the jokes of the world! No Hindu joke, as such, exists. What is the reason? Again, very intellectual people; they have been weaving and spinning theories. From the Vedas to Sarvapalli Radhakrishnan they have been just weaving and spinning theories and theories and they have got into it so deeply that they have forgotten how to tell a beautiful story or how to create a joke.

The Rabbi started telling this story – the disciples must have become relaxed, must have become relaxed *and* attentive. That's the beauty of a story: when a story is told you are attentive and yet not tense. You can relax and yet you are attentive. A passive attentiveness arises when you listen to a story. When you listen to a theory you become very tense. If you miss a single word you may not be able to understand it. You become more concentrated. When you listen to a story you become more meditative – there is nothing much to be lost. Even if a few words are lost here and there, nothing will be lost because if you just have the feel of the story you will understand it, it does not depend so much on the words.

The disciples must have relaxed, and the master told this story.

So the king gave this verdict:
A rope was to be stretched over a deep chasm,
and, one after another, the two were to walk across it.
Whoever reached to the other side
was to be granted his life.

Now, this sentence is very pregnant: *Whoever reached to the other sidewas to be granted his life.* Jesus says many times to his disciples, "Come unto me if you want life in abundance. If you want life in abundance, come to me." But life in abundance happens only to people who go beyond birth and death, who go beyond duality, to the other shore. The other shore, the other side, is just symbolic of the transcendental. But it is just a hint. Nothing is particularly said, just a hint is given.

And then the story moves on...

It was done as the king ordered,
and the first of the friends got safely across.

Now these are the two types of people. The first simply got safely across. Ordinarily we would like to inquire how to go on a rope. A tightrope stretched over a chasm – it is dangerous. Ordinarily we would like to know the ways and means and method, how to go. We would like to know how. The technique – there must be a technique. For centuries people have walked on tightropes.

But the first one simply walked without inquiring, without even waiting for the other. This is the natural tendency: to let the other go first. At least you will be able to watch and observe and that will be helpful for you. No, the first simply walked. He must have been a man of tremendous trust; he must have been a man of undoubting confidence. He must have been a man who has learned one thing in life: that there is only one way to learn and that is to live, to experience. There is no other way.

You cannot learn tightrope walking by watching a tightrope walker – no, never. Because the thing is not like a technology that you can observe from the outside, it is some inner balance that only the walker knows. And it cannot be transferred. He cannot just tell you about it; it cannot be verbalized. No tightrope walker can tell anybody how he manages.

You ride a bicycle. Can you tell anybody how you ride it? You know the balance; it is a sort of tightrope walking, just on two wheels, straight in one line. And you go fast and you go so trustingly. If somebody asks what the secret is, can you reduce it to a formula, just like H_2O? Can you reduce it to a maxim? You don't say, "This is the principle, I follow this principle." You will say, "The only way is for you to come and sit on the bike and I will help you to go on it. You are bound to fall a few times, and then you will know the only way to know is to know." The only way to know swimming is to swim – with all the dangers involved in it.

The first man must have come to a deep understanding in his life – that life is not like a textbook. You cannot be taught about it, you have to experience it. And the man must have been of tremendous awareness. He did not hesitate, he simply walked, as if he had always been walking on a tightrope. He had never walked before; it was for the first time.

But for a man of awareness everything is for the first time, and a man of awareness can do things perfectly, even when he is doing them for the first time. His efficiency does not come out of his past; his efficiency comes out of his presence. Let this be remembered: you can do things in two ways. You can do something because you have done it before – so you know how to do it, you need not be present to it, you can simply do it in a mechanical way. But if you have not done it before and you are going to do it for a first time, you have to be tremendously alert because now you don't have any past experience. So you cannot rely on the memory, you have to rely on awareness.

So these are the two sources of functioning: either you function out of memory, out of knowledge, out of the past, out of the mind; or you function out of awareness, out of the present, out of no-mind.

The first man must have been a man of no-mind, a man who knows that you can simply be alert and go on and see what happens, and whatsoever happens is good. A great courage.

...the first of the friends got safely across.
The other, still standing on the same spot, cried to him,

"Tell me, friend, how did you manage to cross?"

The second is the ordinary mind, the majority mind, the mass mind. The second wants to know first, how to cross it. Is there a method to it? Is there a technique to be learned? He is waiting for the other to say.

"Tell me, friend, how did you manage to cross?" The other must be a believer in knowledge. The other must have been a believer in others' experiences.

Many people come to me. They say, "Osho, tell us. What happened to you?" But what are you going to do about it? Buddha has told it, Mahavira has told it, Jesus has told it – what have you done about it? Unless it happens to you it is futile. I can tell you one more story and then that story can also join your record of memories, but that is not going to help.

Waiting for others' knowledge is waiting in vain because that which can be given by others has no worth, and that which is of any worth cannot be given and cannot be transferred.

The first called back,
"I don't know anything but this..."

Even though he had crossed he still said: *I don't know anything but this...* Because, in fact, life never becomes knowledge; it remains a very suffused experience, never knowledge. You cannot verbalize it, conceptualize it, you cannot put it into a clear-cut theory.

"I don't know anything but this:
whenever I felt myself toppling over to one side,
I leaned to the other."

"This much only can be said: that there were two extremes, left and right, and whenever I felt that I was going too much toward the left and the balance was getting lost, I leaned toward the right. But again I had to balance because then I started going too much to the right and again I felt the balance was getting lost. Again I leaned toward the left."

So he said two things. One, "I cannot formulate it as knowledge. I can only indicate. I don't know exactly what happened, but this much I can give as a hint to you. And that is not much; in fact, you need not have it. You will come across the experience yourself. But this much can be said."

Buddha was asked again and again, "What has happened to you?" And he would always say, "That cannot be said, but this much I can say to you – in what circumstances it happened. That may be of some help to you. I cannot tell about the ultimate truth, but I can tell how, on what path, with what method, in what situation I was when it happened, when the grace descended on me, when the benediction came to me."

The man says, *"...whenever I felt myself toppling over to one side, I leaned to the other."*

"That's all. Nothing much to it. That's how I balanced, that's how I remained in the middle." And in the middle is grace.

The Rabbi is saying to his disciples, "You ask how we should serve God?" He was indicating with this parable: remain in the middle.

Don't indulge too much and don't renounce too much. Don't be only in the world and don't escape out of it. Go on keeping balance. When you feel that now you are falling into too much indulgence, lean toward renunciation, and when you feel that now you are going to become a renunciate, an ascetic, lean back again to indulgence. Keep in the middle.

On the road in India you will find boards saying "Keep to the Left" – in America you will find "Keep to the Right". In the world there are only two types of people: a few keep to the left, a few keep to the right. The third type is the very pinnacle of consciousness. And there the rule is "Keep to the Middle". Don't try it on the road, but on life's way keep to the middle: never to the left, never to the right, just to the middle.

And in the middle there will be glimpses of balance. There is a point – you can understand, you can feel it – there is a point when you are not leaning to either extreme, you are exactly in the middle. In that split second suddenly there is grace, everything is in equilibrium.

And that's how one can serve existence. Remain in balance and it becomes a service to existence; remain in balance and existence is available to you and you are available to existence.

Life is not a technology, not even a science; life is an art – or it would even be better to call it a hunch. You have to feel it. It is like balancing on a tightrope.

The Rabbi has chosen a beautiful parable. He has not talked about God at all; he has not talked about service at all; he has not really answered the question at all directly. The disciples must have themselves forgotten about the question – that's the beauty of a parable. It doesn't divide your mind into a question and an answer, it simply gives you a hunch that this is how things are.

Life has no "know-how" about it. Remember, life is not American, it is not a technology. The American mind, or to be more specific, the modern mind, tends to create technologies out of everything. Even when there is meditation the modern mind immediately tends to create a technology out of it. Then we create machines, and man is getting lost, and we are losing all contact with life.

Remember, there are things which cannot be taught, but which can only be caught. I am here, you can watch me, you can look into me and you will see a balance and you will see a silence. It is almost tangible, you can touch it, you can hear it, you can see it. It is here. I cannot say what it is, I cannot specifically give you techniques how to attain to it. At the most I can tell you a few parables, a few stories. They will be just hints. Those that understand will allow those hints to fall into their hearts like seeds. In their time, in the right season, they will sprout and you will understand me really only on the day you also experience the same that I am experiencing. I have crossed to the other shore, you are shouting from the other side: *Tell me, friend, how did you manage to cross?* I can tell you only one thing: *"I don't know anything but this: whenever I felt myself toppling to the one side, I leaned to the other."*

Keep to the middle. Keep continuously alert that you don't lose the balance, and then everything will take care of itself.

If you can remain in the middle you remain available to existence, to its grace. If you can remain in the middle you can become a Hasid; you can become a receiver of grace. And exisence is grace. You cannot do anything to find it, you can only do one thing: not stand in its way. And whenever you move to an extreme you become so tense that that very tension makes you too solid; whenever you are in the middle tension disappears, you become liquid, fluid. And you are no more in the way. When you are in the middle you are no longer in the way of existence – or let me tell you it in this way: when you are in the middle you are not. Exactly in the middle that mircle happens – that you are nobody, you are a nothingness.

This is the secret key. It can open the lock of mystery, of existence, to you.

Enough for today.

4

Let It Be So

The first question:

Osho,
Something has happened to me through you, but it is
something which is inexpressible. What it is I don't
know. But even then it is there.

T he human mind tends to convert every experience into a
question. That is a very destructive step. Please avoid it. Here
near me the whole purpose is to know that which is not know-
able, to know that which is not expressible, to know that which
cannot be put into words. When it starts happening don't make
a problem out of it, don't create a question out of it, because
your very questioning will become a stopping. Then your mind
will have started something else. Then you are distracted.

When it starts happening, enjoy it, love it, be nourished by
it, savor it, dance it, sing it, but don't make a question about it.
Just *be* it. And allow it total space. It will grow. It needs space in
you to grow.

Don't be in a hurry to make a theory out of it. Theories

are very dangerous. They can kill the child in the womb. The moment you start thinking in terms of analyzing, knowing what it is and what it is not, comparing, labeling, you are moving toward an abortion. You will miss something that was going to grow – you killed it. Don't be suicidal, don't be analytical, just allow it. Feel its presence – but not with the mind. Feel its presence with your totality. Let your heart be open to it and it will grow.

And in that very growth, by and by understanding will come. Understanding is not going to come through analysis, through thinking, through brooding, through logic. Understanding is going to come by deeper and deeper experience.

You say something has happened to you through me, but it is something which is inexpressible. Let it be so. Be happy. You are blessed. When something inexpressible starts happening then you are on the right track, you are moving toward godliness, the ultimate mystery. Whenever you have something within you which you cannot understand, that simply shows something bigger than you has entered in you – otherwise you could have understood it, you could have figured it out. Something bigger than the mind has penetrated you, a ray of light in the dark soul, a ray of light in the dark night of the mind. The mind cannot comprehend it; it is beyond its understanding. But not beyond understanding, remember. Beyond the understanding that is possible for the mind, but not beyond understanding – because there is understanding which is not of the mind: the understanding of the total organism, of your total being, of your totality.

But that comes not by analysis, not by dissection; it comes by absorbing the experience. Eat it! That which is inexpressible has to be eaten by you. Jesus says to his disciples, "Eat me." That's what he means: eat the inexpressible, eat the unknown. Digest it, let it circulate into your blood. Let it become part of you. And then you will know. And the knowing will arise as suddenly as the experience has arisen. Now a ray has entered in you. Allow it to become part of you – only then will you understand it.

This understanding is not the understanding you have been acquainted with up to now. You have known only the mind and its ways. It labels things very immediately. Whenever you ask what is this, what are you asking really? You see a bush and a flower and you say, "What is this?" Somebody says "a rosebush," and you think you have understood. Somebody has just uttered the word "rose" and you think you have understood.

But if you don't know the name you feel a little disturbed. That unknown flower confronts you, challenges you. You feel your prestige is at stake. Because that unknown flower continuously says, "You don't know me, so what kind of knowledge is yours? You even don't know me?" That flower goes on hitting hard at you and you start feeling disturbed. You want to know so that you can finish with this challenge. You go to the library, you look at the books, at the *Encyclopedia Britannica;* you find out what the name of this rose is. It is *rose* – okay, you have labeled it. Now you can be at ease.

But what have you done? Just by putting a word to the rosebush do you think you have understood it? You have lost an opportunity of understanding. You have lost a great challenge. Because remember well – the name 'rose' is given by man to the rosebush, the rosebush does not know the name at all. If you talk about the rosebush to the rosebush, the rosebush will not understand it. What are you talking about? What nonsense are you talking about? The rosebush has no name as far as the bush itself is concerned – the name is given by others, given by people like you who cannot tolerate the unknowable anywhere.

The unknowable is such an uneasy thing, it creates so much discomfort. You see somebody; you say, "Who is this man?" And then somebody says he is a Chinese, or an African, or a Japanese, and you feel at ease. What have you known? Just by saying that he is a Chinese… There are millions of Chinese – one billion – and no other Chinese is like him. In fact, nothing exists like *the* Chinese. There are millions and millions of Chinese; each individual is unique, different; each has his own signature, his own being. What have you understood by labeling a man as a Chinese? But you feel at ease.

What religion does he belong to? He is a Buddhist. Another label has come into your hand. You know a little more now. To what party does he belong? He is a communist. Still a few more labels you gather – and then you think you have known the man.

Is knowledge as cheap as the mind thinks? Labeling is not knowledge. Labeling is a way to avoid the opportunity that was open. You could have known the man if you had got involved with him. You could have known the rosebush if you had meditated alone with it, if you had allowed its fragrance to enter into your nostrils and into your heart; if you had touched it with love. If you had a communion with this rosebush you might have known something.

I don't say you can know the rosebush totally. If you can know a single rosebush totally then you have known the whole universe – because in the single rosebush the whole universe is involved: the sun and the moon and the stars and the past and the present and the future. All time and all space is converging on that small roseflower. If you can know it in its totality you will have known the whole universe. Then nothing is left behind. Each small thing is so great.

And when something like an unknown flower starts blooming within you, don't be in a hurry to dissect it; don't put it on the table and cut it and start looking for the ingredients. Enjoy it. Love it. Help it to grow. A grace has descended upon you. You have become a Hasid.

That is the meaning of *hasid* – grace.

The second question:

Osho,
Lord Shiva disclosed many techniques of equilibrium

unto Devi, his consort in *Vigyan Bhairav Tantra*. Will
you please say something about those techniques in
reference to the Hasidic art of equilibrium, balance?

No, I will not say anything about those techniques – because
Hasidism is absolutely non-technical. The whole approach is non-
technical. Hasidism has no technique – just a sheer joy in life.

Hasidism is not a path of meditation, it is a path of prayerfulness. Prayerfulness has no techniques. Meditation can have
millions of techniques because meditation is a scientific approach
to inner reality. Hasidism is not a science, it is an art. Hasidism
does not believe in techniques, but in love.

Remember well, the technological mind is a mathematical
mind. The mind of the lover is non-mathematical; the mind of
the lover is the mind of the poet. Love is a romance, not a technique. Love is a dream not a technique. Love has a totally
different approach to life.

Hasidism has no techniques; it has no yoga, no tantra in it.
It simply says: trust life, trust existence, and whatsoever has
been given to you, enjoy it. Enjoy it so deeply and with such
gratitude that every ordinary thing becomes hallowed, becomes
holy, each small thing in life becomes sacred. Transform everything into a sacred thing – the profane disappears. You bring
your energy of love, grace, gratitude.

Love is not a technique, so nobody can teach you how
to love. And if you come across books which say that they can
teach you how to love, beware of those books. If you once learn
the techniques of love you will never be able to love again. Those
techniques will become a barrier. Love is a natural spontaneous
phenomenon. Even animals are loving – they don't have Kinseys
and Masters and Johnsons and they are achieving orgasm perfectly, without any scientific help. They don't have any sex ther-
apists and they don't go to any guru to be taught how to love. It
is an inborn quality. Each being born brings it with himself.

There are a few things which you bring with your birth.

A child is born; nobody can teach the child how to breathe. If it depended on teaching then nobody would be able to be alive, because time would be needed to teach the child. He would first have to be sent to school, taught language, disciplined, and then finally, after at least seven, eight or ten years, we would be able to teach him how to breathe – he doesn't understand even the word *breathe*. No, it doesn't depend on any teaching. The child is born with the capacity to breathe; it is inborn. It is as inborn as a flower on a bush. It is as inborn as water rushing toward the ocean – naturally.

The moment a child is born the whole being of the child hankers, becomes hungry for breath – not knowing what is happening because the child has never breathed before. Nobody has ever taught him, he has never done it, he has no experience about it – it simply happens.

In exactly the same way, one day, at the age of fourteen, the child starts feeling a tremendous attraction toward the other sex. Nobody has taught it; in fact, teachers have been teaching against it. The whole human history seems to be a teaching against sexuality, against sex energy. Religions, cultures, civilizations, priests and politicians – they have all been teaching how to suppress sex. But still it cannot be suppressed. It seems it is impossible to suppress it.

It is a natural phenomenon. It arises. It arises even when you are against it – see the truth of it. Even when you are against it, it arises in spite of you. It is bigger than you. You cannot control it. It is natural.

Hasidism says that if a man starts living a natural life, one day, suddenly, the love of existence arises as naturally as love for the woman or love for the man arises; as naturally as breathing arises after birth. That precious moment cannot be managed; you cannot plan for it, you cannot prepare for it, there is no need. You simply live a natural life. Don't fight with nature, float with it, and one day suddenly you will see that the grace has descended on you. A tremendous urge has arisen in your being, a new love toward existence – call it godliness. Because when love arises, existence becomes personal. Then it is no more "it"; it becomes "thou". Then it is a relationship between "I" and "thou".

Hasidism simply says don't be unnatural and prayerfulness will be born on its own accord. It has no techniques. And that's the beauty of it.

If you have missed the natural flowering of prayerfulness – then techniques are needed. Meditation is a substitute for prayerfulness; it is second to prayerfulness. If you have missed prayer then meditation is needed, but if prayerfulness has arisen in you then there is no need for any meditation. Prayerfulness is spontaneous meditation; meditation is prayerfulness with effort. Prayerfulness with technique is meditation; meditation without technique is prayerfulness.

Hasidism is the religion of prayerfulness, that's why in Hasidism there is no renunciation. A Hasid lives the natural life that existence has conferred on him. Wherever existence has placed him, he lives, he loves; he enjoys the small pleasures of life. And once you start enjoying the small pleasures, the total accumulative effect is a great bliss in your being.

This has to be understood. Don't wait for some great bliss to descend on you. It never happens. Great bliss is nothing but small pleasures accumulating in your being. The total of all the small pleasures is the great bliss. Eating, enjoy it. Drinking, enjoy it. Taking a bath, enjoy it. Walking, enjoy it. Such a beautiful world, such a beautiful morning, such beautiful clouds... What else do you need to celebrate? The sky full of stars... What more do you need to be prayerful? The sun rising from the east... What more do you need to bow down? And amidst a thousand and one thorns a small roseflower arises, opening its buds, so fragile, so vulnerable, yet so strong, so ready to fight with the wind, with the lightning, with the thunder. Look at the courage. What more do you need to understand trust?

Techniques are needed when you have missed these small

openings toward godliness. If you go on looking in the small openings, the total effect is a great door. And suddenly you start seeing
what prayer is. Not only seeing, you start living it.

Hasidism is a totally different approach from Tantra. And
Hasidism is far superior to any Tantra, because it is the natural
Tantra, it is the natural way. It is the way of Tao.

But the mind is very cunning. The mind wants to manipulate. The mind wants to manipulate even the relationship of love;
the mind wants to manipulate even the mysterious phenomenon
of prayerfulness. The mind is a great controller. The obsession of
the mind is to control everything, not to allow anything beyond
control – hence technique. The mind is always asking for techniques and the mind goes on planning for every possibility.

If you plan for every possibility, if you manage for everything on your own, you never give a chance to existence to penetrate you, to take control onto his shoulders. You never allow
existence to help you. You think you have to be independent;
you think there is no other way than self-help. You remain
unnecessarily poor.

A small child was playing around his father, who was sitting
in the garden, and the small child was trying to pull up a big
rock. It was too big and he could not do it. He tried hard. He
was perspiring.

The father said, "You are not using all your energies."

The child said, "Wrong. I am using all my energy. And I
don't see what more I can do."

The father said, "You have not asked me to help. That too
is your energy. I am sitting here and you have not asked me to
help. You are not using all your energy."

A man who lives through techniques may think he is using
all his energies, but he has not asked for existence's help. A man
who is simply meditating with a technique is a poor man. A
Hasid is tremendously rich because he is really using all his

energies. A Hasid is open; a technique-oriented mind is a closed mind. It goes on planning everything. If your plans are fulfilled then too you will not be happy, because they are your plans. They are as small as you are. Even if you succeed you will be a failure; even in your success you will have the taste of frustration. Because what will you get? Or, if you fail, you will of course be frustrated. When you fail you are frustrated, but when you succeed then you are frustrated too.

Open yourself to the divine. You live naturally – not trying to improve, not living through ideals, not living through moral disciplines – just living a natural life. Nature should be your only discipline, and whatsoever is natural is good because that's how existence wills it to be, wants it to be. If you can accept your life with such gratefulness, that this is how existence wants it to be. If it has given sex to you, it has given sex to you – it knows better. You need not try to enforce any celibacy on yourself. An enforced celibacy is ugly, uglier than natural sex. And if you accept natural sex you will find that beyond a certain point natural sex becomes natural celibacy. Then *brahmacharya* arises. Then you start living in a totally different way. But it comes floating with the river of life.

Do you see? A river descends from the mountains, moves thousands of miles, then one day disappears into the ocean. If the river were a great thinker, and it started thinking, "This is going downward. I should not do that. My abode is on the mountains. A river is first just the snow peaks of the Himalayas – there is my abode. And I am falling. This is sin: falling down in a glacier, moving toward the earth from the height of the heaven." If rivers were thinkers they would go crazy, because this is going down, descending into hell. But rivers are not thinkers, they are very fortunate. They accept it. It was the will of existence to be on the hilltop, it is its will now to explore the depths.

And a person who really wants to know the height also has to know the depth, otherwise he will not be able to know. Depth is the other part of the height. The higher the peak of the mountain, the deeper the valley. If you want to know the tree, you have to know the roots also. The tree goes upward and the roots go downward. And the tree exists between this: the upward movement and the downward movement. This is the tension that gives life to the tree.

The river moves, trusting, not knowing where she is going. She has never gone before and she has no road map available, no guide to guide. But she goes trusting: if this is how it is happening it must be good. She goes singing and dancing. And then one day every river – whether it runs toward the East or whether it runs toward the West or the South or the North, it makes no difference – every river finally, eventually, reaches the ultimate, disappears into the ocean. In the ocean she has attained the final depth.

Now the journey is complete. She has known the peaks of the Himalayas, now she has known the depth of the ocean. Now the experience is total; now the circle is complete. Now the river can disappear into nirvana; now the river can disappear into *moksha*. This is what liberation is.

A Hasid lives like a river. He trusts. A man who is too much obsessed with techniques is a non-trusting man, a doubting man. He cannot trust in life, he trusts in his own techniques.

I have heard a very beautiful anecdote:

A gorilla collector was anxious to collect some more gorillas, so he went to Africa. Soon he found himself in the hut of a Great White Hunter.

"And how much do you charge for each catch?" asked the collector.

"Well," said the hunter, "I get five hundred dollars for myself, five hundred dollars for that little pygmy over there with the rifle, and five hundred dollars for my dog."

The collector couldn't figure out why the dog should get five hundred dollars, but being a practical man he reasoned that fifteen hundred dollars was reasonable and he didn't care how it got divided up.

On safari, the Great White Hunter spied a gorilla up a tree, whereupon he climbed up the tree and hit the gorilla over the head. As the gorilla fell to the ground, the dog ran over and grabbed it by the testicles with his teeth, rendering it motionless. Meanwhile the hunter climbed down the tree, brought a cage over, and pushed the gorilla in it.

The collector was flabbergasted. He said to the hunter, "This is simply fantastic! I have never seen anything like it in my life. You are certainly earning your five hundred dollars, and that dog – well, what can I say? – he's simply terrific. But that pygmy with the rifle – he doesn't seem to be doing a thing."

The hunter said, "Don't you worry about the pygmy. He earns his money."

So on and so forth it went, catching gorilla after gorilla, until finally he came across a gorilla who had been watching the whole proceedings. The Hunter climbed up the tree, and just as he was about to bash the gorilla over the head, the gorilla turned and bashed him first.

As the hunter was falling from the tree he yelled to the pygmy, "Shoot the dog! Shoot the dog!"

Now this is the technique-oriented mind. It arranges for everything, for every possibility. It does not leave a loophole in a system.

A religious man cannot be in such a planned way, it is not possible. He has to leave many loopholes for godliness to enter in. In fact, if you understand rightly, a religious man is one who plans nothing – because how can we plan? And what are our capacities for planning? We are limited. We have a small light of intelligence, but it is too tiny. Trusting it totally creates a very mediocre life. The vast never enters into this mediocre life; the infinite never enters into this mediocre life; the endless never enters into this mediocre life.

Hasidism is a very revolutionary step – a great risk is involved. The risk is in dropping the mind which seems to be our only security; dropping the mind which seems to be our only certainty; dropping the mind which seems to be our only capacity. And then trusting the no-mind – call it godliness – trusting existence, not trusting oneself. Hasidism is a great surrender.

The third question:

Osho,
Only one master at a time.

I can understand and appreciate your difficulty. I am talking about too many masters and too many paths and too many doors – and it is natural that you may start getting confused.

But you can get confused only if you cling to my words. If you don't cling to my words I am saying the same thing again and again and again, even though the words may be different and I may be using different approaches. And when I use any approach, any path, I am totally with it. Then I don't care about anything else. Even things that I have said before, I don't care about.

When I am talking about Hasids, I am a Hasid. And then I am totally involved in it. That's the only way to reveal its secret to you. If I remain uninvolved, if I remain without any passion, if I am just a spectator, a professor just explaining things to you, it won't give you the insight that is intended, it won't give you the vision. Then you will collect information and you will go home – you will become more knowledgeable, but not wise.

So whenever I am speaking about any master or any path or any scripture, I am totally with it, my involvement is absolute. In those moments nothing else exists for me because I am in a passion, I am passionately in love with that teaching.

Of course, I can understand your difficulty, because when I say passionately that Hasidism is the way, you become disturbed because one day I was saying Tantra is the way, another day I was saying Zen is the way, and another day I was saying Tao is the way. So now what is the way?

When I am talking about one way, I am that way. Don't cling to my words, listen to the wordless message. And if it hits your heart, if it sings in your heart, then you have found your way. Then forget whatsoever I have said before or whatsoever I am going to say in the future. Then you need not worry. You have found your key. Now you can open the lock.

I will go on talking because I am talking for millions. When you have found your key, enjoy whatsoever I say, but don't get disturbed by it again and again. You have found your key; now I must be talking for somebody else who has not yet found his key. When you have found your peace, your silence, your bliss, you have got what you were needing, but there are many others who have not got it. I will be talking for them and I will be using all the possibilities.

For example, when I am talking on Hasidism it may hit your heart deeply and your love may arise for this path. My passion may inflame you. That's why I speak with passion. If I speak with indifference as professors do… I am not a professor. When I am speaking on Hasidism I am a Hasid rabbi. Then it is my path that I am talking about. It is not somebody else's path that I am describing to you, it is my path that I have traveled, that I have loved, that I have known, that I have tasted. I am talking about my own experience, and if it hits and something clicks in your heart and prayer becomes your path, then forget whatsoever I am saying, then you need not reconsider again and again.

If it has not happened then you have to consider. If it has not happened then don't bother about it, forget all about it, I will be talking about something else, I will be opening another door – maybe that is the door for you. But when you have found the door then don't be worried about other doors that I will be opening because all the doors lead to the same. Don't you be worried that you should enter this door. "Maybe Osho is going to open another bigger and golden door." But they are all the same, and the door that you have fallen in love with is the golden door for you.

Now there is no other door if you have fallen in love with this door. And you will find others entering from other doors, but when you reach to the very center of existence, you will all be meeting there in tremendous love and brotherhood. Somebody will be a Hasid and somebody will be a Zen monk and somebody will be a Tibetan lama and somebody will be a Sufi and somebody has come through sitting silently and somebody has come dancing – but in deep brotherhood all seekers meet at the center.

I know it is very difficult. If you start choosing two masters you will be in conflict. Never choose two masters – one is enough, more than enough.

When Mulla Nasruddin was dying he called his son, told him to come close, and said to him, "My son, I have one thing to say to you – even though I know you will not listen, because I didn't listen to my own father when he was dying. He told me, 'Nasruddin, don't chase women too much.' But I could not resist; the temptation was too much. And I got involved with one woman, another woman…" He married nine women – the maximum that the Koran permits.

And he said, "I have created a hell. I suffered much. I know you don't listen, but still I am saying it, because now I am departing and there will be no chance to say it to you. I know you will fall in love with women, but at least remember one thing from your old man: My son, one at a time, one at a time. At least do that much."

One at a time. If you fall in love with two women at a time, what does it show? It shows you have a split personality. You are schizophrenic, you are not one, you are two. If you fall in love with three women at a time then you are three. And there are people who fall in love with any woman they see. Whosoever is passing, suddenly they are in love. Every woman is their love object. They are a crowd. You can count how many persons live in you by counting how many women you fall in love with simultaneously. That's a very beautiful way to measure how many persons live in you, a very easy criterion.

But to fall in love with one woman makes you a unity, gives you a unison, you become total. You become sane because then there is no conflict.

I have heard:

The bride and bridegroom stepped into the hotel elevator and the pretty girl operator said, "Hello, darling" to the bridegroom. Not another word was spoken until the couple alighted at their floor, when the bride exclaimed, "Who was that hussy?"

"Now, don't you begin anything," said the bridegroom quite worriedly. "I'm going to have enough trouble on my hands explaining you to her tomorrow."

Even to fall in love with two women is dangerous – but to fall in love with two masters is a million-fold more dangerous. Because the love of the woman may be only of the body, so the spirit goes only that far. Or at the most, the love of the woman may be of the mind, and the spirit goes only that far. But the love of the master is of the soul, and if you fall in love with two masters your soul will be divided, you will be totally disintegrated, you will start falling in parts, you will not be able to remain together. You will simply lose all shape and all form, all integrity. And the whole point in being with a master is to attain to integration.

Once you fall in love with a master, remain. I am not saying that even when you are disillusioned remain with him. When you are disillusioned, he is no longer your master. Then there is no point in remaining with him. Then seek another.

But never be with two masters in your mind simultaneously. Be decisive about it – because this decision is no ordinary decision, it is very momentous. It will decide your whole being: its quality, its future.

The fourth question:

Osho,
You are really mischievous. You tell us that you want
to break our houses so that we can enter in your
house, but I have seen it. Your house has no floor, no
walls, no ceiling. So I go on looking from the porch
grabbing onto a pillar, afraid to be sucked in.

That's true. My whole effort is to trick you in; to trick you
in for something you have never desired.

A disciple and the master are in a great conflict; a great
struggle goes on. And the disciple can win only if he is unfortunate. If the master wins it, the disciple is blessed, very fortunate.
The struggle is because the disciple has come to the master for
wrong reasons; maybe he has come to seek some sort of spiritual
ego. He has failed in life – money, power, prestige, respectability,
success in the marketplace, ambitions in the political world –
he has failed there. He could not attain to the very peak of his
egoistic journey; he could not become a president or a prime
minister. Now life is running out of his hands and he wants to be
somebody. It is very, very uncomfortable to remain a nobody.

Finally people start seeking and searching into the dimension of religion. There it seems easier. There it seems easier to
attain to a certain ego, a certain crystallization of the ego. At
least you can become an Osho sannyasin – so simple. And you
can feel great. You can feel that you have become special.

The so-called religious people are trying to attain some
thing which they have not been able to attain in the world.
Sometimes they try by austerities, asceticism. Somebody fasts for
days together, he becomes special – nobody can fast that much.
He may be a masochist, he may be a self-torturer – he has to be.
Or he may be suicidal. He has to be. But he starts getting respect
from people, he is a great mahatma. He fasts so much; he is
against the body, he is against comfort. He can lie down on a bed

of thorns, or he can stand for years. Or he can sit on a pillar in a desert for years – just sitting there on a pillar. Very uncomfortable. He cannot sleep, he cannot rest, but then he attracts people.

Suddenly he has become very important. Even those prime ministers and presidents that he wanted to become and failed to, start coming to him because they think that if such a great ascetic can bless them, they can rise more in the world of power. He feels very gratified, contented. Now the ego is at the supermost. Even kings and prime ministers and presidents are coming to him.

The disciple comes for wrong reasons. Or a disciple comes to attain a certain sort of peace because he is in much turmoil. Why does he want to attain to peace? He wants to attain to peace so that he can work out his ambitions in a better way.

Just the other day I was looking at an advertisement for Maharishi Mahesh Yogi's Transcendental Meditation. It promises everything: a good job, proficiency in your work, health – mental health, physical health – longevity; everything that a man can desire it promises. It is a long list: economic, spiritual, social, physical, psychological. All these benefits just for sitting for twenty minutes and repeating something stupid: "Coca-Cola, Coca-Cola," or something like that.

So simple! That's why it is said that you should not tell your mantra to anybody – otherwise they will laugh! It has to be kept private. If you say to somebody that I repeat "Coca-Cola, Coca-Cola," they will think you have gone mad. So a mantra has to be kept absolutely private. You will keep it private anyway because it will look so absurd to tell it to anybody.

Just twenty minutes repeating any nonsense word and you get so many benefits? It appeals to the mediocre mind immediately. This Maharishi Mahesh Yogi's meditation is neither meditation nor transcendental; it is simply an effort to exploit the gullible, to exploit the people who are searching and seeking for everything, searching for a panacea, searching for a remedy.

When you come to a real master he says there is no remedy, he says there is no panacea. And he does not say that he will make you peaceful and healthy and this and that and then you can go into the world and rush after your ambition in a more efficient way. No, he will say you are disturbed, you are in a turmoil *because* of the ambition. Drop the ambition! A real master can only promise you that he will take away your ambition, he will take away your ego. He can only promise that he will kill you. You have come to be protected, you have come to attain to some security, you have come to find some props – but a real master is one who takes your props, prop by prop, away from you. One day you simply collapse. And in that very collapse, out of the ashes, arises a new being. That new being has nothing to do with you. That new being is so new it is discontinuous with you. It has no past, it has no future, it has only a pure presence, herenow.

The question is from Krishna Radha. She is right. "You are really mischievous." I am. So beware of me. And if you can escape in time, good. Otherwise how long can you cling to the porch? If you have entered the porch it is not very far to the house.

And the porch is also imaginary because the house has no floor, no roof, no walls – how can such a house have a porch? Just think about it. The porch is just imaginary.

I help you to see the porch so you can at least enter the porch – then the journey becomes easier. I sometimes promise you things which you ask for, simply to help you to be here a little longer. Your very understanding will tell you by and by that you were asking for foolish things. And then one day suddenly you will find that the porch has disappeared and, of course, that the house had never existed.

But the house that has no walls to it and no roof and no floor is the house of existence – because the very sky is its roof and the very earth is its floor and the no-boundaries are its boundaries.

Yes, I am not taking you into any house which has boundaries because then that house will prove again another imprisonment, it will be another prison. Maybe a little more comfortable, a little more decorated, maybe furnished in a little more modern way and a modern style, but still a prison.

My house is a house of freedom. It is exactly what Radha says "...Your house has no floor, no walls, no ceiling, so I am looking from the porch, grabbing a pillar." Look again. The pillar exists not. Because you want to grab, you believe in the pillar. Look again. Open your eyes. There is no pillar and there is no point in grabbing. Relax. Let go. And suddenly you disappear and you become the infinity, you become the space. That is what godliness is – space with no boundaries.

My house is the house of existence, it is not a man-made temple.

I have heard an anecdote:

Two office workers had a drink or two at a midtown bar after the labors of the day. One offered a third round, but his friend refused, saying he'd better get home and explain to his wife.

"Explain what?" asked the friend.

"How do I know? I'm not home yet."

Don't go on standing on the porch. You will not know by standing on the porch. Come home. Disappear in this infinity that I am making available to you. Only then will you know. And there is no need for any explanation then, no need for any theory then, no need for any rationalization then – because the experience itself is self-evident proof. You have lived in small houses and small dark cells up to now and you cannot believe that one can live in such absolute freedom. You have lost the capacity to be free.

That capacity has to be relearned, that capacity has to be reclaimed. I am not here to discipline you, I am not here to give you principles – my whole effort is to give you an unprincipled life, a spontaneous, undisciplined life. The only gift that I can present to you is freedom. And freedom has no walls to it, it is as infinite as the sky. Claim the whole sky – it is yours.

The fifth question:

Osho,
Who can become a better disciple: a learned fool or
an unlearned fool? And for the intelligentsia please
explain your dictum: Blessed are the fools.

I don't see any intelligentsia here – except blessed fools.
Maybe the questioner can be excluded – Pundit Swami Yoga
Chinmaya. He can be excluded. But otherwise I don't see any
intelligentsia here.

There is a very strange saying of Mohammed – that heaven
is mostly occupied by fools. When I came across it even I was
surprised. I had never expected Mohammed to be so revolutionary. A tremendous saying! What does he mean by it – that
heaven is mostly occupied by fools? But by and by, looking
at you, I felt that he is right! Here also it is mostly occupied
by fools.

Let me explain to you how many types of fools there are.
The first: one who knows not, and knows not that he knows
not – the simple fool. Then the second: one who knows not but
knows that he knows. The complex fool, the learned fool. And
the third: one who knows that he knows not – the blessed fool.

Everybody is born as a simple fool – that is the meaning of
simpleton. Every child is a simple fool. He knows not that he
knows not. He has not yet become aware of the possibility
of knowing – that is the meaning of the Christian parable of
Adam and Eve.

God said to them, "Don't eat the fruit of the Tree of
Knowledge." Before that accident of eating the fruit of the Tree
of Knowledge they were simple fools. They knew nothing. Of
course, they were tremendously happy, because when you know
not, it is difficult to be unhappy. Unhappiness needs a little

training; unhappiness needs a little efficiency to create it; unhappiness needs a little technology. You cannot create hell without knowledge. How can you create hell without knowledge?

Adam and Eve were like small children. Every time a child is born an Adam is born. And he lives for a few years, at the most four years; that time is becoming less and less every day. He lives in paradise because he knows not how to create misery. He trusts life; he enjoys small things: pebbles on the shore, or seashells, and gathers them as if he has found a treasure. Ordinary colored stones look like *Kohinoors*. Everything fascinates him – the dew-drops in the morning sun, the stars in the night, the moon, the flowers, the butterflies – everything is a sheer fascination.

But then by and by he starts knowing: a butterfly is just a butterfly, a flower is just a flower. There is nothing much in it. He starts knowing the names: this is a rose, and that is a *champa* and that is a *chameli* and this is a lotus. And by and by those names become barriers. The more he knows, the more he is cut off from life as such. He becomes heady. Now he lives through the head, not through his totality. That is the meaning of "the fall". He has eaten of the Tree of Knowledge. Every child has to eat of the Tree of Knowledge.

Every child is so simple that he has to become complex – that is part of the growth. So every child moves from simple foolishness toward complex foolishness. There are different degrees of complex foolishness – a few people only matriculate, a few people become graduates, a few become postgraduates, a few become doctors and PhD's – there are degrees. But every child has to taste something of knowledge because the temptation to know is great. Anything that is standing there unknown becomes dangerous, a danger. It has to be known because with knowledge we will be able to cope with it. Without knowledge how are we going to cope with it? So every child is bound to become knowledgeable.

So the first type of fool necessarily, out of necessity, has to become the second type of fool. But from the second the third may happen or may not happen, there is no necessity. The third is possible only when the second type of foolishness has become such a burden: one has carried knowledge too much, to the extreme; one has become just the head and has lost all sensitivity, all awareness, all living; one has become just theories and scriptures and dogmas and words and words whirling around in the mind. One day, if the person is aware, he has to drop all that. Then he becomes the third type of fool – the blessed fool.

Then he attains to a second childhood; again he is a child. Remember Jesus' saying, "In my kingdom of God only those who are like small children will be welcomed." But remember, he says *like* small children, he does not say "small children". Small children cannot enter; they have to learn the ways of the world, they have to be poisoned in the world and then they have to clean themselves. That experience is a must.

So he does not say "small children" he says those who are like small children. That word *like* is very significant. It means those who are not children and yet are like children. Children are saints, but their sainthood is only because they have not yet experienced the temptations of sin. Their saintliness is very simple. It has not much worth in it because they have not earned it, they have not worked for it, they have not yet been tempted against it. The temptations are coming sooner or later. A thousand and one temptations will be there and the child will be pulled in many directions. I am not saying that he should not go in those directions. If he inhibits himself, represses himself from going, he will remain always the first type of fool. He will not become part of Jesus' kingdom, he will not be able to fill Mohammed's paradise – no. He will simply remain ignorant. His ignorance will be nothing but a repression, it will not be an unburdening.

First he has to attain to knowledge, first he has to sin, and only after sin and knowledge and disobeying God and going into the wildness of the world, going astray, living his own life of the ego, will he become capable one day to drop it all.

Not everybody will drop it all. All children move from the first foolishness to the second, but from the second only a few blessed ones move to the third – hence they are called blessed fools.

The blessed fool is the greatest possibility of understanding because he has come to know that knowledge is futile, he has come to know that all knowledge is a barrier to knowing. Knowledge is a barrier to knowing, so he drops knowledge and becomes a pure knower. He simply attains to clarity of vision. His eyes are empty of theories and thoughts. His mind is no more a mind; his mind is just intelligence, pure intelligence. His mind is no longer cluttered with junk, his mind is no longer cluttered with borrowed knowledge. He is simply aware. He is a flame of awareness.

Tertullian has divided knowledge into two categories: one he calls "ignorant knowledge" – that is the second fool, the ignorant knowledge. The pundit knows and yet does not know, because he has not known it as his own experience. He has listened, memorized; he is a parrot, a computer at the most.

Just yesterday I received a letter from a sannyasin, from America. He says, "Osho, I am very happy. And in the office where I work, the computer welcomes me every morning. The computer says, 'Swamiji, Namaste.'" Now he is very happy. And he knows well it is a computer which is saying, "Swamiji, Namaste." There is nobody. But even the word makes him happy. He knows it is just a machine – there is nobody, there is no heart in it. Nobody is saying it.

When a pundit says something he is a computer. He says, "Swamiji, Namaste." It is parrot-like. Tertullian says this is the knowledge which is really not knowledge, but ignorance in the garb of knowledge, ignorance in the disguise of knowledge. It is a fall, a fall from the childhood innocence. It is a corruption. It is a corrupt state of mind. Cunning, clever, but corrupt.

Then, Tertullian says, there is another type of knowledge which he calls "knowing ignorance". This is when a person drops all knowledge, theories, looks directly, looks into life as it is, has no ideas about it, allows reality as it is, encounters reality immediately, directly, with no knowledge about it, faces and encounters reality, allows that which is to have its flowering. He simply listens to reality, looks into reality – and he says, "I don't know." He is the child Jesus talks about – he is not really a child, he is like a child. And I say, "Yes, blessed are the fools because they shall inherit all the blessings of existence."

From the first, the second is automatic; from the second, the third is not automatic. From the second to the third the leap has to be a decision – that's what sannyas is. You decide that you have had enough of knowledge; now you would like to be ignorant again, you would like to be a child again, reborn. I am a midwife here. I can help you to become fools. And remember, unless you have attained to the third, your whole life is a sheer wastage.

Adam disobeyed God: every Adam has to disobey. Adam fell from grace: every Adam has to fall. Adam ate the fruit of the Tree of Knowledge: every Adam has to become knowledgeable, it is a natural process. I have come across thousands of parables, but nothing to compare with this parable of Adam's fall. It is the most pregnant parable ever. That's why I come to it again and again with new meanings; it goes on revealing new meanings.

And when Adam turned into Christ he became the third type of fool. Christ is the third type of fool – the blessed fool. What Adam did, Christ undid. Christ returns back in tremendous obedience, innocence.

The rabbis, the Jewish religious people, the priests of the temple of Jerusalem, they were learned fools. They could not tolerate Jesus. The learned fools are always disturbed by the blessed fools. They had to murder him because his very presence was uncomfortable; his very presence was such a pinnacle of peace, love, compassion and light, that all the learned fools became aware that their whole being was at stake. If this man lived then they were fools, and the only way to get rid of this man was to destroy him so they could again become the learned people of the race.

Socrates was killed by knowledgeable people; Mansoor was killed by other knowledgeable people. There has always been a great conflict whenever the third type of fool arises in the world. All the pundits gather together; their whole business is at stake. All that they know, this man says is foolish. And they also know deep in their hearts that it is foolish because it has done nothing for them. No bliss, no benediction has come out of it. They are as they always have been – their knowledge has not touched their hearts, has not become a transformation at all. They know it deep in their hearts, that's why they become even more uncomfortable. They want to destroy such men because with the very possibility of such a man they are nobodies. Without Jesus they were the great priests of the temple; with Jesus suddenly they were nobodies. In the presence of Jesus there was godliness itself and all the priests felt their glory had been taken away.

Only very courageous people take the jump from the second to the third. It is a quantum leap. Religion is only for the very courageous, in fact, for daredevils. It is not for cowards.

A few anecdotes:

The elderly man who liked his drink, but was also learned and bookish, was hauled before the bar of justice in a country town.

"You're charged with being drunk and disorderly," snapped the judge. "Have you any reason why sentence should not be pronounced?"

"Man's inhumanity to man makes countless thousands mourn," began the prisoner in a flight of oratory. "I am not so debased as Poe, so profligate as Byron, so ungrateful as Keats, so intemperate as Burns, so timid as Tennyson, so vulgar as Shakespeare, so…"

"That'll do," interrupted the judge. "Ninety days – and, officer, take down those names he mentioned and round up those guys also. They're as bad as he is."

Now the judge is the first type of fool and the judged is the second type of fool. And the earth is mostly inhabited by these two types of fools. The third type – a Jesus, a Buddha – rarely happens.

The Indian term for fool is *buddhu* – it comes from buddha. When Buddha renounced his kingdom and many, many people started following him, the whole country was in a turmoil. People started saying to others, "Don't be a *buddhu*, don't be a fool, don't follow this man." People started calling those who followed Buddha, *buddhus*. He is a *buddhu*, he is a fool, because he renounced the kingdom. Who else would renounce a kingdom? People hanker, desire, dream for the kingdom, and he has renounced it – he must be a fool.

The third type is a very rare phenomenon. But it happens. And if you are courageous enough you can take the jump.

The second anecdote:

When somebody tells me that he did the best he could and I figure that it was not good enough, I put this fellow in the same class as the motorcycle cop who stopped a motorist and started to write a ticket.

"Officer," this motorist protested with great indignation, "I was not speeding! You are permitted to go fifty miles an hour, and I was only going forty."

"I know that," the motorcycle cop answered defensively, "but I can't catch up with the really fast ones."

The third fool is very fast. Where angels fear to tread, there too he goes unheeded. The third fool is very fast, that's why I call his leap the quantum leap. The third fool rushes out of sheer courage and energy. The second fool is not so courageous. He goes on collecting pieces from here and there. He does not have that much courage or that great a speed. He borrows knowledge – rather than knowing it himself, he borrows knowledge. That way it is cheaper and he can purchase it wholesale.

If you want to know reality directly, it is very arduous. It asks for total sacrifice. The second fool only tries up to a certain limit. The limit is: if he can get knowledge cheaply he is ready, but if there is anything to be put at stake then he recoils back.

Be courageous. Unless you have infinite courage you will not be able to become the third type, the blessed fool.

And the last anecdote. Wherever you are – because ordinarily nobody remains in the first state, that is only a theoretical state, everybody has to pass out of it, more or less – the difference is of degrees, of quantity but not quality, so people are almost always found in the second category. From the second to the third, wherever you are, remember this rule:

Don't have a closed mind. Be like the old maid who caught a burglar in her room. He pleaded with her, "Please, lady, let me go. I ain't never did anything wrong."

The old maid answered him, "Well, it is never too late to learn."

And that's what I would like to say to you. If you are in the second category, if you think you are the intelligentsia, then it is never too late to learn. Knowledge you have enough, now learn knowing. Knowledge clutters the mind as dust gathers on the mirror. Knowledge is not knowing – knowing has a totally different quality and flavor to it. It has the flavor of learning.

Let me tell you the distinction. Knowledge means that you go on gathering information, experience, categorizing, memorizing; learning means you don't gather anything, you simply remain available to whatsoever is happening or is going to happen. Learning is a state of open mind. The more you know, the more you become closed because then you cannot avoid the knowledge that you have, it always comes inbetween.

If you are listening to me and you are a knowledgeable man, a pundit, then you cannot listen to me directly, simply. You cannot listen to me. While I am speaking, deep inside you are judging, evaluating, criticizing – there is no dialogue, there is a debate. You may look silent, but you are not silent, your knowledge goes on revolving. It destroys everything that I am saying. It distorts. And whatsoever reaches you is not the real thing, whatsoever reaches you is only that which your knowledge allows to reach to you.

A learning mind is one which listens attentively with no interference from the past, which is just an opening, a mirror-like phenomenon, which simply reflects whatsoever is. If you start learning, you will attain knowing. And knowing will help you to see that you don't know at all. A person who has come to know reality becomes aware of his ignorance – he knows that he knows not. In this knowing, ignorance is the mutation, the transfiguration, the revolution.

So take a jump from the second state of foolishness to the third state of being a blessed fool. All my blessings are for those who are blessed fools.

Enough for today.

Having and Being

Rabbi Visakhar Baer met an old peasant
from the village of Oleshnya
who had known him when he was young.
Not being aware of his rise in the world
the peasant called to him, "Baer, what's new with you?"
"And what's new with you?" asked the rabbi.
"Well," answered the other, "I shall tell you.
What you don't get by your own work, you don't have."
From that time on, whenever Rabbi Baer
spoke of the proper way to conduct one's life,
he added, "And the old man of Oleshnya said:
'What you don't get by your own work, you don't have.'"

Consciousness has two dimensions: one is that of having and the other is that of being. And there are only two categories of human beings: one who is struggling hard to have more and more, and one who has understood the futility of it and has changed their life into the other direction, the direction of being. These people are trying to know who they are.

In the world of having you only believe that you have

something, but really you don't have anything. You come alone empty-handed and you go alone empty-handed. And all that happens in between is almost like a dream. It appears to be true, while it is there it appears to be real, but once it is gone then you understand that nothing was really happening. The reality has remained untouched by your dreaming. The world of having is nothing but a world of dreaming.

The religious person is one who has become aware of the futility of it all. You cannot have anything except yourself. And all that you have except yourself is a deception. It is an illusion. And, in fact that which you have possesses you more than you possess it. The possessor finally becomes the possessed. You think you have so many things – riches, power, money – but deep down you are being possessed by those same things, you are being encaged, enchained, imprisoned by those same things.

Look at the rich people. They don't possess riches – they are as poor as any other poor man in the world, they are as beggarly as any other beggar. In fact, whatsoever they possess possesses them. They are burdened by it.

So the first thing to be understood is that these are the two doors: having, being. If you are still lost in the dream of having, you are in the world. You may be sitting in a cave in the Himalayas; that makes no difference – the world is still there because the world is in the very desire to possess. And nobody has ever possessed anything.

Only one thing can be possessed and that you already have with you – your own self, your own consciousness. But to have that being, one has to work hard. You cannot get to it easily because first you will have to detach yourself from the world of having. That will be almost like a death because that's where you have got identified – you are your car, you are your house, you are your bank balance. And when you start awakening out of this dream, you start feeling as if you are disappearing because all your old identities start disappearing. One identity disappears, one part of your being disappears. There is emptiness left behind.

When all your identities disappear and you are simply left, there is only pure space – as pure as life, as pure as death, nothing else is there – that is your being. Only that being can be possessed because it is already there. You can possess only that which is already there; you cannot possess anything else. All desiring is desiring for the futile. It leads only into frustration.

Ordinarily, even when people become religious, they go on thinking in terms of having – possessing heaven or possessing the pleasures of heaven – but still they go on thinking in terms of having. Their heaven is nothing but their projected desire of having everything. All that they have missed here they would like to have in the afterlife. But it is the same desire.

The really religious person is one who has become aware of the futility of desiring, of the impossibility of having anything here in this world or thereafter in the other world. You can only possess yourself. You can only be the master of your own being. If you are not trying for that... It is hard work, there is no shortcut to it; notwithstanding what Timothy Leary says, there is no shortcut to it. Acid, drugs, are not going to help you there. That is very cheap, it is very cunning. It is a chemical deception. You want to get into the world of your innermost being without any effort. It is a dishonesty. You want to possess it without earning it.

When a Mahavira possesses it he has worked hard for it; when a Baal Shem possesses it he has worked hard for it. He has sacrificed his whole being for it. His whole being has become just a prayer, a devotion, a sacrifice to the divine. He is not there, he has simply offered himself totally. Then he possesses. Or a Kabir or a Zarathustra: they have all worked the hard way. The hard way is the only way. There exists no shortcut.

But man has tried to invent shortcuts always, in many ways. The drug trip is the latest invention of the cunningness of the human mind. Just by taking a tablet or injecting a certain chemical into your body you think you can become a buddha, you think you can attain to that total possession of your being. You will simply become a slave of the chemical, not the master of your being. Now there will arise a craving for the chemical – more and more, again and again. Bigger and bigger quantities will be needed. Soon you will be a wreck, soon you will be a wasteland, soon you will be deserted by all that is beautiful and true and all that is divine. But the lure is there. The human mind thinks it can find some shortcuts.

You may all remember certain dreams. In dreams, if you are traveling in the train, you skip many stations. You are in London and then suddenly you are in Tokyo – you skip the whole journey. The unconscious continually craves shortcuts. In dreams it is okay, but in real life it is not possible – you cannot skip any stage and you cannot skip any station on the way. Howsoever fast you go, there is no way to skip anything. Faster or slower, it eventually does not make any difference. But you have to go all the way and you have to go the hard way.

Acid and drugs have always lured man. It is nothing new. It is as old as man himself. In the Vedas they used to have *soma*. In India they have continued to use drugs down the centuries: *charas* and *ganja* and opium; they have tried everything. Now the madness is spreading all over the world. Now people are trying to find a shortcut – a very easy and cheap thing – that you can possess, that you can just swallow. *Samadhi* cannot be swallowed. And godliness is not a chemical phenomenon; you have to earn it, only then can you have it.

Then there are others – there are other methods also. It is not only drugs that are a shortcut, there are other methods also. They all guarantee you that, with very little effort, in fact with no effort at all, you can reach to the goal – for example, just chanting a mantra a few minutes every day. Chanting a mantra can only dull your mind; all repetition dulls the mind, makes you silly and stupid. If you simply go on chanting a mantra it kills your sensitivity, it creates boredom, it brings a sort of slumber to your consciousness; you become more unconscious than conscious, you start slipping into sleep.

That is why mothers have always known that when a child

is restless and cannot go to sleep they must sing a lullaby. A lullaby is a mantra. The mother repeats something again and again and again and the child feels bored. The constant repetition creates a monotonous atmosphere. The child cannot escape anywhere – the mother is sitting by the side of the bed and repeating a lullaby. The child cannot escape; the child cannot say, "Shut up!" The child has to listen. The only escape available is to go into sleep. So he tries that – to avoid this lullaby and to avoid this mother.

The mantra works in the same way: you start repeating a certain word and then you create a monotonous state for yourself. All monotony is deadening; all monotony dulls you, destroys your sharpness.

It has been tried in many ways. In the old monasteries all over the world – Christian, Hindu, Buddhist – in all the monasteries they have tried the same trick on a bigger scale. The life of a monastery is routine, absolutely fixed. Each morning you have to get up at three o'clock or five o'clock, and then the same circle starts. Then you have to do the same monotonous activity the whole day for your whole life. This is spreading a mantra all over your life, making a routine.

By and by, doing the same thing again and again, a person becomes more like a somnambulist. Whether he is awake or asleep makes no difference, he can simply go on making the empty gestures and empty movements. He loses all distinction between sleeping and waking.

You can go to the old monasteries and watch monks walking in their sleep. They have become robots. Between when they get up in the morning and when they go to sleep there is no distinction – the territories are overlapping. And it is exactly the same every day. In fact, the word *monotonous* and the word *monastery* come from the same root. They both mean the same.

You can create such a monotonous life that intelligence is not needed. When intelligence is not needed you become dull.

113

And when you become dull, of course you start feeling a certain sort of peace, a certain silence – but it is not real, it is pseudo. The real silence is very alive, throbbing. The real silence is positive; it has energy in it, it is intelligent, aware, full of life and zest. It has enthusiasm in it.

The false silence, the pseudo silence, is simply dull. You can see it. If a stupid person is sitting there – an idiot, an imbecile – you will feel a certain silence around him; it is the same silence as you can feel near a cemetery. He has a space around him which is very dull. He seems to be very indifferent to the world, not in contact at all, disconnected; he is sitting there like a lump of mud. There is no vibration around him of any life, of any energy; there is nothing streaming around him. This is not real silence. He is simply stupid.

When you come close to a buddha... He is silent because of his intelligence, he is silent because of his awareness; he is silent, not because he has forced himself to be silent, he is silent simply because he has understood the pointlessness of being disturbed in any way. He is silent because he has understood that there is no point in being worried and there is no point in being tense. His silence is out of understanding. It is overflowing understanding. When you come near a buddha you will have a totally different fragrance – the fragrance of consciousness.

And not only will you feel a freshness, a breeze around him, you will feel that you have also become more alive, aflame. Just by being close to him your own inner being is lit; a lamp starts burning within you. When you are close to him, with just the very affinity, the closeness, you suddenly feel you are no longer so depressed. His presence is pulling you out of the mud in which you had established yourself perfectly. His very presence is uplifting – you will feel life, love, compassion, beauty, reality.

A person who goes on chanting a mantra and living a monotonous life of routine is dead; he just goes into the gestures and motions because he has to. And he has done the same things so many times that there is no need to be alert about it –

he can do it in his sleep. He has become very efficient, but his efficiency simply means that he has become mechanical. That's why he is silent. You will see this type of silence if you come across people who practice Transcendental Meditation. They have stilled themselves by repeating a certain mantra; they have forced their mind to keep quiet. But this is cheap and you cannot get the real with such cheap measures. The real becomes available only when you work for it with your totality.

But remember, I am not saying that the real becomes available by your work. There is a paradox in it: you have to work hard, you have to work in a total, passionate way, and yet you have to remember that it does not happen by your work alone. It happens by grace. That is the message of Hasidism.

You work hard – it never happens without you working hard, that is certain; it happens only when you have worked hard. But that only creates the situation for it to happen. It is not like cause and effect. It is not that you heat water to a hundred degrees and then it has to evaporate; it is not like that. It is not a natural law; it has nothing to do with the world of gravitation. It is a second law, a totally different law: the law of grace. You work hard, you come to a hundred degrees, then you wait there – throbbing, expectant, alive, happy, celebrating, singing, dancing. You wait there at the hundred-degree point. It is a must, you must come to the hundred-degree point – but now you have to wait, you have to wait patiently, lovingly.

When the right moment comes, when your work is complete and your waiting is also complete, then the grace descends. Or, you can say that the grace ascends. Both mean the same because it comes from the deepest core of your being. It looks like it is descending because you have not known your innermost core up to now. It seems as if from somewhere above it is coming to you, but it really comes from somewhere within you. The within is also the beyond.

Hard work is needed to attain to grace, but the real thing finally happens only because of grace. This is a paradox. It is difficult to understand it. Because of this paradox millions of people have lost their way. There are a few who say – and they are very logical, their logic is impeccable – there are a few who say that if it comes only by our effort then why bother about grace and godliness? If it happens only by our effort, then okay, they will make all the effort, they will make it happen. So they don't talk about grace or godliness. They will miss, because it never happens only by your own effort.

Then there are people who say that if it happens only by grace and never happens by our own effort, then why bother? We should wait – and whenever existence wills it, it is going to happen.

They both miss. One misses because of egoism – "Only my effort is enough. Only I am enough" – the other misses because of laziness, lethargy. Both miss.

The one who arrives home has to follow the paradoxical path. This is the paradox: I have to work hard, not only hard, I have to put myself totally at the stake – only then will I become capable of receiving grace. But it happens through grace. A moment comes when I have done all that I can do and then I pray that now no more is possible from my side, now something is needed from the other end, now you also do something. And existence starts working on you only when you have done all that you could have done. If something is still lacking and a part of your being is still not involved, then existence cannot come to your help. Existence helps only those who help themselves.

This is the paradox of the Hasid. He works hard and still he trusts that the ultimate flowering is going to be only by his grace, by the grace of existence.

And it is beautiful. We are very small. Our effort cannot create much. Our fire is very small – by this fire alone we cannot set the whole existence aflame. We are just drops. We cannot create oceans out of these drops. But if the drop can drop into a deep prayerfulness, the ocean becomes available. When the drop relaxes, it becomes capable of containing oceans in itself. It is small if you look only at its periphery; it is tremendously vast if you look at its center. Man is both, man is a paradox. He is the tiniest particle of consciousness, an atom, very atomic, and yet he contains the vast. The whole sky is contained in him.

So first these two languages have to be understood: the language of having and the language of being. And you have to change your gears from the language of having to the language of being.

Let me tell you a few anecdotes:

A Japanese high official confronted his daughter, "I have been told that you are going out on dates with a foreigner. Furthermore, he is an American soldier, and what's more, he is Jewish."

The girl shot back, "What schmuck told you that?"

Now the word *schmuck* tells everything. There is no need for anybody to say anything anymore.

The person who knows only the language of having has a totally different quality to his being: the way he walks, the way he sits. the way he talks, the words that he uses, the words that he avoids using, the people he mingles with and the people that he avoids, the places that he visits and the places that he does not visit – everything indicates something. Even single, ordinary words indicate something. Even if he comes to a master, a man who is always trying to have more and more and more can be seen by the way he comes, by the desire with which he comes. Even if he surrenders, in his very surrender you can find his language.

A man came to see me. By the way he came, I could see that he was absolutely indifferent toward me. It was so clear, it was so loud. He was not flowing toward me, he had no flow in his being; he was a stagnant pool of energy.

I was surprised. I wondered why he had come to me. And

then he started talking about God. The word *God* was simply irrelevant on his tongue. It made no sense. He was speaking some language which he did not know how to use. I was waiting, because there must have been something else behind these words about God. He was saying, "I want to realize God and I want to realize myself." But by the way he was saying it and by the way he was expressing it, it was absolutely clear that he had not come for these things. Maybe just to be polite toward me or just to start a dialogue, he was using these props.

And then by and by he said, "I will come one day and become a sannyasin also."

So I said, "If you have come, and you are a seeker, and you want to realize godliness, then why waste any more time? As it is, you have wasted enough already." He must have been almost sixty-five.

He said, "That's right. But right now I am contesting the election." There was a by-election going on. "So I have come for your blessings."

I said, "Then why did you waste so much time talking about God, talking about the soul, talking about meditation?"

Indians are very proficient about such things – just by tradition they have learned these words. These words are in the air, they have caught them. They don't have any roots in their being, they just float in their heads. These words exist in them without any roots, unrelated to them.

I said, "Why did you waste so much time talking about God and the soul? You should have said the real thing in the beginning." He was a little embarrassed. And I told him, "From the very beginning I was wondering why you have come to me – because you were coming toward me and yet you were not coming toward me. Your language was clear and loud. You were sitting here and yet you were not sitting here, and I could see that your presence was false, only physical. And I could see the politician in you; in fact, you were talking about God as a political strategy. It was your politics."

There are those people who say, "Honesty is the best policy." Even honesty they have made into a policy. Policy means politics. "It pays to be honest," they say. So honesty is also a useful instrument to earn more money, to earn more prestige, to be more respectable. But how can honesty be a policy? Just to say such things – that honesty is the best policy – is to utter a profanity. It is almost saying that God is the best policy, or that meditation is the best policy, or that love is the best policy.

If your language is of having, you can use God and meditation and things, but they will be just garbs, masks, and something else will be hidden behind them.

"I'm afraid it's bad news," said the doctor to the husband of a nagging wife. "Your wife has only a few hours left to live. I hope you understand there's nothing more to be done. Don't let yourself suffer."

"It's all right, Doc," said the husband. "I've suffered for years – I can suffer a few more hours."

People have different languages. Even if they use the same words they don't use them with the same meaning. Listen to the meaning and never listen to the words. If you listen to the words you will never understand people. Listen to the meaning – the meaning is a totally different thing.

The woman lion tamer had her beasts under perfect control. At her summons, the fiercest lion came meekly to her and took a piece of sugar out of her mouth. The circus crowd marveled – all except one man, Mulla Nasruddin.

"Anybody could do that," he yelled from the audience.

"Would you dare to do it?" the ringmaster yelled back scornfully.

"Certainly," replied Nasruddin, "I can do it just as well as the lion can."

Whenever you are listening, listen to the meaning. Whenever you are listening to a person, listen to his whole personality – and you will immediately be able to see whether the person lives in the dimension of having or in the dimension of being.

And that will be very helpful for your own inner growth and your own change of gears. Just watch people. It is easier to watch people than to watch yourself in the beginning, because people are more objective, and there is a little distance between you and them. And you can be more objective about people because you are not involved in them. Just watch. Make it a point.

Buddha used to say to his disciples, "Watch everybody passing by; coming and going in the streets, watch people." See exactly what is happening. Don't listen to their words because they are very cunning, they have become very deceptive. When somebody is saying something listen to his face, to his eyes, to his being, to the gesture, and you will be simply surprised how, up to now, you have lived only with words. A person may be saying, "I love you," and his eyes may be simply denying it. A person may be smiling with his lips and his eyes may be ridiculing you, rejecting you. A person may be saying "Hello" and holding your hand, and his whole being may be condemning you.

Listen to the language of the body, the language of the gesture – the language behind the language. Listen to the meaning. And first become alert about it in others. Let everybody who comes to you be an experiment of awareness. Then by and by you will become able to watch yourself. Then turn your whole flood of life upon yourself; then use the same with yourself. When you say to somebody "I love you," listen to what you really are saying – not these words. Words are almost always fake.

Language is very tricky and can garb things so beautifully that the container becomes so important and you lose sight of the content. People have become very sophisticated as far as their surface is concerned, but their innermost core remains almost primitive. Listen to the center of the circumference. Go into each word.

First others have to be watched, then watch yourself. And then by and by you will see that there are a few moments when you also move into the dimension of being. These moments are the moments of beauty, the moments of happiness. In fact, whenever you see that you are feeling very happy, you have come in contact with the dimension of being – because there is no other happiness possible.

But if you don't observe it accurately, you may misunderstand it. You are sitting with a woman you love, or with a man you love, or with a friend, and suddenly you feel a deep well-being arising in you, a deep joy – for no reason at all, for no visible cause. You are just aglow. You start finding causes outside: you think maybe it is because the woman is sitting by your side and she loves you so much. Or it is because you have met the friend after so many years. Or it is because the full moon is so beautiful. You will start finding causes.

But those who have become alert in listening to their heart, to their real meanings, will not be looking for causes outside. They will look inside. They have come in contact with their being. Maybe the woman you loved functioned as a situation, as a jumping-board, and you jumped into yourself.

It is difficult to jump into yourself when there is some antagonism outside. You have to be outside then. When somebody loves you, you can drop all defense measures, you can drop all your strategies, you can drop your politics, you can drop your diplomacy. When somebody loves you, you can be vulnerable; you can trust that he or she is not going to take advantage of it, that you can be defenseless and you will not be killed and crushed, that you can be defenseless and the presence of your friend will be soothing, it will not be poisoning you.

Whenever there is a situation where you can leave yourself defenseless and you can drop your strategies and your armors, suddenly you are in contact with your being – you have moved from the dimension of having to the dimension of being. Whenever it happens there is happiness, there is joy, there is

121

rejoicing. Even if it is only for a split second, suddenly the doors of heaven are open. But again and again you lose it because you are not aware. It happens only accidentally.

Remember, a religious person is one who has understood this accidental happening and who has understood the innermost key of it. And now he does not move into his dimension of being only accidentally, he has the key – and whenever he wants to move, he opens the door, he unlocks the door and goes into it.

This is the only difference. In ordinary happiness and the happiness of a religious person, the only difference is this: that the religious person has become capable of moving any time, any place, into his being. Now he knows the direct route and he does not depend on outside props.

You depend too much on outside props. Sometimes you are in a beautiful house; it feels good. You are traveling in a beautiful car – the car is humming and everything is going beautifully – it feels good. In that feeling you start coming closer to your being. But you misunderstand; you think it is because of this car, so you have to possess this car. Maybe the car functioned as a situation, but the car is not the cause. Maybe a beautiful house functioned as a situation, but it is not the cause.

If you think it is the cause then you move into the world of having; then you must have the most beautiful car – you have to have it. Then you have to have the best house, you have to have the best garden, you have to have the best woman and the best man. And you go on collecting and collecting and collecting and one day suddenly you recognize or realize that your whole life has been a wastage. You have collected much, but you have lost all sources of happiness. You got lost in collecting things. The basic logic was that with whatever you felt good and happy, that thing had to be possessed.

Listen to me: that thing need not be possessed. You just watch what is happening inside you and you can start having that happening without any outside help. That's what a sannyasin is.

It is not that you have to have all, that you have to possess all, but you have to remain alert that you cannot possess *anything* in this world. All that you possess can function only as a situation – it is not the cause. The cause is inside. And you can open the door without any outside prop at any time, in any place, and you can go in and you can rejoice.

You are no longer attached. You can use things, they are useful; I am not against things, remember. Neither are the Hasids against things, remember. Use things, but don't believe that things can cause you happiness. Use things, they have a utility, but don't believe that they are the goals. They are not the ends, they are only the means. The goal is within you, and the goal is such that one can move directly into it without any outside help. Once you know it, you become a master of your being.

This – whatsoever I am saying – has to be experienced by you. Just by my saying it and just by your listening to it and understanding it intellectually, it is not going to help much.

Mulla Nasruddin refused the cow-puncher's command to drink, for three reasons.

"Name them!" roared the terror of the town.

"First," said the Mulla, "it is prohibited in my religion. Second, I promised my grandmother on her deathbed that I would handle not, touch not, taste not, the accursed stuff."

"And the other reason, the third?" insisted the bully, somewhat softened.

"I have just had a drink," said Nasruddin.

If you only listen to me, if you only understand me intellectually and never experiment in your own inner lab of consciousness, whatsoever I am saying will remain just in your head. It will never become a lived experience. And unless it becomes a lived experience it is worthless knowledge, it is junk. Again you can start collecting knowledge, then again you are into the same trap – the dimension of having. And you can go on collecting as much knowledge as is available.

It is one of the misfortunes of modern man that so much knowledge has become available. It was never so. The only thing that has proved the greatest calamity for modern man is the tremendous amount of knowledge which has become available. It was never available before. A Hindu used to live with Hindu scriptures; the Mohammedan used to live with Mohammedan scriptures; the Christian used to live with the Bible – and they were all secluded and nobody went into the other's world of knowledge. Things were clear-cut; there was no overlapping.

Now everything is overlapping and a tremendous amount of new knowledge has become available. We are living in a "knowledge explosion". In this explosion you can start gathering information, you can become a great scholar very cheaply, very easily, but it is not going to transform you at all.

Again, remember, knowledge belongs to the dimension of having; knowing belongs to the dimension of being. They look alike, but they are not. Not even are they not alike, they are diametrically opposite to each other. A man who goes on collecting knowledge goes on losing knowing. Knowing needs a mirror-like mind: pure, uncorrupted. I am not saying that knowledge is useless. If you have your knowing – clear, mirrorlike, fresh – you can use your knowledge in a tremendously useful way. It can become beneficial. But the knowing has to be there in the first place.

Knowledge is very easy; again, knowing is very difficult. For knowing you have to pass through many fires. For knowledge nothing is needed – as you are you can go on adding more and more knowledge to yourself.

A jovial man-about-town, long on charm but short on cash, surprised his friends by his sudden marriage to an extremely ugly woman whose only virtue was her well-padded bankroll. After the marriage, his friends were doubly mystified by his insistence on taking his wife everywhere with him.

"I can understand your marrying that painfully ugly woman for her money," one of his close friends remarked frankly, "but why do you have to bring her with you every time you go out?"

"It's simple," the husband explained. "It's easier than kissing her good-bye."

It is easier to have knowledge – very cheap, costs nothing. It is very difficult, arduous, to attain to knowing. That's why very few... Very rarely people try to meditate, very rarely people try to pray, very rarely people ever make any effort toward knowing what truth is. And whatsoever you have not known on your own is meaningless. You can never be certain about it, the doubt never disappears; the doubt remains like a worm underneath it, sabotaging your knowledge. You can shout loudly that you believe in God, but your shouting does not prove anything. Your shouting only proves one thing: that there is doubt. Only doubt shouts loudly. You can become a fanatic believer, but your fanaticism simply shows one thing: that there is doubt.

Only a man who has doubt within himself becomes a fanatic. A fanatic Hindu means one who does not really trust that Hinduism is right. A fanatic Christian simply means one who has doubts about Christianity. He becomes fanatic, aggressive – not to prove anything to others, he becomes fanatic and aggressive to prove to himself that whatsoever he believes he *really* believes. He has to prove it.

When you really know something, you are not a fanatic at all. A man of knowing, one who has come to know even glimpses of godliness, glimpses of his being, becomes very, very soft, sensitive, fragile. He is not fanatic. He becomes feminine. He is not aggressive. He becomes deeply compassionate. And, by knowing, he becomes very understanding of others. He can understand even the diametrically opposite standpoint.

I have heard about a Hasid rabbi:

He was saying, "Life is like a river."

A disciple asked, "Why?"
The rabbi said, "How can I know? Am I a philosopher?"

Another day the rabbi was saying, "Life is like a river."
Another disciple asked, "Why?"
And the rabbi said, "Right you are. Why should it be?"

This is tremendous understanding. No fanaticism. A man of knowing attains to a sense of humor. Let this always be remembered. If you see someone who has no sense of humor, know well that that man has not known at all. If you come across a serious man, then you can be certain that he is a pretender. Knowing brings sincerity, but all seriousness disappears. Knowing brings a playfulness; knowing brings a sense of humor. The sense of humor is a must.

If you find a saint who has no sense of humor, then he is not a saint at all. Impossible. His very seriousness says that he has not achieved. Once you have some inner experiences of your own you become very playful, you become very innocent, childlike.

The man of knowledge is very serious. The man of knowledge always carries a serious, gloomy atmosphere around him. Not only does he carry a serious atmosphere, he makes anybody he comes into contact with serious. He forces seriousness on them. In fact, deep down, he is worried that he does not know anything. He cannot relax, his seriousness is a tension. He is anguished. He knows that he knows only for its name's sake, he knows that his knowledge is all fake – so he cannot laugh at it.

Now listen to it:

The rabbi said, "Life is like a river."
And a disciple asked, "Why?"
And the rabbi said, "How can I know? Am I a philosopher?"

And another day the rabbi said again, "Life is like a river."

Another disciple asked, "Why?"

And the rabbi said, "Right you are. Why should it be?"

You see the non-seriousness? You see the tremendous sense of humor?

Hasidism has created a few of the greatest saints of the world and my respect toward them is immense because they are not serious people. They can joke and they can laugh – and they can laugh not only at others, they can laugh at themselves, that's the beauty. If you go on collecting knowledge, you can have a great amount of knowledge, but it is not going to be of any help when the need arises. You can go on throwing it around and showing and exhibiting it, but whenever the need arises and the house is on fire you will suddenly see you have forgotten all that you knew – because you never knew in the first place. It was just in the memory.

Wherever there is an emergency situation... For example, when a person is dying, he will forget all his knowledge. In that moment he will not remember that the soul is immortal. That was advice for others. In that moment he will not remember that he is going back to the source and that one should go happily, and dancing. In that moment he will start clinging to life; all his knowledge will be gone.

I used to know a very learned man, a very intellectual man, famous all over the country. He was not only learned, he was a follower of J. Krishnamurti. He used to come to see me sometimes and he would say that there is no need for any meditation because Krishnamurti says so.

I used to listen to him and laugh. He would ask me, "Why do you laugh whenever I say these things?"

I told him again and again, "I listen to *you*, I don't listen to what you say. Your being gives me a totally different message. If there is really no need for meditation, there is no need for scriptures, there is no need for any methods, there is no need even for

prayer, and you have understood it, then this would have transformed you totally."

He would answer seriously, "That's right. I have understood
intellectually, but some day I will understand it non-intellectu-
ally also. I have taken the first step, the second will be coming."

Then one day his son came running to me to tell me,
"Father is very ill, it seems like a heart attack and he remembers
you." So I rushed to him.

He was lying on the bed repeating "Rama, Rama, Rama."

I shook his head and I said, "What are you doing? Your
whole life you said there is no meditation – what are you doing
repeating Rama, Rama, Rama…?"

He said, "Now don't disturb me at this moment. Death is
at the door. I am dying. Who knows? – maybe God is. And
who knows, maybe the people who have always said remember
his name and he will forgive you, are right. This is no time to
create a debate or an argument; let me repeat it."

For forty years he had not said a single mantra, but now,
suddenly, forty years of knowledge is discarded, it is of no use.
In this dangerous situation when death is there, he forgets
Krishnamurti completely. He becomes again an ordinary Hindu.
It was okay for an ordinary Hindu villager to repeat "Rama,
Rama" – he can be forgiven – but this man? He had written
books, he had lectured all over the country, he had helped many
people to drop their mantras and to drop their meditations and
their scriptures. And now suddenly he is repeating a mantra.

But he survived the heart attack and he came to see me after
two or three months – and again he was back to his knowledge. I
said, "Now stop your foolishness. Death will come again and you
will repeat 'Rama, Rama, Rama'. So what is the point of it all?"

A very rich old man had remained a bachelor. Now he was
nearing seventy-five. Then suddenly a friend, a married friend,
convinced him that he should get married. "You should not
miss this pleasure," he said.

So he decided to get married. Because he had so much money he immediately found a beautiful girl. Off they went on their honeymoon.

He took the married friend and his wife with him as guides in this new exploration. The next morning they met in the motel at breakfast. The friend had fed him every bit of information about sex and how to make love and what to do and what not to do. "What a fantastic time I had last night," said the married man. "We went to bed last night. My wife was eager, I was eager, and we had a marvelous night of love. What about you, old man?"

"Oh, my God!" said the old rich man. "I clean forgot about it!"

After a whole life of bachelorhood, even if somebody guides you, tells you things and you memorize them, they don't have any deep contact with your being, they simply float above your head. They don't touch you.

The old man said, "Oh my God! I clean forgot about it!" Seventy-five years of sleeping alone creates a mechanical habit of its own.

If you go on accumulating knowledge, it creates a habit; it never gives you any knowledge, but it gives you a habit, a habit for accumulating more, a very dangerous habit. Even if you come across a Buddha or a Jesus you will miss, because there also you will be accumulating. You will be taking notes inside the mind – "Yes, this is right, worthy of being remembered." Your accumulation will become bigger and bigger, but you will be just a dead museum, or a museum of dead things.

And the more you are covered with this "having knowledge", the less will be the possibility for the real knowledge to be there; the knowledge that comes by knowing being, by *being*, will be missed.

Remember, the mind is nothing but that which you have collected up to now. The mind is all that you have inside your being. Beyond the mind is your real being, beyond having is your real being. Outside you have collected things, inside you have collected thoughts – both are in the dimension of having.

When you are no longer attached to things and when you are no longer attached to thoughts – suddenly the open sky, the open sky of being. And that's the only thing worth having and the only thing that you can really have.

Now the story:

> *Rabbi Visakhar Baer met an old peasant*
> *from the village of Oleshnya*
> *who had known him when he was young.*
> *Not being aware of his rise in the world*
> *the peasant called to him, "Baer, what's new with you?"*
> *"And what's new with you?" asked the rabbi.*
> *"Well," answered the other, "I shall tell you.*
> *What you don't get by your own work, you don't have."*

A tremendously significant saying. Maybe the peasant hasn't meant it in such a significant way, but the rabbi took it. It was a precious stone. Out of that ordinary peasant… He may not have meant it the way the rabbi understood it – you understand only in the way that *you* can understand.

> *From that time on, whenever Rabbi Baer*
> *spoke of the proper way to conduct one's life*
> *he added, "And the old man of Oleshnya said:*
> *'What you don't get by your own work, you don't have.'"*

The old man must have meant it in the ordinary way. He was saying that in this life you can have only that which you have worked for. There is no other way. One has to work hard to have something.

That is the experience of an ordinary farmer. The farmer was not a king; a king can have much that he has not earned by his own labor.

A very great, rich man was once asked by a poor man, "What is the best way to get rich in the world?"

The rich man said, "The best way is to find the right parents."

You can have much without ever having earned it if you were clever enough to find the right womb. Very few people are that clever. They simply rush into any womb available.

You can rob, you can cheat, you can exploit; there are a thousand ways. But the farmer, the peasant really lived by his own earning. He was not a king, he was not a politician, he was not a rich man – whatsoever he earned, that's all he had. The farmer must have said it in the very ordinary sense, but look at the beauty of it.

Whatsoever you hear, you hear from your dimension. The rabbi heard it in a totally different way. It became a very illuminated saying in his being. It was a simple, ordinary statement, but the rabbi himself was in a deep meditation, the rabbi himself was in his other dimension – the dimension of being.

When you are in the dimension of being, small things, ordinary pebbles, become precious stones. Ordinary things take on so much color, become so colorful. Ordinary events become so psychedelic. It depends on you, on your vision.

From that time on, whenever Rabbi Baer
spoke of the proper way to conduct one's life,
he used to add, "And the old man of Oleshnya said:
'What you don't get by your own work, you don't have.'"

This is true. In the innermost world it is absolutely true – although it may not be so true in the outside world. In the outside world there are a thousand and one ways to be dishonest, to cheat, to rob, to steal, to exploit. In fact, in the outside world the workers don't have much, only the cheaters. The cunning people have much. Those who work don't have much. Those who don't work, they have much.

But in the inside world the statement is absolutely true. You cannot have anything there in your being that you have not earned. And it is earned the hard way; there are no shortcuts. So don't try to cheat existence.

A man who is deluded by having things, loses all opportunities of attaining to the state of being.

I have heard:

A husband took a shot at his mother-in-law, so she brought charges against him.

"You were drinking," said the judge, "so I must tell you something. It was liquor that inflamed you. It was liquor that made you hate your mother-in-law. It was liquor that got you to buy the revolver to shoot her. It was liquor that made you go to your mother-in-law's house, point the revolver, pull the trigger and fire. And note, it was liquor that made you miss her!"

It is the same story, the same liquor. Throughout your whole life it is your ambition to have, that functions like the liquor. So watch it. Beware of it. That is the only illusion in the world.

One day when you will go, then you will realize – but then it will be too late.

I have heard about a man. He went to Florida with his wife, and became fascinated by the spectacle of eight horses chasing each other around a track. He and his wife bet heavily, and after a few days they had only two dollars left between them. But he was a hopeful type and he convinced his wife that everything would be all right if she let him go out to the track alone.

A friend drove him out. There was a forty-to-one shot in the first race, and he decided to bet on it. The horse came in.

In every race the man backed the long shot, and in every race he won. By the end of the last race he had over ten thousand dollars, and he decided to press his lucky streak. On the way back to the hotel he stopped off at a little gambling club and ran his stake up to forty thousand on the roulette wheel. One more play, he decided, and he would leave. He put the entire forty thousand on black.

The wheel spun. The croupier announced, "Number fourteen, red."

The man walked back to the hotel. His wife called him from the verandah. "How did you make out?" she asked eagerly.

The husband shrugged: "I lost the two dollars."

In the end, when death comes, the whole game of thousands and thousands of dollars, achieving this, attaining that, becoming this, becoming that, the power, the prestige, the money, the respectability – nothing counts. Finally, you have only to say, "I have lost my being."

In running, rushing into the dimension of having, only one thing happens – you lose your being. Life is a great opportunity – a great opportunity. In fact, there are millions of opportunities in it to attain to yourself, to know who you are. But that comes the hard way. You have to work for it.

Don't try to borrow. Nothing can be borrowed in that inner world. And don't try to become just knowledgeable. Attain to a clarity, attain to a vision where no thought exists in your mind. This is the hardest thing in the world. To drop thoughts is the hardest thing in the world, the greatest challenge. All other challenges are very small. This is the greatest adventure that you can take and those who are courageous, they accept the challenge and go into it.

The greatest challenge is how to drop the mind, because only when the mind ceases, the godliness can be. Only when the known disappears, the unknown can be. Only when there is no mind, no *you*, nothing of you left, suddenly there is that which you have been seeking and seeking forever and forever. Godliness is when you are not. This is the hardest thing to do.

The last anecdote:

Rabbi Grossman and Father O'Malley were seated beside each other at a banquet.

"Have some ham," offered the priest.

"I'm afraid not," answered the rabbi.

"C'mon, try some," the priest encouraged. "It's real good!"

"Thanks, but I don't eat that kind of meat because of my religion."

"It's really delicious!" said Father O'Malley five minutes later. "You oughta try this ham, you'd like it."

"No thank you!" replied Rabbi Grossman.

After dinner, the two men shook hands. "Tell me," said the Jewish clergyman, "do you enjoy sex with your wife?"

"Oh, Rabbi, you should know I'm not allowed to be married," said the priest. "I can't have sex."

"You ought to try it," said the rabbi. "It's better than ham."

That's all that I can say to you. You ought to try the state of no-mind, the state of being. It is better than all the worlds put together.

The world of being is the only real world, the world of truth. And unless you have come to it you go on wandering in foreign lands. You can never come home. You come home only when you have come into the innermost core of your being – which is possible. It is difficult, but not impossible; arduous, but not impossible. It is difficult certainly, but it has happened. It has happened to me, it can happen to you.

But don't cling to cheap remedies. Don't try to cheat, chemically or otherwise. Don't try to borrow knowledge. Don't go on accumulating.

It is already there, accumulations only hide it. It is already there. Once you stop accumulating and you drop all the junk you have accumulated inside you – that's what your mind is, the junk. If you drop that junk, suddenly it is there in its absolute purity, in its absolute beauty, in its absolute benediction.

A wise man, the wonder of his age, taught his disciples from a seemingly inexhaustible store of wisdom. He attributed all his knowledge to a thick tome that was kept in a place of honor in his room. The sage would allow nobody to open the volume.

When he died, those who had surrounded him, regarding themselves as his heirs, ran to open the book, anxious to possess what it contained. They were surprised, confused and disappointed when they found that there was writing on only one page.

They became even more bewildered, and then annoyed, when they tried to penetrate the meaning of the phrase that met their eyes. It was: "When you realize the difference between the container and the content, you will have knowledge."

Let me repeat it: "When you realize the difference between the container and the content, you will have knowledge."

The container is your consciousness, the content is your mind. The container is your being, the content is all that you have accumulated. When you realize the distinction between the content and the container, between the mind and the being, you will have knowledge. In a single split moment, when you remember and you recognize that you are not the content, you are the container, there is a mutation, there is a revolution. And that is the only revolution there is.

Enough for today.

6

The Art of Living

The first question:

Osho,
Today at the lecture you extolled the virtues of
Hasidism. But if they are so praiseworthy, so full of
feeling of brotherhood, etc., why do they exclude
women from their religious practices, and particularly
their ecstatic religious dancing?

A woman has asked the question. It is very relevant, and
has to be understood. The first thing to remember, to always
remember, is never to judge the past by present standards. That
is not compassionate. For example, when Hasidism was arising,
to allow women into an ecstatic religious dance would have
been impossible. Not that Hasidic mystics were not aware, not
that they would not have liked to allow it – they would have
loved it – but it was impossible.

Even Buddha was afraid to initiate women into his order.
What was the fear? Was he an orthodox person? No, you cannot
find a more revolutionary mind, but he insisted for many years

on not allowing women into his order. The reason is to be found somewhere else.

A religion has to exist in the society. If the society is too much against a certain thing, even the founder has to make a few compromises otherwise the religion as such will not exist at all. The society is not in a condition of perfection, the society is not yet as it should be, but a religion has to exist in this society, in the framework that this society allows it. Revolutionaries try to go a little further than the boundary, but even they cannot go too far. If they go too far they will be uprooted.

For example, I have no objection if you go naked when meditating. I have no objection. In fact I will support it, because clothes are part of the repressive culture. I know it, but still I have to insist on you not being naked in the meditations because that creates such trouble that even meditation will become impossible. That will be too much. To destroy the whole possibility of meditation just for clothes or nudity would be foolish. It would have been good if I had been able to allow you to be absolutely free – free from clothes also. But then society will not allow us to exist at all, and we have to exist in society. So we have to choose the lesser evil.

Or, take the question of drugs. I am not in support of drugs, but I am not against them either. I am not in support of Timothy Leary, I don't think that you can attain *samadhi* by drugs – about that I am absolutely certain. No one has ever attained *samadhi* by drugs, notwithstanding what Aldous Huxley and others say. It is too cheap, and there is no possibility to attain the ultimate through chemicals. But I am aware that drugs can help in a certain way. They can give you a glimpse; they cannot give you the reality, but they can give you a glimpse of the reality, and that glimpse can become a breakthrough. That glimpse can uproot you from your past and can send you on a search for the real. Even if you have seen God, even in your dream, your whole life will be transformed. Of course, the God in a dream is a dream, but the next morning you will start looking into the world – where can you find this phenomenon that has happened in your dream?

So many people start their journey toward godliness, truth, *samadhi*, because they have had a certain glimpse somewhere – maybe through drugs, maybe through sexual orgasm, maybe through music, or sometimes accidentally. Sometimes a person falls from a train, is hit on the head and he has a glimpse. I'm not saying make a method of that! But I know this has happened. A certain center in the head is hit by accident and the person has a glimpse, an explosion of light. Never again will he be the same; now he will start searching for it. This is possible. The improbable is no more improbable; it has become possible. Now he has some inkling, some contact. He cannot rest now.

I am not for drugs, I am not against drugs. But still, in this community, in my commune, drugs cannot be allowed, because politicians have never been very intelligent and one should not expect too much from them. In fact, only stupid people become interested in politics. If they were intelligent they would not be in politics at all.

So just for some ordinary, small thing the whole movement cannot be destroyed. That would be foolish. After a hundred years my attitude that drugs cannot be allowed in the Commune will be thought anti-revolutionary. Naturally, I know it is anti-revolutionary. So let it be on the record.

The Hasidic masters knew it well. It is inhuman, anti-revolutionary, not to allow women to participate in ecstatic religious ceremonies, in ecstatic dances. But that society was very much against it. Because of this the whole movement would have died. So they had to prohibit it.

Buddhism died in India. Do you know why? It was because Buddha finally allowed women into his order. He himself is reported to have said, "My religion would have lived at least five thousand years, but now it will not live more than five hundred, because I am taking a very great risk." Just allowing woman into his order was such a risk that Buddha said, "The life of my religion is reduced by four thousand, five hundred years – at the most it will last only five hundred years." And it happened exactly that way. Buddhism lived for only five hundred years, and that life was also not at the climax, not at the optimum. Every day the life was slowing down, every day death was coming closer and closer. What happened?

The society. The society has long been male-dominated. To allow women into a religious order was to destroy the old hierarchy, the superiority of man. Even a man like Mahavira, a very revolutionary man, is reported to have said that women cannot enter *moksha* directly as women. First they will have to be born as men and then... So no woman has entered into the Jaina *moksha*, into nirvana, directly as a woman. First she has to change her body, take a male shape and form, and then she can enter.

Why should Mahavira say this? Society, the politics of the country, the priests and the politicians, they were too male chauvinistic. Some compromise was needed, otherwise they would not allow anything. Mahavira lived naked, but he himself did not allow any women to go naked because the society was not ready to accept even him in his nudity. By and by people accepted him, grudgingly, reluctantly, but to accept the idea that women could go naked would have been too much.

And because Mahavira said, "Unless you leave everything – even clothes – unless you are as innocent as a child, as you were on the first day you were born, you cannot enter into my kingdom of God," he had to say that women could not enter directly. If he had said that women could enter directly then a few courageous women would have come forward and would have thrown off their clothes also, would have become naked. Just to avoid nude women he had to make a very false statement, untrue. And I know he knew that it was untrue – I know because I make many untrue statements.

But we have to exist in a society, in a particular state, in a particular confused state, in a particular neurotic state. If you live with mad people you have to make a few compromises.

If you live with mad people at least you have to pretend that you are also mad.

Narendra is here. His father went mad thirty or forty years ago. He escaped from the house. After a few months he was caught in Agra and put into jail with mad people all around. There was a special jail in Lahore, only for mad people. He said that for nine months everything went okay because he was also mad.

After nine months, just by accident, he drank a whole jug of phenol – a mad man, he found it in the bathroom and he drank it. That made him vomit, gave him nausea, diarrhea. Because of that diarrhea he was throwing things out for fifteen days continuously, and his madness also disappeared. It helped, it helped like a catharsis. When his madness disappeared then the real problem began, because he was among mad people.

Now for the first time he became aware of where he was – somebody was pulling his leg, somebody was hitting him on his head, and people were talking and dancing. And he was no longer mad. Those three months when he was not mad and was living with mad people, were the most painful; they were deep anguish and anxiety. He couldn't sleep.

And he would go to the authorities and he would say, "Now let me out because I am no longer mad!" And they wouldn't listen because every mad person says that – that he is no longer mad. So that was not proof. He had to complete his sentence of one year.

He told me that he could never forget those three months; they were a continuous nightmare. But for nine months he was perfectly happy because he was also mad.

You cannot conceive of what happens to a person when he becomes a Buddha or a Baal Shem in a country, in a world, which is absolutely mad. He is no longer mad, but he has to live with you, he has to follow your laws, otherwise you will kill him. He has to make compromises. Of course he cannot hope that you will make compromises with him. You are not in a state in which you can think. But he can think. Only the higher can make compromises with the lower, only the greater can make compromises with the lower, only the wise person can make compromises with stupid people.

So it happened that women have never been accepted. It is only just in this century, very recently, that women are coming out of the dark night of the past history.

I have heard:

It happened that when Golda Meir was Prime Minister of Israel, Indira Gandhi, Prime Minister of India, went to Israel. And when Indira Gandhi visited Israel she was welcomed by Golda Meir.

After seeing all the historical sights, Mrs. Gandhi said, "I would like to visit a synagogue."

"By all means," answered the Israeli Prime Minister.

Two weeks later, Mrs. Gandhi stood before her cabinet.

"What did you learn in Israel?" asked one of the members.

"Many things," answered the Indian Prime Minister. "But most of all I learned that in Israeli synagogues the men pray on the first floor and the prime ministers worship in the balcony."

Two women, but she thought that prime ministers worship in the balcony and men on the floor. Once a thing settles it is very difficult to change it, even for a prime minister. Even for a prime minister it is difficult to change the traditional way.

The Hasids were a wave; but rather than destroying the whole movement they chose to go with the society and its rules and its regulations. At least let the message reach to men. If it cannot reach to women right now, later on it will – but at least let the message be rooted on the earth.

I exist here in a very alien and strange world. I would like to give you many things, but I cannot because you yourself will resist. I would like to make you aware of many things in your being, but you will be against me. I have to go very slowly,

I have to be very roundabout; it cannot be done directly.

Just see: I have done what the questioner was inquiring about in relation to Hasidism. I have done it. In my community, men and women are no longer separate. That's why Indians have stopped coming to my ashram. They cannot come. When they used to come, their questions were more or less all concerned about what type of ashram this was – men and women mixing and meeting, holding each other's hands, going together? Even after meditations hugging, kissing each other? What type of things were these? This is not good.

They used to come to me and say, "This is not good, this should not be allowed. Osho, you should interfere." I never interfered because to me there is nothing wrong – man and woman should not be made in any way distinct. They are not separate, nobody is higher and nobody is lower. They are different but equal. Difference is beautiful, it has to be there. The difference has to be enhanced, but the equality has to be saved. And to me, love is a way toward godliness.

I didn't listen to them. By and by they disappeared. Now only very courageous Indians can enter here. Now only a few Indians can enter here, those who have no repressed mind in them, who are post-Freudians – only they can enter here. But India as a whole is pre-Freudian. Freud is still unknown in India. Freud has not yet entered into the Indian soul.

But I have done it. And I am a Hasid, so you can forgive the old Hasids. Time was not ripe at that time; even now it is very difficult. I have to encounter difficulties every day; for every small thing there are difficulties. Those difficulties could be avoided if I behaved in an orthodox way. I cannot behave in an orthodox way – because then there is no point in my being here, then I could not deliver the message to you – and I cannot be absolutely revolutionary because then there would be no possibility of something happening between you and me.

And I am not in any way interested in being a martyr because that too seems to me to be a sort of masochism. People who are always seeking to become martyrs are not really aware of what they are doing – they are seeking suicide. I am not a martyr. I love life, I love all that is implied in life, and the original Hasid masters were as much in love with life as I am. That's why I have chosen to talk about them. When I choose to talk about some path, I choose it only because that path appeals to me tremendously.

The Hasids were not people who wanted to become political revolutionaries. They were not reformists. They were not trying to reform the society; they were trying to bring a mutation to the individual soul. And they had to exist in the society. Remember that always.

But then what happens whenever a tradition gets settled? Now Hasidism is a settled tradition, now it itself has become an orthodoxy. Now the time is ripe. If the community exists in New York – a Hasidic community exists in New York – now the time is ripe, but now they themselves have become orthodox. They have their own tradition, they cannot go against Baal Shem. And these people who are now Hasids are not really masters, they are simply followers of the followers of the followers.

You are here with me. You are face to face with something original. When you tell it to somebody else it will not be the original. You have heard it from me, then you will tell it to somebody else and much of it is lost – and then that person goes to somebody else and delivers the message. Again much is lost. Within a few years, within a few transfers, the truth is completely destroyed, only lies are left. And again a revolutionary movement becomes an orthodox tradition.

The second question:

Osho,
Can't you do it for me? Can't you cut my head off?
Because I can't drop it. I know that because I have
tried.

I can do that but there will be much trouble. Let me tell you an anecdote:

St. Peter returned to the new arrival waiting impatiently outside the gates. "I can't find your name," he reported. "Would you please spell it for me?" The man did so, and St. Peter left to check his reservation lists again. In a few moments he returned, "Say, you are not due for ten years. Who is your doctor?"

If I cut your head off, then St. Peter will ask you, "You are not due for many lives. Who is your guru?"

It cannot be done by another. It is not something that can be done from the outside. In fact you also cannot do it. You have to grow into it. It is not something that you can do or force; it comes through deeper understanding.

The dropping of the head is one of the most difficult things because you are identified with the head. You are the head! Your thoughts, your ideologies, your religion, your politics, your scriptures, your knowledge, your identity – everything is in your head. How can you drop it? Just think of dropping the head – then who are you? Without the head you are nobody.

You have to grow into understanding. When you can grow a new head above this head, only then can you drop this head. That's the whole effort of meditation – to help you grow a new head, a new head which does not need thoughts, does not need ideologies; which is pure awareness and enough unto itself; which needs no external influence to live; which lives from its own innermost core. When you have grown a new head, the old will be dropped very easily. It will drop on its own accord.

If I force anything upon you, you will resist it, you will become afraid, you will be scared. And nobody wants to die. It is a great art to be learned.

I have heard:

It was the day of the hanging, and as Mulla Nasruddin was

led to the foot of the steps of the scaffold, he suddenly stopped and refused to walk another step.

"Let us go," the guard said impatiently. "What is the matter?"

"Somehow," said Nasruddin, "those steps look mighty rickety. They just don't look safe enough to walk up."

He is going to be hanged, but those steps look "mighty rickety" – not safe enough to walk on! Even at the moment of death a person goes on clinging – to the very end. Nobody wants to die, and unless you learn to die you will never be able to live, you will never be able to know what life is. A person who is able to die is a person who is able to live, because life and death are two aspects of the same coin. You can choose both or you can drop both, but they both come together in one parcel, they are not different things.

Once you are afraid of death you are bound to be afraid of life. That's why I am talking about this Hasidic approach. The whole approach consists of methods, ways and means of how to die – the art of dying is the art of living also. Dying as an ego is being born as a non-ego; dying as a part is being born as a whole; dying as man is a basic step toward being born as a god.

But death is difficult, very difficult. Have you watched it? Except man, no animal can commit suicide. It is not possible for any animal even to think about committing suicide. Have you thought about it? Have you heard of any tree committing suicide, any animal committing suicide? No, only man, man's intelligence, can make it possible that a man can commit suicide.

And I am not talking about ordinary suicide – because that is not really suicide, you simply change the body – I am talking of the ultimate suicide. Once you die the way I am teaching you to die, you will never be born again in life. You will disappear into the cosmos, you will not have any form anymore, you will become the formless.

I have heard:

The man was charged with trespassing on the farmer's property and shooting quail. The Counsel for Defense tried to confuse the farmer.

"Now," he asked, "are you prepared to swear that this man shot your quail?"

"I didn't say he shot them," was the reply. "I said I suspected him of doing it."

"Ah, now we are coming to it. What made you suspect this man?"

"Well," replied the farmer, "firstly, I caught him on my land with a shotgun. Secondly, I heard a gun go off and saw some quail fall. Thirdly, I found four quail in his pocket, and you can't tell me them birds just flew in there and committed suicide."

Only man is capable of committing suicide. That is the glory of man. Only man can be capable enough to think that life is not worth living, only man is capable enough to reflect that this life is simply futile. Ordinarily when people commit suicide, they don't do it because they have understood life's futility, they do it only because they have understood *this* life's futility – and they are hoping that in another life somewhere else things will be better.

The spiritual suicide means that a man has come to understand that not only *this* life is futile, but life as such is futile. Then he starts thinking of how to get rid of being born again and again, how to get rid of getting into the tunnel of the body and of being confined and encaged; then he starts thinking of how to remain absolutely free without any form. This is what *moksha* is, this is what liberation is – or you can call it salvation.

A man can never be happy in the body because it is such a confinement. All around are walls; you are forced into a prison. It does not look like a prison because the prison walls with you – wherever you go it goes with you, so you don't feel that it is like a prison. Once you have known a life without the body, once you have become capable of getting out of the body – even for a single split moment – then you will see how you are confined, how you are imprisoned.

The body is a bondage, the mind is a bondage, but you have to understand, I cannot force you free. Remember one thing: you can be forced into bondage from the outside, but you cannot be forced into freedom from the outside. Somebody can force you into a prison cell, that can be done, but nobody can take you out of a prison cell. If you want to remain in a prison cell, you will find some other prison cell somewhere else. You may escape from one prison, but you will get into another – from the frying pan into the fire. You can easily change your prisons, but that doesn't make any difference. That's what everybody has been doing for millennia. Each life you have been in a prison – sometimes a man, sometimes a woman, sometimes black, sometimes white, sometimes Indian, sometimes Chinese, sometimes American. You have moved in all the forms possible.

When people come to me and I look into them, it is a surprise in how many forms they have moved in, how many bodies, how many shapes they have lived in, how many names and religions and countries... And still they are not fed up. And they go on repeating the old circle again and again.

Remember one thing more. Just as I said to you that suicide is absolutely human, no animal commits it, the same is true about boredom. Boredom is also absolutely human. A buffalo is never bored, a donkey is never bored – only man, only a highly evolved consciousness. If you are not bored with your life, it simply shows that you live in a very low state of consciousness.

A Buddha is bored, a Jesus is bored, a Mahavira is bored – bored to death! Just repetition all around and nothing else. Out of boredom comes renunciation. A man who is bored with the world becomes a sannyasin. The search is not for another world, it is for an end of the search. It is suicide, total, ultimate.

The third question:

Osho,
Listening to you I feel as if I am dying, as if you are
continuously pushing me farther away. You are my
peak, my Everest, so beautiful and so far away and yet
incredibly close. Is there anything I can do to open
myself to you?

My whole purpose here is to push you toward death, to
push you into the abyss of the unknown, to push you into a
zero experience. We in India call it *samadhi*. It is a zero experience – where in a way you are and in a way you are not; where
you are empty of all content, just the container has remained;
where all writing from the book has disappeared, just the book
remains, empty. That's the real Bible, the real Veda. When all
writing has disappeared and the book is absolutely empty; when
all the content, all the thoughts, mind, emotions, desires, have
disappeared and there is only a pure consciousness, empty of all
content – this is what I call the abyss.

You say, "You are my peak, my Everest…" Yes, that's true,
but the peak will come only later on. First comes the abyss. I
am also your abyss. Let me tell you one very, very beautiful
anecdote. Listen to it very attentively, and later on when you
are sitting silently at home, meditate over it.

A man went to a ranch to buy a horse, pointed at one and
said, "My, that's a beautiful pony right there. What kind is it?"

"That's a palomino," said the rancher.

"Well, any friend of yours is a friend of mine. I would like
to buy that pony," said the man.

The rancher replied, "I gotta tell you sir, it was owned by a
preacher-man. If you want the horse to move you say, 'Good
Lord'; if you want the horse to stop you gotta say, 'Amen.'"

"Let me try that horse," said the buyer.

He mounted and said, "Good Lord." The horse promptly
moved out and was soon galloping up in the mountains. The

man was yelling, "Good Lord! Good Lord!" and the horse was really moving. Suddenly he came to the end of a cliff, and panic-stricken he yelled, "Whoa! Whoa!" That didn't work and then he remembered and said, "Amen!" The horse stopped right on the end of the cliff.

And wiping his brow with relief, the man said, "Good Lord!"

You ask, "Is there anything I can do to open myself to you?" Say "Good Lord" and then all else will happen on its own accord.

The fourth question:

> Osho,
> I love every time I hear you speak, but my favorite
> thing I ever heard you say was the other day when you
> asked us if we could hear you.

I would like to ask it every day, every moment. Can you hear me? But just out of politeness I don't ask it. That day the mike failed and I could gather courage. But remember, you lied to me. When I said, "Can you hear me?" you said, "No." You lied. If you had not heard my question how could you answer it? Again because of politeness I remained quiet. I had to.

A young lady went to Mulla Nasruddin for advice. She said to the Mulla, "Should I marry a fellow who lies to me?"

"Yes, unless you want to remain unmarried forever," said Nasruddin.

I have to accept you liars as my disciples because there is no other way, unless I decide to remain a master without disciples. You lied to me absolutely that moment. You had heard me, you immediately said, "No." Not only did you like my asking you, "Can you hear me," I also loved your answer.

The fifth question:

Osho,
You call the Hasidim a joyous, enlightened
community, yet the Hasidism of modern New York
appears to be so rigid, austere, dogmatic and
contemptuous of both goyim and other Jews.
How did this transformation take place?

It always takes place.

Truth cannot remain long on the earth; it comes and it disappears. If you are available it hits you, and then it is gone. You cannot hold it on the earth. The earth is so false and people are so much engrossed in their lies that truth cannot remain here long. Whenever a buddha walks on the earth, truth walks for a few moments. When the buddha is gone, truth also disappears. Only the footprints are left and you go on worshipping the footprints. The footprints are not the buddha, and the words uttered by the buddha are just mere words. When you repeat them they are just words, they mean nothing.

It was Buddha who was the meaning behind the words. You can repeat exactly the same words, but they will not mean the same, because the person behind the words is no longer the same.

The Hasidim were a joyous community when Baal Shem was there. When he walked on the earth, the Hasidim were one of the most beautiful communities on the earth – they flowered. A master is needed, a living master is needed. Only in a living master's presence does your innermost bud open, blossom.

After Baal Shem disappeared, there was only a tradition left. What he said, what he did, the legends about him, are many. And then people go on repeating them, people go on imitating them. These people are bound to be false.

But this is natural, so don't be angry at them. Once I am gone from here this community will not be so joyous, cannot be. It is just natural. Then the words will be there and people will be repeating them and they will try to follow them religiously, but there will be effort. Right now there is no effort. You are simply flowing with me. Right now it is spontaneous, right now it is a love affair. Then it will be a sort of duty to be fulfilled. You will feel an obligation.

You will remember me. You will want to live the same way, but something very vital will be missing – the life will be missing. Whenever a master departs only a dead corpse of his teaching remains.

So always seek a living master. A dead master is of no use – because a dead master means nothing but a dead teaching. Always seek a living master. But it is very difficult because people's minds are very slow. By the time you come to recognize somebody as a master he is gone. This is the difficulty. By the time you recognize that Jesus is a master, Jesus is no longer there. Then there are only Christians, then there are churches, then there are the pope and the priest, and they catch hold of you.

Yes, Hasidism has become orthodox but the Hasids were not. They were a living religion, a very living river.

I have heard:

A rabidly anti-Catholic Jew was on his deathbed. All the family were gathered round as he gasped, "Fetch a priest."

They were all thunder-struck, but his wife said to their eldest son, "Go on, it is his dying wish. Fetch a priest." So the son fetched a Catholic priest, who received the old man into the Church, gave him the last rites and left.

The eldest boy, with tears in his eyes, whispered to his father, "Dad, all your life you have brought us up to believe that the Church of Rome is the anti-Christ. How come in your last moments you can bring yourself to join them? You are a Jew, and you have always believed in the Judaic tradition. How can you do this at the last moment?"

And with his last breath the old man muttered, "Another one of the bastards dead."

He converted himself to be a Catholic so that a Catholic dies in the world. "Another one of the bastards dead!"

People always become that way because people live through the mind. Mind is a tradition.

I have heard:

"Is your grandfather a religious man?" asked the young co-ed of her date.

"He's so orthodox," replied the boy, "that when he plays chess he doesn't use bishops, he uses rabbis!"

The ego functions in a very traditional way. To be revolutionary, one needs to be beyond the ego. And it is not that you can do it once and forever, you have to do it every moment again and again because the ego goes on closing in on you, it goes on caving in on you. Each moment that you pass through, whatsoever you have lived, whatsoever you have experienced, becomes your ego. You have to discard it. Renunciation is not once and for all. You have to renounce every moment; whatsoever is gathered you have to renounce it, only then renunciation remains a revolution. And not only do you have to renounce ordinary things of the world, you have to renounce ordinary ideologies also – Jewish, Christian, Hindu, Mohammedan. You have to renounce thoughts so that you can remain in a pure mirrorlike reflection. Then your consciousness can remain undisturbed, uncolored by any thought, you can see into things directly and your consciousness is not distracted or distorted by any prejudice.

Once a tradition settles, once a religion is no longer revolutionary, you start interpreting it in your own ways. Then you don't bother what Buddha means, then you start reading your own thoughts into Buddha's assertions. Then you don't bother what Krishna says, you go on reading into the Gita whatsoever you want to read. Then the perversion settles. That's why I insist again and again: if you can find a living master, be with him – because you cannot distort a living master. You will try! But you cannot distort him because a living master can stop you from distorting his message. But a dead book, a scripture – Holy Bible, Holy Koran, Holy Gita – what can they do? They may be holy, but they are completely dead, you can do whatsoever you want to do with them. And man is very cunning and very clever.

When aged Fennessy collapsed on the street, a crowd soon gathered and began making suggestions as to how the old fellow should be revived.

Maggie O'Reilly yelled, "Give the poor man some whiskey."

No one paid any attention to her and the crowd continued shouting out suggestions. Finally Fennessy opened one eye, pulled himself up on an elbow, and said weakly, "Will the lot of ye hold your tongues and let Maggie O'Reilly speak?"

Whatsoever we want to hear, whatsoever we want, becomes our scripture, becomes our interpretation. People are rigid. So whether they are Hasids or Buddhists or Sufis or Zen Buddhists does not matter – people are rigid, people's minds are rigid. Wherever they belong they create rigidity there. You can move from being a Hindu and you can become a Christian, or from Christian you can become a Mohammedan, but it will not make much difference because you will remain you. And you will do the same by being a Christian, you will do the same by being a Mohammedan or by being a Hindu. What ideology you believe in does not matter much. The real thing that matters is you, your consciousness, your state of consciousness.

You are here with me. Your children, the next generation, will believe in me simply because their father or their mother believed in me. They will not have any direct contact with me, they will simply believe; it will not be a trust, it will be just a mental thing, a formal thing.

It happens that sometimes the children come and when the mother takes sannyas, the child also wants to take sannyas.

The child does not know what he is doing, not knowing where he is moving; he is just imitating the mother. The mother has come on her own, but the child has come just as a shadow. For the mother I have a totally different meaning, for the child I have no meaning at all. If the mother had gone to another master, the child would have been initiated there. If the mother had become Mohammedan or Christian, the child would have become Mohammedan or Christian.

There is no relevance for the child, it is not significant for the child – and it may become part of his ego that he is a sannyasin. Later in his life he may wear orange, may wear a mala, and he will do the formal thing, but he will be as ordinary a mind as there are all over the world. And he will do with his belief what the ordinary mind has always been prone to do: he will become rigid about it, fanatical about it. He will start declaring that *here* is truth and nowhere else.

When you declare that only your belief is true and all else is false, you are not concerned with truth at all. You are simply concerned with the assertion of your ego. It is an ego declaration, "*My* country has to be right, *my* religion has to be right. Wrong or right, *my* country has to be right, *my* religion has to be right – because it is *my* religion."

Deep down it is my "I" that has to be right.

The sixth question:

Osho,
Last night, in the early morning, I saw two dreams
one after another. In one, you were sitting in a room
in complete silence. I entered the room very slowly,
came closer and closer to you, bowed down, touched
your feet. You placed your hands on my head. I felt
very blissful, ecstatic, very, very light. In the other
dream there was a beautiful room, very cool,
soothing, blue-colored. You were lying on the bed.

Laxmi, some other disciples and myself were sitting
there – very few disciples were there. Laxmi beckoned
to me to come closer near your bed. You were
indicating something not indicated before. Your
fingers were making very different gestures. It looked
as if you were giving your final message. I could even
hear it very clearly and distinctly. It was, "Drink me,
eat me, breathe me. Don't leave me undrunk,
uneaten, unbreathed." And we all were weeping.

There you missed. You should have been laughing. Correct
your dream. Next time don't commit that mistake.

The seventh question:

Osho,
"Shall the day of parting be the day of gathering? And
shall it be said that my eve was in truth my dawn?
Shall my heart become a tree, heavy-laden with fruit
that I may gather and give unto them? Am I a harp
that the hand of the Mighty may touch me, or a flute
that his breath may pass through me? A seeker of
silences am I, and what treasure have I found in
silences that I may dispense with confidence?"

Yes, a million, million times, yes. Let this be your guide.
You just allow the divine and he will start singing through your
flute. Just don't hinder his way.

Only one thing is needed – don't hinder existence. It is not
a question of God playing on your flute or not. It is only a
question of whether you will allow him or not. If you allow
him, this very moment the song begins. If you don't allow him
and you go on praying, "Play on my flute," then it is never
going to begin.

Man has nothing else to do but surrender – in deep trust, in deep love. Don't be a doer, just surrender. Let there be a let-go. And whatsoever you have asked, I say yes, a million, million times, yes.

The eighth question:

> Osho,
> I was a sad child, a frightened adolescent, and an angry young man. Yet all my life I have felt deep within that everything was funny, absurd, ridiculous. When I was in the seminary some years ago, a friend told me that we have such a limited capacity for divine things that if God told us a joke, we would die laughing. I remember my friend's statement because since coming to Pune I have felt a great belly-laugh welling up inside of me. I feel that God has told me a joke, and the punch-line is slowly dawning on me. I am a little afraid that I will not catch it fully until I have left Pune in December, and then I will laugh so loud and hard that you will be able to hear me all the way from Texas. Please tell me, will I survive this joke?

It is impossible to survive *this* joke. The laughter that I am teaching to you is something that is going to destroy you completely. The laughter that I am teaching to you is very destructive, it is a crucifixion. But only after this destruction is there creation. Only out of chaos are stars born and only after crucifixion is there resurrection.

No, you will not be able to survive this laughter. If you really allow it, you will be drowned by it, you will disappear and only laughter will remain. If *you* laugh then the laughter is not total. When there is only laughter and you are not, then it is total. And only then have you heard the joke that God is telling.

Yes, this whole cosmos is a joke; Hindus call it *leela*. It is a joke, it is a play. And the day that you understand then you start laughing, and that laughing never stops. It goes on and on. It spreads all over the cosmos.

Laughter is prayer. If you can laugh you have learned how to pray. Don't be serious; a serious person can never be religious. Only a person who can laugh, not only at others but at himself also, can be religious. A person who can laugh absolutely, who sees the whole ridiculousness and the whole game of life, becomes enlightened in that laughter.

No. You ask: "Please tell me, will I survive this joke?" No, if you have heard the joke you cannot survive. If you have not heard, then it is very unfortunate because you will survive.

The last question and the most important:

Osho,
Why do Jews have long noses?

Now don't be afraid. I am not going to give you a long talk, a ninety-minute talk, no, because I know the answer. When you don't know the answer you have to give a very long answer. You see, that's why I go on talking so long. When I don't know the answer I have to talk very long. In my talking you forget your question. But when I know the answer, then there is no need. And I know the answer. I happen to know the answer.

How I came upon the answer – about that I must tell you something.

One day – just a few days ago – Vivek asked me this question early in the morning: "Why do Jews have long noses?" I settled in my chair, in my posture. I made my towel comfortable, looked at the clock and I was just going to start a great discourse on the philosophy and the physiology of the Jewish nose. But then she became apprehensive and afraid. Naturally – because once I take off, then it takes ninety minutes at least for me to land again on the earth. So she said, "Stop! Stop! I happen to know the answer! You need not give me the answer!"

I was very shocked because I was already on the way. In a hurried way she said, "Because the air is free!"

It is a beauty. I loved it. It explains everything. The Jews have long noses because the air is free!

Enough for today.

7

The Treasure

Rabbi Bunam used to tell young men
who came to him for the first time
the story of Rabbi Eisik, son of Rabbi Yekel in Cracow.
After many years of great poverty,
which had never shaken his faith in God,
he dreamed that someone bade him look for treasure
under the bridge which leads to the king's palace in Prague.
When the dream recurred the third time he set out for Prague.
But the bridge was guarded day and night
and he did not dare start digging.
Nevertheless he went to the bridge every morning
and kept walking around it until evening.
Finally, the captain of the guards,
who had been watching him, asked in a kindly way whether he
was looking for something or waiting for someone.
Rabbi Eisik told him of the dream
which had brought him from a faraway country.
The captain laughed, "And so to please your dream you wore out
your shoes to come here! You poor fellow.
And as far as having faith in dreams, if I had had it I should
have had to go to Cracow and dig for treasure under the stove in

the room of a Jew – Eisik, son of Yekel!
That's what the dream told me. And imagine what it would
have been like; one half of the Jews over there are called Eisik,
and the other half Yekel!" And he laughed again.
Rabbi Eisik bowed, traveled home,
dug up the treasure from under his stove,
and built the house of prayer which is called Reb Eisik's Shul.
Rabbi Bunam used to add,
"Take this story to heart and make what it says your own. There
is something you cannot find anywhere in the world, not even at
the zaddik's,
and there is, nevertheless, a place where you can find it."

Life is a search, a constant search, a desperate search, a hopeless search, a search for something one knows not what. There is a deep urge to seek, but one knows not what one is seeking.

And there is a state of mind in which whatsoever you get is not going to give you any satisfaction. Frustration seems to be the destiny of humanity, because whatsoever you get becomes meaningless the very moment you have got it. You start searching again.

The search continues whether you get anything or not. It seems irrelevant what you have got, what you have not got – the search continues anyway. The poor are searching, the rich are searching, the ill are searching, the well are searching, the powerful are searching, the powerless are searching, the stupid are searching, the wise are searching – and nobody knows exactly what.

This very search – what this search is and why it is there – has to be understood. It seems that there is a gap in the human being, in the human mind; in the very structure of the human consciousness there seems to be a hole, a black hole. You go on throwing things into it, and they go on disappearing. Nothing seems to make it full, nothing seems to help toward fulfillment. It is a very feverish search. You seek it in this world, you seek it in the other world; sometimes you seek it in money, in power, in prestige, and sometimes you seek it as God, bliss, love, meditation, prayer – but the search continues. It seems that man is ill with search.

The search does not allow you to be here and now because the search always leads you somewhere else. The search is a project, the search is a desire: that somewhere else is what is needed, that it exists, but it exists somewhere else, not here where you are. It certainly exists, but not in this moment of time, not now – and somewhere else. It exists "then-there", never here-now. It goes on nagging you; it goes on pulling you, pushing you, it goes on throwing you into more and more madness; it drives you crazy and it is never fulfilled.

I have heard about a very great Sufi mystic woman, Rabiya al-Adabiya:

One evening people found her sitting on the road searching for something. She was an old woman, her eyes were weak and it was difficult for her to see. So the neighbors came to help her. They asked, "What are you searching for?"

Rabiya said, "That question is irrelevant, I am searching. If you can help me, help."

They laughed and said, "Rabiya, have you gone mad? You say our question is irrelevant, but if we don't know what you are searching for, how can we help?"

Rabiya said, "Okay. Just to satisfy you, I am searching for my needle, I have lost my needle."

They started helping her – but immediately they became aware of the fact that the road is very big and a needle is a very tiny thing. So they asked Rabiya, "Please tell us where you lost it – the exact, precise place. Otherwise it is difficult. The road is big and we can go on searching and searching forever. Where did you lose it?"

Rabiya said, "Again you ask an irrelevant question. How is it concerned with my search?"

They stopped. They said, "You have certainly gone crazy!"

Rabiya said, "Okay. Just to satisfy you, I have lost it in my house."

They laughed, they asked, "Then why are you searching here?"

And Rabiya is reported to have said, "Because here there is light and there is no light inside."

The sun was setting and there was a little light still left on the road.

This parable is very significant. Have you ever asked yourself what you are searching for? Have you ever made it a point of deep meditation to know what you are searching for? No. Even if in some vague moment, dreamy moment, you have some inkling of what you are searching for, it is never precise, it is never exact. You have not yet defined it.

If you try to define it, the more it becomes defined the more you will feel that there is no need to search for it. The search can continue only in a state of vagueness, in a state of dream; when things are not clear you simply go on searching, pulled by some inner urge, pushed by some inner urgency. One thing you do know: you need to search. This is an inner need. But you don't know what you are seeking.

And unless you know what you are seeking, how can you find it? It is vague – you think it is in money, power, prestige, respectability. But then you see people who are respectable, people who are powerful – they are also seeking. Then you see people who are tremendously rich – they are also seeking. To the very end of their life they are seeking. So richness is not going to help, power is not going to help. The search continues in spite of what you have.

The search must be for something else. These names, these labels – money, power, prestige – these are just to satisfy your mind. They are just to help you feel that you are searching for something. That something is still undefined, a very vague feeling.

The first thing for the real seeker, for the seeker who has

become a little alert, aware, is to define the search; to formulate a clear-cut concept of it, what it is; to bring it out of the dreaming consciousness; to encounter it in deep alertness, to look into it directly; to face it. Immediately a transformation starts happening. If you start defining your search, you will start losing your interest in the search. The more defined it becomes, the less it is there. Once it is clearly known what it is, suddenly it disappears. It exists only when you are not attentive.

Let it be repeated: the search exists only when you are sleepy; the search exists only when you are not aware; the search exists only in your unawareness. The unawareness creates the search.

Yes, Rabiya is right. Inside there is no light. And because there is no light and no consciousness inside, of course you go on searching outside – because outside it seems clearer.

Our senses are all extrovert. The eyes open outward, the hands move, spread outward, the legs move into the outside, the ears listen to the outside noises, sounds. Whatsoever is available to you is all opening toward the outside; all the five senses move in an extrovert way. You start searching there where you see, feel, touch – the light of the senses falls outside. And the seeker is inside.

This dichotomy has to be understood. The seeker is inside, but because the light is outside, the seeker starts moving in an ambitious way, trying to find something outside which will be fulfilling.

It is never going to happen. It has never happened. It cannot happen in the nature of things – because, unless you have first sought the seeker, all your search is meaningless. Unless you come to know who you are, all that you seek is futile because you don't know the seeker. Without knowing the seeker how can you move in the right dimension, in the right direction? It is impossible. The first things should be considered first.

So these two things are very important: first, make it absolutely clear to yourself what your object is. Don't just go on stumbling in darkness. Focus your attention on the object –

what you are really searching for. Because sometimes you want one thing and you go on searching for something else, so even if you succeed you will not be fulfilled. Have you seen people who have succeeded? Can you find bigger failures anywhere else? You have heard the proverb that nothing succeeds like success. It is absolutely wrong. I would like to tell you: nothing fails like success. The proverb must have been invented by stupid people. Nothing fails like success.

It is said about Alexander the Great that the day he became the world conqueror he closed the doors of his room and started weeping. I don't know whether it really happened or not, but if he was even a little intelligent it must have happened.

His generals were very disturbed. What has happened? They had never seen Alexander weeping. He was not that type of man, he was a great warrior. They had seen him in great difficulties, in situations where life was very much in danger, where death was very imminent, and they had not seen even a tear coming out of his eyes. They had never seen him in any desperate, hopeless moment. What has happened to him now – now when he has succeeded, when he is the world conqueror?

They knocked on the door, they went in and they asked, "What has happened to you? Why are you crying like a child?"

He said, "Now that I have succeeded, I know it has been a failure. Now I know that I stand in exactly the same place as I used to be in when I started this nonsense of conquering the world. And the point has become clear to me now because there is no other world to conquer anymore – otherwise I could have remained on the journey, I could have started conquering another world. Now there is no other world to conquer, now there is nothing else to do, and suddenly I am thrown to myself."

A successful man is always thrown to himself in the end and then he suffers the tortures of hell because he wasted his whole life. He searched and searched, he staked everything that he had, now he is successful – and his heart is empty and his soul is meaningless and there is no fragrance, there is no benediction.

So the first thing is to know exactly what you are seeking. I insist upon it, because the more you focus your eyes on the object of your search, the more the object starts disappearing. When your eyes are absolutely fixed, suddenly there is nothing to seek; immediately your eyes start turning toward yourself. When there is no object for search, when all objects have disappeared, there is emptiness. In that emptiness is conversion, turning in. You suddenly start looking at yourself. Now there is nothing to seek, and a new desire arises to know who this seeker is.

If there is something to seek, you are a worldly man; if there is nothing to seek, and the question, "Who is this seeker?" has become important to you, then you are a religious man. This is the way I define the worldly and the religious.

If you are still seeking something – maybe in the other life, on the other shore, in heaven, in paradise, in *moksha,* it makes no difference – you are still a worldly man. If all seeking has stopped and you have suddenly become aware that now there is only one thing to know: "Who is this seeker in me? What is this energy that wants to seek? Who am I?" – then there is a transformation. All values suddenly change. You start moving inward.

Then Rabiya is no longer sitting on the road searching for a needle that is lost somewhere in the darkness of one's own inner soul. Once you have started moving inward… In the beginning it is very dark – Rabiya is right. It is very, very dark because for lives together you have never been inside, your eyes have been focused on the outside world.

Have you watched it? Observed? Sometimes when you come in from the road where it is very sunny and the sun is hot and there is bright light – when you suddenly come into the room or into the house it is very dark because the eyes are focused for the outside light, for much light. When there is much light, the eyes shrink. In darkness the eyes have to relax. A bigger aperture is needed in darkness; in light a smaller aperture is enough. That's how a camera functions and that's how your eye functions. The camera has been invented along the lines of the human eye.

So when you suddenly come from the outside, your own house looks dark. But if you sit a little while, by and by the darkness disappears. There is more light; your eyes are settling.

For many lives together you have been outside in the hot sun, in the world, so when you go in you have completely forgotten how to enter and how to readjust your eyes. Meditation is nothing but a readjustment of your vision, a readjustment of your seeing faculty, of your eyes. In India that is what is called the third eye. It is not an eye somewhere; it is a readjustment, a total readjustment of your vision. By and by the darkness is no longer dark; a subtle, suffused light starts being felt.

And if you go on looking inside – it takes time – gradually, slowly, you start feeling such a beautiful light inside. But it is not aggressive light; it is not like the sun, it is more like the moon. It is not glaring, it is not dazzling, it is very cool; it is not hot, it is very compassionate, it is very soothing, it is a balm.

By and by, once you have got adjusted to the inside light, you will see that you are the very source. The seeker is the sought. Then you will see that the treasure is within you and the whole fault was that you were seeking for it outside. You were seeking for it somewhere outside and it has always been there inside you, it has always been here within you. You were seeking in a wrong direction, that's all.

Everything is available to you as much as it is available to anyone else, as much as it is available to a Buddha, to a Baal Shem, to a Moses, to Mohammed. It is all available to you, you are only looking in the wrong direction. As far as the treasure is concerned you are not poorer than Buddha or Mohammed – no, existence has never created a poor man. It does not happen, it cannot happen – because existence creates you out of its richness. How can it create a poor man? You are its overflowing, you are part of its being, how can you be poor? You are rich, infinitely rich, as rich as existence itself.

But you are looking in a wrong direction. The direction is wrong; that's why you go on missing. And it is not that you will not succeed in life, you can succeed, but still you will be a failure. Nothing is going to satisfy you because nothing can be attained in the outside world which can be comparable to the inner treasure, to the inner light, to the inner peace, to the inner bliss. Now this story. This story is tremendously meaningful.

Rabbi Bunam used to tell young men
who came to him for the first time,
the story of Rabbi Eisik, son of Rabbi Yekel in Cracow.
After many years of great poverty,
which had never shaken his faith in God,
he dreamed that someone bade him look for treasure
under the bridge which leads to the king's palace in Prague.
When the dream recurred the third time he set out for Prague.
But the bridge was guarded day and night
and he did not dare start digging.
Nevertheless he went to the bridge every morning
and kept walking around it until evening.
Finally, the captain of the guards,
who had been watching him, asked in a kindly way whether he
was looking for something, or waiting for someone.
Rabbi Eisik told him of the dream
which had brought him from a faraway country.
The captain laughed, "And so to please your dream you wore out
your shoes to come here! You poor fellow.
And as far as having faith in dreams, if I had had it I should
have had to go to Cracow and dig for treasure under the stove in
the room of a Jew – Eisik, son of Yekel!
That's what the dream told me. And imagine what it would
have been like; one half of the Jews over there are called Eisik,
and the other half Yekel!" And he laughed again.
Rabbi Eisik bowed, traveled home,
dug up the treasure from under his stove,

and built the house of prayer which is called Reb Eisik's Shul.
Rabbi Bunam used to add,
"Take this story to heart and make what it says your own. There
is something you cannot find anywhere in the world, not even at
the zaddik's,
and there is, nevertheless, a place where you can find it."

The first thing to be understood about the story is that he dreamed. All desiring is dreaming and all dreaming takes you away from yourself – that is the very nature of the dream.

You may be sleeping in Pune and you may dream of Philadelphia. In the morning you will not wake up in Philadelphia, you will wake up in Pune. In a dream you can be anywhere; a dream has a tremendous freedom because it is unreal. In a dream you can be anywhere: on the moon, on Mars. You can choose any planet, it is your game. In a dream you can be anywhere, there is only one place you cannot be – that is where you are.

This is the first thing to be understood about the dreaming consciousness. If you are where you are, then the dream cannot exist, because then there is no point in the dream, then there is no meaning in the dream. If you are exactly where you are and you are exactly what you are, then how can the dream exist? The dream can exist only if you go away from you. You may be a poor man and you dream about being an emperor. You may be an ordinary man and you dream about yourself being extraordinary. You walk on the earth and you dream that you fly in the sky. The dream has to be a falsification of reality; the dream has to be something else than reality.

In reality there is no dreaming, so those who want to know the real have to stop dreaming.

In India we have divided human consciousness into four stages. We call the first stage the ordinary waking consciousness. Right now you are in the ordinary waking consciousness. What is an ordinary waking consciousness? You appear to be awake, but you are not. You are a little bit awake, but that little bit is so small that it doesn't make much difference.

You can walk to your home, you can recognize your wife or your husband, you can drive your car – that little bit is only enough for this. It gives you a sort of efficiency, that's all. But it is a very small consciousness, exhausted very easily, lost very easily. If somebody insults you it is lost, it is exhausted. If somebody insults you, you become angry, you are no longer conscious. That's why after anger many people say, "Why did I do it? How did I do it? How could I do it? It happened in spite of me." Yes, they are right – it happened in spite of you because you lost your consciousness. In anger, in violent rage, people are possessed; they do things they would never do if they were a little aware. They can kill, they can destroy; they can even destroy themselves.

The ordinary waking consciousness is only "waking" for name's sake – deep down dreams continue. Just a small tip of the iceberg is alert – the whole thing is underneath, in darkness. Watch it sometimes. Just anywhere close your eyes and look within: you will see dreams floating like clouds surrounding you. You can sit on a chair any moment of the day, close your eyes, relax, and suddenly you see that the dreams have started. In fact they have not started, they were continuing – just as during the day stars disappear from the sky. They don't really disappear, they are there, but because of the light of the sun you don't see them. If you go into a deep well, a very deep, dark well, from the dark well you can look at the sky and you will be able to recognize a few stars, even at midday. The stars are there; when night comes they don't reappear, they have always been there, all twenty-four hours. They don't go anywhere, the sunlight just hides them.

Exactly the same is the case with your dreaming: it is just below the surface, it continues just underground. On the top of it is a little layer of awareness, underneath are a thousand and one dreams. Close your eyes any time and you will find yourself dreaming.

That's why people are in great difficulty when they start meditating. They come to me and they say, "This is something funny, strange. We never thought that there were so many thoughts." They have never closed their eyes, they have never sat in a relaxed posture, they have never gone in to see what was happening there because they were too engaged in the outside world, they were too occupied. Because of that occupation they never became aware of this constant activity inside.

In India, the ordinary waking consciousness is called the first state. The second state is that of dreaming. Any time you close your eyes you are in it. At night you are continuously in it, almost continuously. Whether you remember your dreams in the morning or not is not of much importance, you go on dreaming. There are at least eight cycles of dreaming during the night. One cycle continues for many minutes – fifteen, twenty minutes, then there is a gap, then there is another cycle, then there is a gap, then again there is a cycle. Throughout the whole night you are continuously dreaming and dreaming and dreaming. This is the second state of consciousness.

This parable is concerned with the second state of consciousness. Ordinarily all desires exist in the second state of consciousness, the dreaming state. Desire is a dream, and to work for a dream is doomed from the very beginning because a dream can never become real. Even if you sometimes feel it has become almost real, it never becomes real – a dream by nature is empty. It has no substance in it.

The third state is sleep, deep sleep, *sushupti*. In it all dreaming disappears – but all consciousness also. While you are awake there is a little awareness, very little; when you are dreaming, even that little awareness disappears. But still there is an iota of awareness – that's why you can remember in the morning that you had a dream, such and such a dream. But in deep sleep even that disappears. It is as if you have completely disappeared. Nothing remains. A nothingness surrounds you.

These are the three ordinary states. The fourth state is called *turiya.* The fourth is simply called "the fourth." *Turiya* means the fourth. The fourth state is that of a buddha. It is almost like dreamless sleep, with one difference – that difference is very great. It is as peaceful as deep sleep, as without dreams as deep sleep, but it is absolutely alert, aware.

Krishna says in his Gita that a real yogi never sleeps. That does not mean that a real yogi simply sits awake in his room the whole night. There are a few foolish people who are doing that. That a real yogi never sleeps means that while he is asleep he remains aware, alert.

Ananda lived with Buddha for forty years. One day, he asked Buddha, "One thing surprises me very much; I am intrigued. You will have to answer me. This is just out of curiosity, but I cannot contain it anymore. When you sleep at night I have watched you many times, for hours together, and you sleep in such a way that it seems as if you are awake. You sleep in such a graceful way; your face, your body – everything is so graceful. I have seen many other people sleeping, and they start mumbling, their face goes through contortions, their body loses all grace, their face becomes ugly, they don't look beautiful anymore..." All beauty has to be managed, controlled, practiced; in deep sleep it all disappears.

"And, one thing more," Ananda said. "You never change your posture, you remain in the same posture. Wherever you put your hand in the beginning, you keep it there the whole night. You never change it. It seems that deep down you are keeping absolutely alert."

Buddha said, "You are right. That happens when meditation is perfect."

Then awareness penetrates your being so deeply that you are aware in all of the four states. When you are aware in all four states then dreaming absolutely disappears, because in an alert mind a dream cannot exist. And the ordinary waking state becomes an extraordinary waking state – what Gurdjieff calls self-remembering. One remembers oneself absolutely, each moment. There is no gap. The remembrance is a continuity. One becomes a luminous being.

And deep sleep is there, but its quality changes completely. The body is asleep, but the soul is awake and alert, watchful. The whole body is deep in darkness, but the lamp of inner consciousness burns bright.

This story says:

> *After many years of great poverty,*
> *which had never shaken his faith in God,*
> *he dreamed that someone bade him look for treasure*
> *under the bridge which leads to the king's palace in Prague.*

After many years of great poverty... it is natural that one should start dreaming about treasures. We always dream about that which we don't have. Fast for one day and in the night you will dream about food. Try to force celibacy upon yourself and your dreams will become sexual, they will have a quality of sexuality.

That's why psychoanalysis says that the analysis of dreams is of tremendous import, because it shows what you are repressing. Your dream becomes a symbolic indication of the repressed content of your mind. If a person continuously dreams about food, about feasts, that simply shows that the person is starving himself. Jaina monks always dream about food – they may say so, they may not. If you fast too much you are bound to dream about food. That's why many religious saints become so afraid of falling asleep.

Even Mahatma Gandhi was very afraid to go into sleep. He was trying to reduce it to as little as possible. Religious people make it a point to try not to sleep for too long – four hours, five hours at the most. Three is the ideal. Why? Because once your need of bodily rest is complete your mind starts weaving and spinning dreams, and immediately the mind brings up things which you have been repressing. Mahatma Gandhi said, "I have become a celibate as far as my waking consciousness is concerned, but in my dreams I am not a celibate." He was a true man in a sense – truer than other so-called saints. At least he accepted that in his dreams he was not yet celibate.

But unless you are celibate in your dreams you are not yet celibate, because the dream reveals whatsoever you are repressing during the day. The dream simply brings it back to your consciousness. Dream is a language, a communication from the unconscious which is saying, "Please don't do this to me. It is impossible to tolerate. Stop this nonsense. You are destroying my natural spontaneity. Allow me, allow whatsoever is potential in me to flower."

When a person represses nothing, dreams disappear. So a buddha never dreams. If your meditation goes deep you will immediately find that your dreams are becoming fewer and fewer and fewer. The day your dreams completely disappear and you attain to clarity in your sleep – no clouds, no smoke, no thoughts; simple, silent sleep, without any interference of dreams – that day you have become a buddha, then your meditation has come to fruition.

Psychoanalysis insists that dreams have to be understood because man is very cunning: he can deceive while he is awake, but he cannot deceive when he is in a dream. A dream is truer. Look at the irony. A dream is truer about you than your so-called waking consciousness. Man has become so false, man has become so fake that the waking consciousness cannot be relied upon; you have corrupted it too much.

A psychoanalyst immediately goes into your dreams, he wants to know about your dreams, he does not want to know about your religion, he does not want to know about your philosophy of life, he does not want to know whether you are a Hindu or a Christian, an Indian or an American – that is all nonsense. He wants to know what your dreams are. Look at the irony – your dreams have become so real that your reality is less real than your dreams. You are living such a pseudo-life, inauthentic, false, that the psychoanalyst has to go to your dreams to find a few glimpses of truth. Only your dreams are still beyond your control.

There are also people who try to control dreams. In the East methods have been invented to control dreams. That means you are not even allowing the unconscious to convey any message to you. You can do that too. You can cultivate dreams if you work hard. You can start planning your dreams. You can give a story to your own unconscious to unfold in your dreams. If you do it consistently, every day, by and by you will be able to corrupt the unconscious.

For example, once a devotee of Krishna stayed with me. He said, "I always dream of Krishna."

I asked him, "How do you manage it? A dream is not something that you can manage. What method have you tried?"

He said, "A simple method which my guru gave to me. Every night when I go to sleep I go on thinking and thinking about Krishna, fantasizing. After three years of continuously practicing fantasy while falling asleep, one day it happened. Whatsoever I had fantasized continued in my dream and it became my dream. Since then I have been having tremendously religious dreams."

I said, "You just go into the details – because you may have managed the story, but the unconscious will be sending messages in the story itself. The unconscious can use your story to send its messages."

He said, "What do you mean?"

I said, "You simply give me the content of your dream, the detailed content."

And he started telling me. It was absolutely sexual. Krishna was his lover and he had become a male *gopi,* a boyfriend. The content was homosexual. And they were dancing together and kissing and hugging and loving each other.

I said, "You have simply changed the figure, but the content still remains. And my understanding is that you are a homosexual."

He was very much disturbed and shocked. He said, "What do you mean? How have you come to know about it?"

I told him, "Your dream is a clear message."

He started weeping and crying. He said, "From my childhood I was never attracted to women, I was always attracted to men. And I thought it was good because women would distract me from my path."

The homosexual content had entered into his religious story. Krishna was nothing but a homosexual partner. He became very disturbed and that very night the dream disappeared and a purely homosexual dream entered. He said, "What have you done to me?"

I said, "I have not done anything. I have simply made your message clear to you. You can fabricate a story, but that doesn't matter, the inner content remains the same."

Just see. Go to a person who is not religious. You will find nude pictures of women in Indian homes, in bachelors' homes. These people are not religious. But go to a religious man. He may have beautiful pictures of gods and goddesses, but just look at the content, at the detail of it. Whether it is a film actress or whether it is a goddess makes no difference. Just look at the breasts! They will indicate exactly the same content. The story is different, somebody has a picture of a goddess on his wall and somebody has Elizabeth Taylor or somebody else's picture, or Sophia Loren – but it makes no difference. Whether you call her a goddess or you call her a film actress makes no difference. Look at the detail and you will see what that man is hankering after.

You can manipulate your dreams, you can destroy the purity of your unconscious's messages, but still the unconscious will go on giving you messages. It has to. It has to scream to you because you are destroying your own nature, your own spontaneity.

This dream happened: *After many years of great poverty, which had never shaken his faith in God, he dreamed that someone bade him look for treasure under the bridge which leads to the king's palace in Prague.* Poor men always dream of kings' palaces and kings' treasure and things like that. If you have very rich dreams it simply shows that you are a poor man. Only very rich people dream of becoming sannyasins – a Buddha, a Mahavira. Living in their palaces they have dreams of becoming sannyasins, because they were fed up with their success. Success is finished for them, it has no charm, it has no allurement, it has no fascination any more. Now they think that a poor man's life is a real life and they seek somewhere else where they are not.

But the dream always goes somewhere else. The rich man thinks that the poor man is living a real life, and the poor man thinks that the rich man is living a real life. But the fallacy is the same: they both think, "Real life is somewhere else where I am not. Somehow I am always excluded from the real life – somebody else is enjoying it. Life is always happening somewhere else. Wherever I go, life simply disappears. Wherever I reach for it I always find emptiness." But it is always happening somewhere else. Life seems to be like the horizon, it is just ahead somewhere. It is a mirage.

When the dream recurred the third time he set out for Prague.

And remember, even if a dream recurs too many times it almost starts looking real. Repetition makes things real.

Adolf Hitler wrote in his autobiography *Mein Kampf* that if you go on repeating a lie it becomes real. Repetition is the key. And he should know, he practiced it. He is not simply asserting something theoretical, he practiced it the whole of his life. He uttered lies, absolutely absurd lies, but one thing he insisted on – he went on repeating. When you go on repeating some lie again and again and again it starts becoming real, because the mind starts getting hypnotized by it.

Repetition is the method of hypnosis. Repeat anything and it becomes engraved in your being – that's how we are deluded in life. If you repeat, "This woman is beautiful, this woman is beautiful..." If you go on repeating it, you will start seeing beauty in her. It may be there, it may not be there, it doesn't matter – if you repeat it long enough it will become true. If you think that money is the goal of life, go on repeating it and it will become your goal of life.

That's how all advertising functions: it just goes on repeating. The advertiser believes in the science of repetition; he simply goes on repeating that this brand of cigarette is the best. When you read it for the first time you may not believe it. But next time, again and again – how long can you remain an unbeliever? By and by the belief will arise. And the belief will be such that you may not even become conscious of it. It will be subliminal, it will be just underneath consciousness. One day suddenly, when you go to the store and the storekeeper asks what brand of cigarette you need, you will say a certain brand. That repetition worked. It hypnotized you.

That's how religions have been functioning in the world – and all politics depends on it. Advertise, go on repeating to the public, and don't be bothered whether they believe or not – that's not the point. Hitler says there is only one difference between truth and lie: the truth is a lie that has been repeated very often. And man can believe any lies. Man's gullibility is infinite. Man can believe in hell, man can believe in heaven, man can believe in angels, man can believe in devils, man can believe in anything! You just go on repeating.

And there is no need to argue. An advertisement never argues – have you observed the fact? There is no need to argue. The advertisement simply persuades you, it never argues. An arguer may not be able to convince you, but a person who persuades you, who simply goes on throwing soft suggestions at you, not direct arguments… Because when somebody argues with you, you may become defensive, but if somebody simply goes on hinting at certain things, not in any direct way, just supposing, you are more prone to be convinced by it.

Dream functions in that way; dream is a salesman. Dream simply goes on repeating itself. It never argues, it simply insists on being repeated. And, often repeated, one starts believing in it.

When it happened thrice: …*he set out for Prague.* He started believing in its reality.

But the bridge was guarded day and night
and he did not dare start digging.

In the world there is too much competition. Every place is guarded and every object has to be fought for – it is not easy. This is something very strange in this world. Nothing is meaningful and yet for everything you have to fight. Nothing seems to be significant, but there is much competition, much conflict. Everybody is rushing toward it; that creates the trouble – it is not that there is something in it. There is nothing in it, but everybody is trying to rush toward it. Everybody is hankering for everybody else's place, that's why the world is so crowded.

In fact it is not as crowded as it seems. Look: we are sitting here, everybody is sitting in his own place. This place is not crowded at all. But if a frenzy suddenly takes hold of your mind and everybody starts trying to reach another's place, then this place would be crowded. Right now you are sitting religiously; in the other situation you would be rushing at each other politically. Right now you are satisfied with your place and you are not hankering for anybody's place – at least not in Chuang Tzu auditorium. But if you start pushing yourself into other's places, others will become defensive, they will start pushing you. A fight, a war, will ensue.

Why are there so many wars in the world? The reason is

that everybody is trying to have another's territory. And the other may be trying the same thing. He may be looking at you.

But the bridge was guarded day and night
and he did not dare start digging.
Nevertheless he went to the bridge every morning
and kept walking around it until evening.

That's what many people are doing. Very few succeed, many simply walk around. But they go on doing it. Even if you cannot succeed, your desires, your hopes, are continuously there. At least you can go to the place, near the palace, and you can simply walk around. The whole day, from morning to evening he was walking around – that's what many people are doing, waiting for some miracle to happen. Someday there may be no guards, someday may be a holiday, someday there may be a possibility to dig… One waits and one goes on waiting. It never happens, but one's whole life is wasted in waiting.

Nevertheless he went to the bridge every morning
and kept walking around it until evening.
Finally, the captain of the guards,
who had been watching him, asked in a kindly way whether he
was looking for something, or waiting for someone.
Rabbi Eisik told him of the dream
which had brought him from a faraway country.
The captain laughed, "And so to please your dream you wore out
your shoes to come here! You poor fellow.
And as far as having faith in dreams, if I had had it I should
have had to go to Cracow and dig for treasure under the stove in
the room of a Jew – Eisik, son of Yekel!
That's what the dream told me. And imagine what it would
have been like; one half of the Jews over there are called Eisik,
and the other half Yekel!" And he laughed again.
Rabbi Eisik bowed, traveled home,

dug up the treasure from under his stove,
and built the house of prayer which is called Reb Eisik's Shul.

It is a beautiful story – and very true. That is how it is happening in life. You are looking somewhere else for that which is already there within you. Rabbi Eisik bowed, thanked the man, traveled home…

This is the journey of religion: traveling back home. And a man who has understood life always pays his respect toward life because it has shocked you out of your dreams. He is not against life; he simply knows that he has nothing to do with life, he simply knows that he was searching in a wrong direction.

Life has always been compassionate, life has been telling you again and again that you can find nothing here – go back home. But you don't listen.

You earn money, and one day money is there – then life says to you, "What have you got?" But you don't listen. Now you think you have to put your money into politics, you have to become a prime minister or a president, then everything will be okay. One day you are a prime minister, and life again says, "What have you got?" You don't listen. You go on thinking of something else and something else and something else. Life is vast – that's why many lives are wasted.

But don't be angry at life. It is not life that is frustrating you, it is you who are not listening to life. And this I call a criterion, a touchstone: if you see some saint who is against life, bitter against life, know well he has not understood yet. Otherwise he will bow down to life in deep respect and reverence, because life has awakened him out of his dreams. Life is very shocking, that's why. Life is painful. The pain comes because you are desiring something which is not possible. It doesn't come from life, it comes from your expectation.

People say that man proposes and God disposes. It has never happened. God has never disposed of anybody. But in your own proposition you have disposed of yourself. Listen to

God's proposition, keep your own proposition to yourself. Keep quiet. Listen to what the whole is willing – don't try to have your private goals, don't try to have your private desires. Don't ask anything individually – the whole is moving toward its destiny. You simply be part of it. Cooperate. Don't be in a conflict. Surrender to it. And life always sends you back to your own reality – that is why it is shocking.

It shocks you because it doesn't fulfill your dreams. And it is good that life never fulfills your dreams – it always goes on disposing, in a way. It gives you a thousand and one opportunities to be frustrated so that you can understand that expectations are not good and dreams are futile and desires are never fulfilled. Then you drop desiring, you drop dreaming, you drop proposing. Suddenly you are back home and the treasure is there.

Rabbi Eisik bowed, traveled home, dug up the treasure from under his stove, and built the house of prayer which is called Reb Eisik's Shul. The treasure had always been waiting there under his stove. In the same room he dreamed that the treasure was somewhere near the palace of the king in Prague. It was just there! In his own room, in his own house, it was just there waiting to be dug up.

This is very indicative. Your treasure is in your own being – don't look for it somewhere else. All palaces and all bridges to the palace are meaningless; you have to create your own bridge within your own being. The palace is there; the treasure is there.

Existence never sends anybody into this world without a treasure. It sends you ready for every situation – how can it be otherwise? When a father sends his son on a long journey he makes every preparation. Even for unexpected situations the father provides. He gives all the provisions.

You are carrying everything that you need. Just go into the seeker and don't go seeking outside. Seek the seeker, let the seeker be the sought.

Because of this, Rabbi Eisik built the house of prayer. It was such a tremendous revelation, such a tremendous experience –

"Existence has put the treasure where I have always lived. I was poor because of myself, I was not poor because existence wanted me to be poor. As far as it is concerned I was a king, always a king." Because of this understanding he made a prayer house, a temple, out of this treasure. He used it well.

Whenever somebody comes to his innermost treasure, prayerfulness arises – that is the meaning of the story. He made a house of prayer called Reb Eisik's Shul. Whenever you understand the grace of existence, the compassion, the love, what else can you do? A great prayer of thankfulness arises into your being, you feel so overpowered by its love, overwhelmed. What else can you do? You simply bow down and you pray.

And remember, if you pray to ask for something, it is not prayerfulness. When you pray to thank existence for something, only then is it prayerfulness. Prayerfulness is always a thanksgiving. If you ask for something, then the prayerfulness is still corrupted by desire. Then it is not prayerfulness yet – it is still poisoned by dreaming. Real prayerfulness happens only when you have attained to yourself, when you have known what existence has given to you already without your asking for it. When you realize what you have been given, what infinite sources have been given to you, prayerfulness arises. You would like to say to existence, "Thank you." There is nothing else in it but a pure thank you.

When a prayer is just a thank you it is prayerfulness. Never ask for anything in a prayer; never say, "Do this, do that; don't do this, don't do that." Never advise existence. That shows your irreligiousness, that shows your lack of trust. Thank it. Your life is already a benediction, a blessing. Each moment is such pure joy, but you are missing it, that I know. That's why the prayerfulness is not arising; otherwise you would build a house of prayer. Your whole life would become that house of prayer; you would become that temple – the shrine of existence. Its song would burst from your being. It would flower in you and its fragrance would spread to the winds.

It does not happen because you are missing something. And you are missing not because of existence, you are missing because of yourself. If you desire, and you think that the treasure is somewhere else, you move into the future. The future is needed because you desire; the future is a by-product of desiring. How can you project desire in the present? The present is already here, you cannot project any desire in it, it does not allow desire. If you desire, the present has already gone; you can desire only in the future, only in the tomorrow.

This has to be understood. Desire is always in the future, but the future is never there. The future is that which is not, and desire is only in the future. And desire comes out of the past which also is not. The past is gone and the future has not yet come. Desire comes out of the past because you must have known what you desire in the past somehow. How can you desire something which is absolutely new? You cannot desire the new. You can only ask for some repetition. You had some money, you will ask for more; but money you know. You had some power, you ask for more; but power you know.

Man cannot desire the unknown. The desire is just a repetition of the known. Just look at it. You have known it and you are not fulfilled, so you are asking for it again. Do you think you will be fulfilled? At the most you can ask for more quantity, but if one rupee is not fulfilling, how can a thousand rupees be fulfilling? If one rupee is unfulfilling, ten thousand rupees will be ten thousandfold more unfulfilling – that is simple logic. If one woman has not fulfilled you, then ten thousand women are not going to fulfill you. If one woman has created such a hell, then ten thousand women... Just think! It is simple arithmetic. You can solve it.

You can ask only out of the past and you can ask only in the future, and both are non-existential. That which exists is the present. This very moment is the only moment there is. You cannot desire in it, you can just be in it. You can just enjoy it.

And I have never come across a person who can be miserable

in the present. You will be surprised. Many times people come to me and they say that they are very miserable and this and that, and I say to them, "Close your eyes and find out right now whether you are miserable or not." They close their eyes, then they open their eyes, and they say, "Right now I am not miserable."

Right now nobody is miserable. There is no possibility. It is not allowed by the nature of things. This very moment are you miserable? This very moment? You may have been miserable a moment before; okay, that is right. Or you may be miserable a moment afterward – that too is allowed. But this very moment, between these two non-existential moments, are you miserable? Nobody has ever been.

This moment is always of pure benediction; this moment is always of joy, of tremendous delight; this moment is God's moment. The past is yours, the future is yours, the present is God's. We divide time into three tenses – past, present, future – but we should not divide it in that way. That division is not right. Time can be divided between the past and the future, but the present is not part of time, it is part of eternity. Existence has no past, remember, you cannot say existence was. Existence has no future – you cannot say existence will be. Existence has only one tense – present. Existence is. Existence always is. In fact God is only another name for "isness". Whenever you are also in the moment, whenever you are also in this "isness," you are happy, blessed. A prayerfulness arises. You become a shrine. You should become Reb Eisik's Shul, you should become a prayer house.

Rabbi Bunam used to add, "Take this story to heart and make what it says your own.
There is something you cannot find anywhere in the world, not even at the zaddik's,
and there is, nevertheless, a place where you can find it."

Zaddik means the master. The word *zaddick* comes from a Hebrew root which means the pure, the purest, purity itself.

The *zaddik* means the master – who has attained to his "presentness", who is no longer in the past and no longer in the future, who is just here-now, who is just a presence. To be in the presence of a master is to be in the presence of a presence. That's all. And to be in the presence of a master can help you to be present because his presence can become infectious.

But Rabbi Bunam says: *There is something you cannot find anywhere in the world, not even at the zaddik's...* He says that there is something which you cannot find anywhere, not even in the presence of a master. But don't feel hopeless: *...there is nevertheless a place where you can find it.*

That place is you, and that time is now. In fact the *zaddik's*, the master's effort is nothing but to throw you to your "presentness", to make you available to existence, or to make existence available to you.

This "presentness" cannot be taught, but it can be caught – hence the value of *satsang*, of being in the presence of a *zaddik*, of a master, of a guru; just to be there doing nothing. In fact a master is not doing anything. He is just there. A master is prayerfulness, a constant thankfulness. With each breath he is thanking existence. Not verbally; his very breathing is a thankfulness, with each beat of his heart he goes on saying thank-you. His thank-you is not verbal, it is existential. His being is prayerfulness. To be in the presence of such a man may help you to have some taste of prayerfulness. That taste will start a new journey in your life – the inward journey.

You have been seeking for centuries, for millennia, and you have not yet found. Now, let the seeker be the sought. You have traveled outside for so long that you are very tired, very exhausted.

Jesus says, "Those who are tired, those whose burden is heavy, they should come to me. I will give them rest." What does he mean? He simply means, "Come to me. I am at rest. Be close to me. Have a taste of it." And that very taste will turn the tide and you will start moving inward.

You are here with me. Have a taste of my being. Don't just

listen to my words, listen to me. Taste me. And then suddenly you will be here and now, and you will be turning inward and you will not ask for anything and you will not desire anything and you will not have any movement into the future and you will not have any clinging with the past. And then this moment is liberation, this moment is enlightenment.

Enough for today.

8

Only the Knower Is Left

The first question:

> Osho,
> Who are you and what type of play are you playing
> with us? And how long will you play? Please explain.

To be frank with you – which usually I am not – I don't
know who I am. Because knowledge is not possible here where
I am. There is only the knower left, the known has disappeared;
only the container is left, the content is no more.

For knowledge to exist, a great division is needed in reality
– the knower and the known. And between the two, knowledge
happens. The known is a must for knowledge to happen.

The space I am in is absolutely undivided and indivisible.
Knowledge is not possible. So, to be exact, I don't know.

And I would like you also to come to this innocent ignorance,
to this state of not-knowing, because the state of not-knowing is
the highest state of knowing – not of knowledge, mind you, but
of knowing. And this knowing is content-less – not that you
know something; there is nothing to know. You simply are. I am,

but I don't know who. All identities have disappeared; just a tremendous emptiness is left behind.

I call it emptiness because you are full of identities – otherwise it is absolute presence, not emptiness, not absence. It is the presence of something which by its very nature is a mystery and cannot be reduced to knowledge.

So I don't know who I am, but I am tremendously content in this not-knowing. And whosoever has ever come to this door of not-knowing has laughed at all knowledge and the stupidity that goes on in the name of knowledge. Knowledge is mediocre. To be in the state of not-knowing is intelligence, it is awareness, it is non-accumulative. Each moment that which happens disappears, it leaves no trace behind, no existential trace. One comes out of it again pure, again innocent, again like a child.

So I am a child on the seashore of time, collecting seashells, colored stones. But I am tremendously fulfilled. I know not who I am because I am not. When I say "I am not" I mean the "I" no longer has any relevance. I use the word – obviously I have to use it and there is nothing in the word to be against it – but it is no longer relevant to my inner world. It is still of use with you, but when I am alone I am not. When I am with you, then this word *I* has to be used as a communicative device. But when I am alone I am not. Aloneness is there, amness is there, but the "I" is not. So who should know, and whom?

First I told you that the content has disappeared. Now I would like to tell you – because the more you get ready and receptive, the more I can tell you – that the container has also disappeared. Because the container is meaningful only with the content; without the content what is the meaning of the container? The content and the container are both not there. Something is, tremendously is, absolutely is, but there is no name to it. In love you call this space *bhagwan,* and in deep respect I also call it *bhagwan.*

Just the other night I was reading a letter in *Current.* The letter-writer asked me who appointed me as a *bhagwan.* Now, a *bhagwan* cannot be appointed. If somebody appoints somebody as a *bhagwan* then the appointer will be the *bhagwan*, not the appointed. It is a recognition, it is a realization. *Bhagwan* simply means that all that we call worldly is no longer there – that's all. The desire to possess, to be possessed, the desire to accumulate, the desire to cling, the desire to be, the libido, the lust for life, has disappeared. When this desire disappears, when the smoke of desire disappears and only the flame remains in its purity, who is going to appoint? Who is there to appoint? It is not an appointment. Or, if you love the word very much, then I will say, "It is a self-appointment." But that too is not very meaningful. It is a declaration.

The letter-writer wants me to say who. Nobody can decide who I am. This is my declaration. Only I know what has happened within me; nobody else can know it. Unless you also come to that state of being divine... The state is hiding behind you; any moment you become courageous enough to enter it, you can – then only will you recognize me, not before it.

I also call this space, in tremendous respect, *bhagwan*. The word *bhagwan* is very beautiful. The English word *God* is not as beautiful. *Bhagwan* simply means the blessed one. That's all. The blessed one. And I declare myself to be the blessed one. And I declare it only so that you can also gain heart and you can also strive for it; so that my presence can become a dream in you; so that my presence can invoke a journey in you; so that my presence can create a fire in you – a fire that will burn you, and through which you are going to be reborn true. A fire that is going to destroy you, annihilate you utterly, and yet out of it you will come absolutely new, with no identity, with no name, with no form.

I have declared myself a *bhagwan* because I would like you also to come to this recognition. You have forgotten the language. Somebody must exist in front of you as a reality, not as a concept, not as someone in the scriptures. Krishna exists in the Gita, Christ exists in the Bible – they may have been, they may not have been, nobody can be certain.

I am just here, confronting you. If you are courageous enough to open toward me, suddenly a sprout will start coming into being in your seed; you will start growing in an unknown dimension. To make that dimension available to you I declare myself a *bhagwan*. This is nobody else's business.

But I can declare myself a *bhagwan* only because I am not. Only one who is not can call himself the blessed one.

Because if *you* are, you remain miserable, your very being is your misery. Hell is not somewhere else; hell is the confined state, hell is the miserable state when you live with the "I". To live with the ego is to live in hell.

You ask me, "What type of play are you playing with us?" Certainly, it is a play. I am not serious. And if you are serious, there is not going to be any meeting with you. Seriousness does not cross my path at all. I am absolutely non-serious. This is a play. And I would like to call this play "the mad game."

I have coined the word *mad*: M stands for the master and *d* stands for the disciple. The master-and-disciple game! It is a mad game. I am an expert in being a master. If you are also ready to become a disciple, here we go!

And it is none of anybody else's business. It is a game between me and you. If you decide to be a disciple, as I have decided to be a master, then we can play the game. And those who have decided to be disciples are enjoying it tremendously.

Once you decide to be a disciple you enter into another world – a totally different world of the heart, of love, of trust. Then it is a play. You are not serious, but still you are very sincere. Never misunderstand seriousness for sincerity. Sincerity is very playful, never serious. It is true, authentic, but never serious. Sincerity does not have a long face, it is bubbling with joy, radiating with an inner joyousness.

Rejoice that I am here! If you decide to be a disciple, then only can you understand what I am doing here, then only can you understand this mad game, this madly mad game. It is a play; in fact it is the ultimate game in life. You have played many other games, this is the last. You have played being a lover, being a friend; being a father, being a husband, being a wife, mother, being rich, being poor, being a leader, being a follower – you have played all the games. And only those who have played all the games can play this game, because they will be mature enough to play it.

This is the last game. After this game, games stop, game playing stops. Once you have played the game rightly – the master-disciple game – by and by you come to a point where all playing disappears. Only you are left – neither the master nor the disciple exists there. This is just a device.

Between the master and the disciple – if the rule of the game is followed rightly – devotion arises. That is the fragrance, the river that flows between the two banks of the master and the disciple. That's why it is so difficult for the outsider to understand. But I am not interested at all in the outsider understanding it; it is a very esoteric game. It is only for the insiders, it is only for mad people. That's why I am not interested even in answering people who are not insiders, because they will not understand. They are not at that altitude of being where understanding can become possible.

Just see. If two chess players are playing and you don't know what chess is, and you start asking questions, they will simply say, "Shut up! First you go and learn the game. It is a complicated game."

And chess is nothing when you start playing *this* mad game! Your whole life – your emotions, your feelings, your intellect, your body, mind, soul, everything – is involved, is at stake. It is the last gamble.

So only those who are insiders can understand; outsiders will always feel uncomfortable about it. They don't know the language.

I am not here playing the game of a priest; I am not here playing the game of a prophet. In fact the prophet is nothing but the politician in disguise. The language of the prophet is the language of the politician – of course, in the name of religion.

The prophet is revolutionary; he wants to change the world, the whole world, to his heart's desire. I have no plans for changing the world. It is perfectly good as it is and it is going to remain as it is. All the prophets have failed. That game is doomed to be a failure.

I am not a priest because I don't belong to any religion; I simply belong to religion as such. I am not a Jew, I am not a Hindu, I am not a Christian, I am not a Mohammedan, I am not a Jaina – I don't belong to any religion. So I am not a priest, I am not a preacher. I simply love pure religion.

Let me tell you an anecdote:

Mr. and Mrs. Goldberg had scrimped and saved to put their eldest son through college. At last they had the money and decided to send him to a fine, highbrow Eastern boarding school. They saw him off on the train and tearfully bade him farewell.

A few months later he returned home for the Christmas holidays. The parents were overjoyed to have their son, Sammy, back with them. The mother greeted him with, "Samelah! Oh, it's so good to see you."

"Mother," replied the son, "stop calling me Samelah. After all, I'm a grown-up man now, and I do wish you would refer to me as Samuel."

She apologized and asked, "I hope you only ate kosher foods while you were away...?"

"Mother, we are living in a modern world, and it's preposterous to hang onto the old world traditions. I indulged in all types of kosher and non-kosher food, and believe me, you would be better off if you did too."

"Well, tell me, did you at least go to the synagogue to offer a prayer of thanks occasionally?"

The son replied, "Really, do you honestly feel that going to a synagogue when you're associating with a large percentage of non-Jews is the proper thing to do? Honestly, Mother, it's unfair to ask it of me, really."

At this point Mrs. Goldberg, fighting back anger, looked at her eldest son and said, "Tell me, Samuel, are you still circumcised?"

I am not interested in whether you are circumcised or not. I am not interested in whether you are a Jew, a Hindu, a Christian or a Mohammedan. To me that sort of thing is sheer stupidity. I am not teaching you any religion. My whole effort, or my whole play here, is to make you aware of the reality as it is; to make you aware of the fact, not to give you any fantasy about it; to make you aware of the truth, not to give you any theory about it. I am not a theoretician, I am not a theologist. In fact theology has killed God, and so many religions have created such confusion in the minds of people that, rather than helping, they have been harmful and poisonous. Rather than helping people to be religious, they have created great politics in the name of religion – great violence, conflict, hatred in the name of religion.

To me, religion simply means a dimension of love. I am here to show you the beauty of life, the grandeur that surrounds you. From that very grandeur you will have your first glimpses of godliness.

I am here to seduce you into a love of life; to help you to become a little more poetic; to help you drown your head into your heart; to help you die to the mundane and to the ordinary so that the extraordinary explodes in your life. But this is possible only if you decide to be a disciple.

Sannyas is a great agreement, a covenant. When I initiate you into sannyas, I am initiating you into the world of my play. And if you are ready to go with me, great doors are waiting to be opened for you. But those doors are not of the mosque, of the church, of the *gurudwara* and the temple – those doors are of life itself. Life is the only shrine of existence and to be playful about it is the only prayer.

"Who are you and what type of play are you playing with us? And how long will you play?" It is not a question of time. If you decide to be a disciple, it can go on and on – in the body and out of the body, with the mind and without the mind, in life and in death, within life and beyond life. This game is an eternal game, that's why I call it the ultimate game. Those who decided to play with Christ, they are still playing; on new planes, in new plenitudes it continues. Those who decided to play with Buddha are still playing. The game is so beautiful, so eternal, who wants to stop it?

I may not be here in the body, but that will be a loss only to those who are not close to me, that will be a loss only to those who were not courageous enough to be with me. When I have gone out of the body it is not going to be a loss to you if you have really been a disciple. The game will continue. I will remain available, you will remain available. It is a question of the heart, it is a question of consciousness. And consciousness knows no time; consciousness is beyond time, consciousness is timelessness.

So the question is meaningful from some outsider – but then I will not answer it. The question is meaningless from an insider – and only then can I answer it. If you are an insider, you know there is a beginning to this play but there is no end to it. You have entered into something which is going to last forever.

"Osho, please explain." A game has to be played, not to be explained, because if you explain it, it loses all charm. Come, be a partner. Get involved in it.

There are a few things which cannot be explained; in the very explanation they die. For example a joke cannot be explained. That's the beauty of a joke: either you understand it or you don't understand it. If you ask, "Please explain," it cannot be explained. If somebody explains it and it becomes completely clear to you, no laughter will come out of it, because it is when the joke suddenly dawns on your being that there is laughter; when there is a jump, a quantum leap, then there is laughter.

You were going along on one plane, the story was moving along on one plane, then suddenly an unexpected turn which you could not have imagined, happened. That very turn, which you could not have imagined happening, gives it beauty. That very turn shocks you. That very turn releases the tension that was building up. You were going along in suspense – "What is going to happen? What is going to happen?" – and everything was just ordinary and then, suddenly, there is an extraordinary turn to the story. The punch line has to be a sudden turn. Then the built-up tension relaxes and you start laughing. The tension is released, explodes. But if somebody explains to you, dissects the joke logically, explains everything to you and then you understand it, then the joke disappears. The joke has to be enjoyed, not understood.

This whole world is a cosmic joke. If you try to understand it you will miss. That is how philosophers have always been missing. They have been trying to solve it, they have been trying to look for clues. It has no clues. It is a sheer mystery. It has no keys and no locks. It is available if you are available. But a mind which wants to understand it becomes tense and becomes unavailable.

Don't try to understand life. Live it! Don't try to understand love. Move into love. Then you will know – and that knowing will come out of your experiencing. That knowing will never destroy the mystery: the more you know, the more you know that much remains to be known. Life is not a problem. To look at it as a problem is to take a wrong step. It is a mystery to be lived, loved, experienced.

In fact the mind that is always after explanations is an afraid mind. Because of great fear he wants everything to be explained. He cannot go into anything before it is explained to him. With explanation he feels that now the territory is familiar, now he knows the geography, now he can move with the map and the guidebook and the timetable. He is never ready to move in an unknown territory, uncharted, without a map, without a guide. But life is like that. And no map is possible, because life goes on changing. Every moment it is new. I say to you there is nothing old under the sun. Everything is new. It is a tremendous dynamism, an absolute movement. Only change is permanent, only change never changes – everything else goes on changing.

So you cannot have a map; by the time the map is ready it is already out of date. By the time the map is available it is useless. Life has changed its tracks. Life has started playing a new game. You cannot cope with life with maps because it is not measurable. And you cannot cope with life with guidebooks because guidebooks are possible only if things are stagnant. Life is not stagnant; it is a dynamism, it is a process. You cannot have a map of it. It is not measurable, it is an immeasurable mystery. Don't ask for explanations.

That's why although I answer when you ask questions – because this is part of the agreement of this mad game: you will ask and I will answer – you should never take my answers as explanations. They are not. They are simply introductions to the mystery, prefaces to the mystery, seductions to the mystery. They are not really answers.

My answers are not answers; my answers are simply to help you to come out of your questions and to start living. An answer is an answer when it simply explains your question and you are satisfied that you have now got some information which you were needing and your question is no longer there. Now the place that the question was occupying is occupied by the answer. My answers are not answers in that way. They will help you to drop the question, but they are not going to answer the question. And once the question is dropped you will find no answer occupying its place. There will be no answer. My whole way of answering is such that I answer and yet I never answer. I answer so that you don't feel offended – your question has to be respected so I respect it – but I cannot answer it because life has no answers.

And this I call maturity of mind: when somebody comes to the point of looking at life without any questions, and simply dives into it with courage and fearlessness.

The second question:

Osho,
Dreams are unreal. But I have heard and read that the
mother of Mahavira saw nine white elephants in her
dreams before Mahavira's birth. Then what does that
mean? And what is the use of answering the dreams
of questioners?

Dreams are unreal, but so is your life. Dreams are unreal,
but that is what your life is. Your life is just a dream because
you are fast asleep. Can't you hear yourself snoring?

You are fast asleep. Whatsoever you call your life is just a
dream seen with open eyes. You see two types of dreams: one
with closed eyes, one with open eyes. But both are dreams.

You say, "Dreams are unreal but I have heard and read that
the mother of Mahavira saw nine white elephants in her dreams
before Mahavira's birth." Your reading is a dream, your hearing
is a dream. Whatsoever you have heard about Mahavira has
nothing to do with Mahavira. It is your dream.

And just look: Mahavira's mother dreamed of nine white elephants. First it is a dream, then it is a dream about a white
elephant. A dream in a dream! White elephant? The story is
beautiful; it says that life is just like a Chinese box: a box within a
box. You go on – it is just like an onion. You peel it, there is
another layer; you peel it, another layer – box within box.

First, Mahavira's being born is a dream; then, being born
out of a mother is another dream. Then the mother dreams.
And the mother dreams about white elephants! Look at the
whole absurdity of it.

Then there are stupid people who start analyzing these
dreams and make much fuss about it. Jainas say that whenever
a *tirthankara* is born, a particular series of dreams has to happen
to the mother. And if those dreams have not happened, then
the man is not a *tirthankara*. So all the mothers *had* to dream –
remember. Twenty-four *tirthankaras* have been born in India,
and all the mothers of the *tirthankaras* had to repeat the same

dream. It is a must, it is a legal thing – you cannot avoid it! If you don't dream, your son cannot be a *tirthankara*. When my mother started dreaming I said, "Stop! There is no need. I am not going to fulfill any legal and formal things. There is no need to dream about white elephants. You can rest."

Foolish people go on finding foolish things, but they decorate them very well. You ask what it means. It means nothing. It simply means that you are more interested in dreams than you are in reality.

People are not interested in Mahavira as such. If Mahavira's mother had forgotten to dream these dreams, Jainas would have not accepted him as the twenty-fourth *tirthankara*. That was one of the most important things to be decided. You may not know it, but there were a few other people who were also claiming that they were *tirthankaras*. In the time of Mahavira there were eight persons who were claiming that they were *tirthankaras* and it was a great problem how to decide because no criteria existed. So people had to invent such foolish criteria. It was only Mahavira's mother, the story says, who dreamed these dreams.

Goshalak's mother erred. Poor Goshalak suffered for it. Mahavira's mother must have been very clever; she must have planned everything very beautifully. At least Mahavira's astrologers must have – the mother died immediately after giving birth. In fact I don't see that she ever told anybody about her dreams, because she died immediately. But that too is a point. Jainas say that when a *tirthankara* is born, the mother dies immediately. They have made things very difficult for the mother. Mahavira's mother's death must have been a pure accident. Goshalak's mother lived. These things are not allowed. Goshalak suffered because his mother lived. Mahavira's mother died. These are foolish criteria. They don't see Mahavira directly; they are looking for other indications.

When Jesus was there, Jews were asking certain questions because he had to fulfill the prophesies in the Old Testament. Were they fulfilled or not? Jesus was there in reality, standing before them, but they were not concerned about Jesus, they were concerned about the prophesies in the Old Testament. If they were fulfilled, then he was the right man; if they were not fulfilled, then he was not the right man. How foolish can humanity be? Jesus is there – but that is not proof of anything, no. And Jews denied him because they thought he had not fulfilled all the criteria. They had to crucify him because they thought he was just a charlatan, a deceiver; he had not fulfilled all the prophesies.

And Christians go on proving that he has fulfilled them. Now it has become just a verbal game of argumentation, of logic. The reality is completely forgotten.

Look at the real. If Mahavira is there, Mahavira is there whether the mother dreamed of white elephants or black elephants. Whether she dreamed or didn't dream doesn't matter; whether she lived or died doesn't matter. These are all irrelevant things. If Mahavira is there, look directly. His presence will be enough proof. And if it is not enough proof, then there is no need to bother about other proofs. Then what can other proofs do?

"And what is the use of answering the dreams of questioners?" The questioners have only dreams, they don't yet have a real life, so by answering their questions I will be pulling them out of their mud of dreams. I am not interested in their dreams, I am interested in the consciousness that is dreaming. That consciousness is not a dream. It is dreaming, it is in a dream, but it is not a dream. It is a reality, and it has to be pulled out of the dreaming state.

So I go on using whatsoever devices are needed. If sometimes I feel that analyzing the dream may help you to come out of it then I analyze it. But remember always and always, I am not interested in the dream, I am not a psychoanalyst. But if I feel that by dissecting the dream I will be able to make you aware that you are not the dream, that you are the witness to it, then I dissect it. The reality is not in the dream, the reality is in the dreamer – and the dreamer has to be awakened. I function like an alarm clock.

The third question:

> Osho,
> For people who have been so clouded by lies and
> deceptions in the waking state, can remembering
> dreams, re-enacting and experiencing them in the
> waking state, be a useful method – the first step on
> the path of higher consciousness and truth? Can this
> method hasten the thirst for godliness until the point
> comes when the dreaming mind is dropped?

Yes, to a limited extent it can be of great help – but remember, only to a limited extent. Otherwise people are such that first they waste their time in dreaming, then they can waste their time in enacting the dream in the waking state; then they can waste their time on some psychoanalyst's couch talking about their dreams – and the psychoanalyst analyzes them. Then dreams become too important. That much importance should not be given to them.

There is a great need of a shift of consciousness from the content to the container. Yes, for the time being, dreams can be used. Enacting them will be useful. If in the night you have seen a dream, then enacting it in the morning can be of tremendous help because in the night you were asleep. The dream was there, the message was there, the message was delivered by the unconscious, but the conscious was fast asleep. So it was as if you were drunk and somebody called you and you took the phone somehow, and you listened, but you cannot remember exactly what the message was because you were drunk. The message was delivered, the unconscious delivered a certain message.

That's what a dream is: a packaged message from the unconscious that you are doing something wrong, that you are moving against nature, that you are going against me, that you are going against yourself. It is a warning from the unconscious that enough is enough, stop! Come back home, be natural, be more spontaneous. Don't be lost in social formalities and moralities and don't become a fake. Be real.

The message is delivered, but you are asleep and in the morning you cannot even remember anything exactly. Have you watched it? When you wake up in the morning, for a few seconds some fragments of the dream float in the consciousness – just for a few seconds, not more than thirty seconds, or at the most sixty seconds, one minute. Then they are gone. You have washed your face, taken a cup of tea; finished with the night, you don't remember now. And even when you awake in the morning, only very fragmentary things are there. And those too are the tail parts of the dream. When you dream, you dream in a certain way: you started the dream at five o'clock in the morning, then you went into it, and at six o'clock you woke up. That was the end part of the dream – it is as if you were seeing a film and you were only awake at the end part. So you remember the end part of the dream, not the beginning, not the middle. Then you have to go upstream. If you want to recollect the dream you have to move in the reverse order, as if you are reading a book backward. It is very difficult.

And then, one thing more. When you are conscious you again start interfering with the dream content, you don't allow the whole message to be received. You will drop many things. If you have murdered your mother in the dream, you will drop it. You may not remember it, you may not allow it to become conscious. Or, at the most, you will allow it in a very deep disguise: you have murdered somebody else. Or, if you have lived in a community which values nonviolence very much, you may not even remember that you murdered – that part will simply disappear. We listen only to that which we want to listen to.

I have heard:

As he lay on his deathbed he spoke, "Sara, I want you to know before I die that Ginsburg the tailor owes me two hundred dollars, and Morris the butcher owes me fifty dollars, and

Klein next door owes me three hundred dollars."

His wife turned to the children and said, "What a wonderful man your father is. Even when he's dying he's got the brains to realize who owes him money."

The old man continued, "And Sara, I want you also to know that I owe the landlord a hundred dollars."

To which his wife cried, "Ho ho, now he's getting delirious."

Whatsoever you want to hear is right, otherwise "ho ho!" Then immediately you become disconnected.

You will remember the dream, now the mechanism has to be understood. The dream is a message from the unconscious to the conscious because the conscious is doing something which the unconscious feels is unnatural. And the unconscious is always right, remember; because the unconscious is your nature. The conscious is cultivated by the society, it is a conditioning. The conscious means society inside you. It is a trick of society. The conscious is doing something which the unconscious feels is too much against nature, so the unconscious wants to give a warning. In the morning, when you remember, again you will remember from the conscious, again the conscious will interfere. Whatsoever is against it will not be allowed; whatsoever is sweet will be allowed. But that is not the point. The bitter part was the real message.

But try it. What they do in psychodrama can be helpful. Rather than remembering a dream, reliving a dream is more useful. And they are different. When you remember, you remember from the conscious; when you relive, you relive from the total. In reliving there is more possibility that the unconscious will again be able to give some messages.

For example: you dreamed during the night that you were walking on a road. You go on walking and walking and walking and the road never ends. The non-ending road creates tremendous fear in you because with anything non-ending the mind cannot cope, the mind becomes afraid. Non-ending? It looks very boring. You go on, you go on, you go on – and the road is non-ending. You become tired, you become frustrated, you are fed up, you fall down – but the road goes on and on and on. You have limitations and the road seems to be unlimited.

If you dream such a dream... Many people dream about it because there is a great message in it. The famous Russian author, Maxim Gorky, used to dream it many times. He said that in his life it was one of the most important dreams – it was repeated continuously, almost every month. It must have had a great message otherwise it wouldn't have been repeated. And it was repeated – that simply shows that Gorky never understood it. Once you understand a dream, once the message is delivered, the dream stops. If a dream is continuously repeated, that simply shows that you have not understood it, so the unconscious goes on knocking at your door. It wants you to understand it.

Remembering is one thing – you can close your eyes and remember the dream and it will be as if you are seeing a film, a movie. Reliving it is totally different. You create the whole situation, you visualize the whole situation. It is not a dream on the screen, you relive it. Again you are on the road. Look around. Close your eyes when you remember it, look around. What type of road is it? Are trees there or is it a desert? What kind of trees? Is the sun there in the sky or is it night? Visualize it, stand on the road and visualize it and let it be as colorful as possible – because the unconscious is very colorful. The conscious is just black and white, the unconscious is very psychedelic.

So let it be colorful. See the greenness of the trees, the redness of the flowers, the brightness of the stars. Feel the road, the touch underneath your feet. Feel the road – rough, smooth, dead, alive? Every road has its own individuality. Smell. Standing there, smell. What type of smell is it? Has it rained just now and a delicate smell from the earth is arising? Or have the flowers bloomed and the fragrance is there? Feel the breeze; feel whether it is cool or warm. Then start moving – as if you are moving in reality. It is not on the screen of the memory, you are reliving it. And through this sensitivity of taste, touch, air, feel, coolness, warmth, greenery, color, it again becomes real. Again the unconscious will start giving you messages. They can be of tremendous value.

But there is a limit to it. Try to understand in this way, but always remember that whether the dream is seen in the night or relived in the day, it is a dream. And below the unconscious – or beyond the unconscious – is still another door of your being that has to be opened.

Freud and the Freudians think that man ends with the conscious and unconscious. Man does not end with the conscious and unconscious, there is a super-conscious element also. And that is truer.

So, don't think that the conscious is the only mind. Before Freud it was thought that the conscious was the only mind. When Freud introduced the concept of the unconscious for the first time, he was laughed at, ridiculed, because people said, and they were linguistically right, "What nonsense! How can mind be unconscious? Mind means consciousness. If it is unconscious, it is not mind; if it is mind, it is conscious." Of course their grammar was right and their language was true – but existentially they were wrong. And Freud by and by became victorious. Truth always wins.

Now another layer has to be introduced into the world of psychology – that layer is of the super-conscious. Psychologists will again be against it. They will say, "What nonsense you are talking! You are bringing religion into psychology. Somehow we have got rid of religion and now you bring it in again from the back door!" But you cannot get rid of religion – religion is not something accidental, it is very essential. You have to recognize it. And you have to recognize its claims.

Man is conscious, unconscious and super-conscious. Man is a trinity – that is the meaning of the old concept of the trinity in Christianity, Judaism. In the East we have the concept of *trimurti* – three faces of God, three faces of being. Man is a triangle. The third has to be remembered.

The questioner has asked: "For people who have been so clouded by lies and deceptions in the waking state, can remembering dreams, reenacting and experiencing them in the waking state, be a useful method?" Yes, a useful method but with a limited possibility. And rather than remembering, emphasize reliving.

"Can it be the first step on the path of higher consciousness and truth?" Certainly, but only the first step. And never be lost in the first step. There are many people who become lost in the first step and then they never take the second. Then the first is useless. Unless the second happens, the first is meaningless. Only with the second does the first become relevant. With the third the second becomes relevant. And only when you have achieved the goal does your journey become relevant. Otherwise it remains irrelevant; the relevance always comes from the beyond, the relevance is transcendental.

So, first relive your dreams. It will be helpful, it will make you more alert. And then start – even in your dreaming, even while you are reliving or when you are awake, walking on the street in an ordinary waking state – start seeing yourself as a witness, not as a participant; as a watcher. The watcher, the observer, the seer, the witness, is the real step which leads you into reality. It is beyond dream.

The dreams can be helpful so that the grip of the dreams on your mind is loosened, but the real step is only when you have started becoming watchful. Try it the whole day. Whatsoever you are doing, remember that you are the watcher. Walking... Remember that the body is walking, you are the watcher. Eating... Remember that the body is eating, you are the witness. If it spreads all over your day, one day, suddenly, you will see that in the dream also the watcher has a little possibility. And when you can also remember that "I am just the watcher" in the dream, then dreams disappear. Then, with the disappearance of the dreams, a new consciousness arises in you. That consciousness I call the super-consciousness. And that consciousness is the goal of the psychology of the buddhas.

The fourth question:

Osho,
How can I come closer? What should I do?

Let me tell you an anecdote:

"Help me," the man demanded of the rabbi. "I have a wife and twelve children and I cannot support them. Every year my wife gives me a new child. What should I do?"
"Do?" screamed the rabbi. "Haven't you done enough?"

You ask me, "What should I do to come closer to you?" Your doing is not going to help – because by doing, you become more of a doer and the doer feeds the ego and the ego is the barrier between me and you. By non-doing you will come closer to me, not by doing. Not by willpower can you come closer to me, but only by surrendering. Only when you recognize that nothing can be done, and you are helpless and you relax, suddenly you will find that you have come close to me. When you surrender you come close to me.

The mind goes on asking "What should I do?" If you do something, that very doing will not allow you to move away from the ego.

Let me tell you another anecdote:

Old man Ginsberg was disgusted with his family. He told them that he was leaving them and going to Japan.
The boys asked, "Papa, how will you get there?"
He said, "Don't worry, I'll row there."
They walked him to the dock and, without their father seeing, tied a very long rope to his row boat. He bade them all farewell and started rowing toward the horizon. They let him stay in the boat all night, but when the sun began to rise they became nervous about his well-being. There was a tremendous

fog and the old man and the boat were not visible. The old man had been rowing away all night when suddenly he heard a voice in the distance shouting, "Abe Ginsberg, are you all right?"

He turned toward the voice and shouted, "Who knows me in Japan?"

Now he thinks he has reached Japan just by rowing the whole night, and the boat is tied with a long rope. He has not gone anywhere. If you want to come close to me by doing something then you may have a little or a long rope, but you will remain tethered to the shore, you cannot go far away.

By doing, nobody can come close to a master. By doing, you can attain things in the world, but by doing you cannot attain anything in existence – only by non-doing, by a tremendous receptivity, passivity. You just leave it to me, you just enjoy being here. You dance, you sing, you celebrate. You forget this nonsense of coming closer and you will be coming; by your dance, by your singing, by your rejoicing, you will be coming close to me.

The question is from Priya. She has asked today, but three weeks ago I gave her a message to go and dance every day. Her question has come today, but it reached me three weeks ago. It may have reached to her self today, to her own conscious it may have come today – but three weeks ago I suddenly felt that a deep desire to come close to me was arising in her unconscious, so I sent her a message to go and dance. And she is dancing, and believe me, she is coming closer.

By your dance, by your laughter, by your joy, you come close to me – because in dance you relax, the doer disappears. In singing you are lost. Whenever you are lost I can penetrate your being; whenever you are there then it is difficult, because you are closed.

The fifth question:

Osho,
I have heard sannyasins say that they are with you for

some benefit to them. They have a motivation of
enlightenment or something likewise. But I do not
have any thoughts of enlightenment or any benefit
which I may get by being with you. I just love to be in
your presence without any motivation whatsoever.
Please comment.

Then why are you asking? In your question there is a motivation. You want me to say, "Good boy. You are absolutely
right. It is you who are going to obtain enlightenment and not
the others, because you have no motivation." This is the motivation in asking the question!

But remember, you cannot deceive me. Your words cannot
deceive me. Your words cannot hide the motivation. Why are
you asking me to comment? If you are really enjoying being
here, no comment is needed. If you are really in love with me, it
is enough – nothing else is needed. In love there is no question,
it is a non-questioning attitude.

But you want me to say, "This is the true way. You are on
the right track. Soon enlightenment is going to happen to you
and others who are here with motivation are going to miss."

Let me tell you an anecdote:

A Jewish couple found themselves in Florida unable to find
a room in a hotel. The only place left to stay in was a hotel that
was notorious in its policy of not allowing Jews.

The husband turned to his wife and said, "Becky, you keep
your big mouth shut; not one word is to come from your lips.
Leave it to me. You'll see, I'll talk good English, the man at the
desk will never know, and we'll get a room."

Sure enough, they walk up to the desk, Dave asks for a
room, the hotel clerk gives them the key to the room, and they
are set.

Becky says, "Dave, it's so hot, maybe we can go down to the
pool for a swim?"

Dave says, "Okay, but remember, not one word is to fall from your mouth."

They walk down to the cabanas. Dave signals the cabana boy and he sets up chairs and towels for them.

Becky turns to Dave and asks, "Now can I go into the pool?"

He answers, "Okay, but remember, not a syllable must you utter."

Becky goes over to the edge of the pool and sticks one toe into the water, which is icy cold, and before she realizes what she is doing, she yells, "Oy vey!" whereupon everyone at the pool turns on her. Without blinking an eye she adds, "Whatever that means."

But you cannot deceive. Howsoever you put it, it will show. Motivation is such a thing you cannot hide. There is no way to hide it; there is no language to hide it. Motivation simply shows.

Now, let me tell you this. This motivation may not be very conscious to you, you may not be very aware of it, but it is there. And I am not saying that something is wrong in it, I am not trying to make you guilty about it. Always remember one thing: never feel guilty about anything.

It is natural to come with a motivation, nothing is wrong in it. It is absolutely natural to come with a motivation, otherwise how else will you come? Without motivation, only a madman can come here. Without motivation, how can you come? You must have some motivation to learn meditation, to have a more silent life, to learn about love, to have more loving relationships, to know what this life is all about, to know what death is, or to know if there is something beyond death. Without motivation you cannot come to me.

So I accept it absolutely, and you have to accept it – you have come to me with motivation.

It is my work here to help you to drop the motivation. You

come with motivation – that's your work, without it you cannot come. Then starts my work: to help you to drop the motivation. Motivation brings you close to me, but then motivation itself becomes the obstacle. You have to come with a motivation and then you have to learn to drop it. And when you drop it, suddenly you are not only close to me, you are one with me – because closeness is still a distance. In closeness also there is a distance. Howsoever close you are, you are distant. The real closeness is only when all distance and all closeness disappear – you are simply one with me, I am one with you; when we only appear as two, but we are not.

Become conscious of your motivation in asking this question and that will help you to drop it. Consciousness helps you to drop it. Anything you become conscious about starts slipping out of your hands. You cannot cling consciously, you cannot be angry consciously, you cannot be greedy consciously, you cannot be motivated consciously.

Consciousness is such a mutation, it brings so much light into your being that darkness simply disappears.

So the only thing to remember is: don't be worried about others' motivations; that is none of your business. If they are motivated, they will suffer for it, they will create their own hell. You simply don't be concerned with it, you simply go on looking at your own motivations, you simply go on penetrating deeper and deeper into why you are here.

And never feel guilty if you have found a motivation. If you come across a motivation, it is natural. But when I say it is natural, I don't mean that it has to be there forever and ever. It is natural but it has to go. When it goes, something supernatural starts happening. If you are not aware about it and if you go on hiding it, then it will never go.

And this may be a trick of the mind – looking for motivation in others. You may be using others as scapegoats. It is one of the great psychological truths about the human mind that whatsoever you want to hide within yourself you start projecting onto others. Whenever you start seeing something in somebody else, remember it as a message. Go immediately withinward – it must be there. The other is functioning only as a screen. When you see anger in others, search for it within yourself. When you see greed in others, go in and dig for it there and you will find it; when you see too much ego in others, just go inside and you will find ego sitting there. The inside functions like a projector; others become screens and you start seeing films on others which are really your own tapes.

The last question:

Osho,
I do not feel I am a man, yet I see a man's face in the mirror.

A great insight has happened to you, a great realization. Let it sink deep, let it become your constant awareness.

No face is yours. All faces are false. Once you had the face of a lion, once you had the face of a donkey, once you had the face of a tree and sometimes the face of a rock. Now you have the face of a man – or a woman, ugly, beautiful, white, black.

But you don't have any face. Your reality is faceless. And that facelessness is what Zen people call the original face. It is not a face at all.

When you were not born, what face had you then? When you die, what face will you carry with yourself? This face that you see in the mirror will be dropped here; it will disappear into the earth – dust unto dust. You will go faceless just as you came faceless.

Right now you don't have any face, the face is just a belief – you have believed in the mirror too much. And when you have come to realize this facelessness, you have seen the face of God.

Enough for today.

9

Belong to the Transcendent

One day, after he had gone blind,
Rabbi Bunam visited Rabbi Fishel.
Rabbi Fishel was famous throughout the land
for his miracle cures.
"Entrust yourself to my care," said his host,
"I shall restore your light."
"That is not necessary," answered Bunam,
"I see what I need to see."

Spirituality is not a question of morality, it is a question of vision. Spirituality is not the practicing of virtues – because if you practice a virtue it is no longer a virtue. A practiced virtue is a dead thing, a dead weight. Virtue is virtue only when it is spontaneous; virtue is virtue only when it is natural, unpracticed – when it comes out of your vision, out of your awareness, out of your understanding.

Ordinarily religion is thought of as a practice. It is not. That is one of the most fundamental misunderstandings about religion. You can practice nonviolence but you will still remain violent, because your vision has not changed. You still carry the old eyes. A greedy person can practice sharing, but the greed will remain. Even the sharing will be corrupted by the greed, because you cannot practice anything against your understanding, beyond your understanding. You cannot force your life into principles unless those principles are of your own experience.

But so-called religious people try to practice virtue – that's why they are the most unvirtuous people on the earth. They try to practice love, and they are the most unloving people on the earth. They have created all sorts of mischief: wars, hatred, anger, enmity, murder. They practice friendship, but friendship has not flowered on the earth. They go on talking about God, but they create more and more conflict in the name of God. The Christian is against the Mohammedan, the Mohammedan is against the Hindu, the Hindu is against the Jaina, the Jaina is against the Buddhist – that's all they have been doing.

There are three hundred religions and they have all created fragments in the human mind; they have not been an integrating force, they have not healed the wounds of the human soul. Because of them humanity is ill, because of them humanity is insane – and the insanity comes out of one thing. That has to be understood as deeply as possible because you can also go in the wrong direction. The wrong direction has a tremendous appeal; otherwise so many people would not have gone in it. The appeal must be great. The magnetic force of the wrong direction has to be understood, only then can you avoid it.

You can try practicing anything you like and you will remain opposite to it. You can enforce a sort of stillness upon yourself: you can sit silently, you can learn a yoga posture, you can make the body still, as if it is without movement, you can make the body like a statue. And by repeating a mantra or just by repressing the mind continuously for a long time, you can enforce a certain stillness upon your being – but it will be the silence of the cemetery, it will not be throbbing, alive, kicking. It will be a frozen thing. You can deceive others, but you cannot deceive yourself and you cannot deceive God. You have got it without any understanding; you forced it upon yourself; it is a practiced silence.

The real silence arises out of the understanding: "Why am I not silent? Why do I go on creating tensions for myself? Why do I go on getting into miserable patterns? Why do I support my hell?" One starts understanding the "why" of one's hell – and by that very understanding, by and by, without any practicing on your part, you start dropping those wrong attitudes that create misery. Not that you drop them, they simply start disappearing.

When understanding is there, things start changing around you. You will love, but you will no longer be possessive. It is not love that creates trouble. If you ask your so-called saints, they say it is love that creates trouble. That is an absolutely false statement. It is based on a deep misunderstanding of the human love life.

It is not love that creates misery – love is one of the greatest blessings, a benediction. It is possessiveness that creates misery. Possess your beloved, your friend, your child, and you will be in misery. And when you are in misery those religious people are there waiting by the corner. They jump upon you. They say, "We told you before: never love, otherwise you will be in trouble. Drop out of all love situations, escape from the world." And of course it appeals because you are already seeing it happening to you. It is now your own experience that they are right – and yet they are not right and it is not your experience. You never analyzed the phenomenon that has happened, you never analyzed that it is not love that has tricked you into misery, it is possessiveness. Drop possessiveness, not love.

If you drop love of course the misery will disappear, because by dropping love you will be dropping possessiveness also – that will be automatically dropped. The misery will disappear, but you will never be happy. Go and see your saints. They will be a proof of what I am saying. They will never be happy.

They are not unhappy, that is true, but they are not happy

either. So what is the point? If happiness does not arise by dropping unhappiness then some mistake has been committed. Otherwise it should be natural. You say, "I have lit the candle and the darkness is still there." Either you are befooling yourself or you are dreaming, hallucinating, about the candle. Otherwise it is not possible – the candle is burning bright and the darkness is still there? No, the darkness is a certain, absolute proof that the light has not entered yet.

When unhappiness drops, suddenly there is happiness. What is happiness? Absence of unhappiness is happiness. What is health? Absence of disease is health. When you are not unhappy then how can you avoid happiness? When you are not unhappy how can you manage not to be happy? It is impossible. It is not in the nature of things. It is against the arithmetic of life. When a person is not unhappy suddenly all his sources are alive, a dance arises in his being, a joy rises in his being. A laughter bursts forth. He explodes. He becomes a Hasid, a Sufi. He becomes a presence of divine ecstasy. By seeing him you will see godliness – a glimpse, a ray of light. By visiting him you will be visiting a shrine, a sacred place, a *teertha*. Just by being in his presence you will be suffused with a new light, a new being; a new wave will arise around you and you can ride on that tidal wave and go to that other shore.

Whenever there is really a dropping of unhappiness, happiness is left – nothing else is possible. One is simply happy without any reason, without any why.

But your saints are not happy, your saints are very sad; your saints are not living, your saints are dead. What has happened? What calamity? What curse? A misstep. They thought love had to be dropped and then there would be no misery. They dropped love – but the misery was not happening because of love, the misery was happening because of possessiveness.

Drop possessiveness! In fact, convert the energy which is involved in possessiveness into love energy. But that cannot be done by enforcing anything – a clear vision is needed, a clarity.

So the first thing I would like to say to you is: spirituality is not the practicing of any virtue, spirituality is the gaining of a new vision. Virtue follows that vision; it comes on its own accord. It is a natural by-product. When you start seeing, things start changing.

In life there are three things – one: the objective world, the world of things. Everybody is able to see that. We are naturally capable of seeing the objective world. But this is only the beginning of the journey. Many have stopped there and think that they have arrived home. Of course they have not arrived so they are miserable.

Beyond the objective is the opening of another world – the world of the subjective. The objective is the world of things, objects; the objective is the world of science, mathematics, physics, chemistry. The objective is very clear because naturally we are born perfectly able to see the objective.

The subjective has to be explored; nobody is born with a vision of the subjective. The subjective has to be explored, one has to learn what it is; one has to taste it by and by and move into it by and by. The world of music, poetry, art – the world of any creativity – is the world of the subjective. The man who starts moving inward becomes more poetic, more aesthetic. He has a different aroma around him, a different aura.

The scientist lives with things; the poet lives with persons. The scientist is not at all aware of who he is, he is simply aware of what surrounds him. He may be able to know about the moon and about Mars and about the stars far, far away, but he is completely oblivious of his own inwardness. In fact the more he becomes concerned with faraway things, the more and more he becomes oblivious of himself. He remains almost in a sort of sleep about himself.

The poet, the painter the dancer, the musician, they are closer to home. They live in the subjective – they know they are persons. And when you know you are a person, suddenly you become capable of looking into other persons. For a poet even a tree is a person, even animals are people; for a scientist even a man or a woman is nothing but an object. A scientist looks at a man as if he is also just an object. And if he is not aware of his own inwardness, how can he be aware of the inwardness of the other?

When I use the word *person*, I mean that there is an inside to it which is not available to outside observation, analysis, dissection. There is a rock, it has no inside; you can break it and you can see everything. If you break a rock nothing is disturbed, nothing is destroyed. Even if it is in pieces, it is the same rock. But if you break a person, something of tremendous value immediately disappears. Now you are left with a dead body, and the dead body is not the person. The broken rock is still the same rock, but the broken person is no longer the same person. In fact the broken person is not a person at all. On the dissection table of a surgeon you are not a person; only when a poet touches you and holds your hand do you become a person.

That's why people hanker for love. The reason for the hankering for love is nothing but this: you would like somebody to see that you are a person, not a thing.

You go to the dentist, he is not worried about you; he is simply interested in your teeth. Even if *I* go to the dentist, I see him… What a miracle! He is not interested in me, he just looks. I am there, sitting in his chair, he is completely oblivious of me. A great space is available just in his room, but he will not even look at me – that's not his concern. He is only interested in the teeth, in his own technique. His knowledge of the objective world is his only world.

People hanker for love because only love can make you a person, only love can reveal your inwardness to you, only love can make you feel that you are not just that which is apparent from the outside. You are something more; you are something totally different from what you appear to be. The reflection in the mirror is not your totality; the reflection in the mirror is just the reflection of your surface, not of your depth. It says nothing about your depth.

When you come to a scientist, or a person who is absolutely absorbed with the objective dimension, he looks at you as if you are just the reflection in the mirror. He does not look at you, he looks around you. His approach is not direct, his approach is not intimate – and you feel something is missing. He is mistreating you because he is not accepting your personality. He is treating you as if you are a thing. He is doing things but he is not touching you at all; you remain almost non-existential to him.

And unless somebody touches you with love, looks at you with love, your own inwardness remains unfulfilled, unrecognized; that is the need to be needed.

The subjective is the dimension, the inward dimension, of poetry, song, dance, music, of art. It is better than the scientific dimension because it is deeper. It is better than the objective dimension because it is closer to home. But it is not yet the dimension of religion, remember. There are many people whose mind is obsessed with the objective – when they think about God, God also becomes an object. Then God is also outside. Ask a Christian where God is and he will look upward, somewhere in the sky – outside. When you ask a person where God is and he looks somewhere else than within himself, then he belongs to the non-religious dimension. People ask, "What is the proof of God?" Proofs are needed only for a thing. God does not need proof. If I love you, what is the proof? For poetry there is no proof, for chemistry there is. But poetry exists. And a world without chemistry would not be very much worse, but a world without poetry would not be a human world at all.

Poetry brings meaning to life, the unproved brings meaning to life – the proved at the most makes you comfortable. God is not an object and cannot be proved. God is more like music. It exists, certainly it exists, but there is no way to grab it. You cannot have it in your fist, you cannot lock it into your treasury, there is no way.

Love exists, but you cannot possess it. If you try to possess it, you belong to the objective dimension and you are killing love – that's why possession is destructive. If you possess a woman, if you say, "She is my wife and I possess her" then she is no longer a person. You have reduced her to be a thing and she will never be able to forgive you. No wife has ever been able to forgive her husband; no husband has ever been able to forgive his wife – because both have reduced each other to things.

A husband is a thing, a wife is a thing, and when you become a thing you become ugly – you lose freedom, you lose inwardness, you lose poetry, you lose romance, you lose meaning. You become simply a thing in the world of things. Utility is there – but who lives for utility? Utility can never be satisfying. You are being used, how can it be satisfying? Whenever you feel you are being used, you feel offended. And you *should* feel offended, because it is a crime to use somebody and it is a crime to allow somebody to use you. It is a crime against existence.

But there are people who try to use God also. When you go and you pray for something you are trying to use existence. You don't know what prayerfulness is, you don't know what love is, you don't know what poetry is, you don't know the subjective realm at all. Your prayer, if it has a motivation in it, a desire in it, is ugly. But we find – we are very cunning people – we find ways and means.

Let me tell you an anecdote:

A minister, a priest and a rabbi were discussing how they decided what part of the collection money each retained for personal needs and what part was turned over to their respective institutions.

"I draw a line," said the minister, "on the floor. All the money I toss in the air. What lands to the right of the line I keep, to the left of the line is the Lord's."

The priest nodded, saying, "My system is essentially the same, only I use a circle. What lands inside is mine, outside is his."

The rabbi smiled and said, "I do the same thing. I toss all

the money into the air and whatever God grabs is his."

We even go on playing tricks with God. In fact God is also our invention, a very cunning invention. It is also somewhere there – and you can pray to him, you can ask things from him, you can find security in him, consolation, comfort. It is a security measure, a sort of other-worldly bank balance. But it remains an object.

God is not an object – that's why Mohammedans, Christians, Jews have all tried not to make any image of God. That is very symbolic and meaningful because when you make an image of God it becomes objective. Let God remain without any image. But it has remained without an image only in theology. Whether you have made an image of God or not, it makes no difference; your mind, if it is just capable of moving in the objective dimension, will treat God as an object. Even a Mohammedan turns toward Mecca for his prayers; that becomes an image. Even a Mohammedan goes to Mecca to kiss the stone; that becomes the image. The Black Stone of Mecca is the most-kissed stone ever. In fact it is very dangerous to kiss it now – it is unhygienic.

But whether you make any image of God or not, if the mind is objective, your idea of God will be objective. When you think of God you start thinking of high heaven, the uppermost boundary of the sky. *There* God is. If you ask a truly religious person where God is, he will close his eyes and go inward. God is there, inward. Your own being is divine. Unless godliness is immanent in you, unless godliness is immersed in your being, you are carrying an image. Whether you have made an image of wood or of stone does not matter – you can make an image with thinking, thought, idea. That too is an image – of a subtler material, but still an image.

Man remains the same unless he changes his dimension. Somebody is an atheist; he says, "There is no God because I cannot see him. Show me and I will believe." And then someday he comes to have an experience, a vision, a dream in which he sees God standing there. Then he starts believing.

In the Gita, Arjuna, Krishna's disciple, goes on asking again and again, "You go on talking about him, but I cannot believe unless I see." Now, what is he saying? He is saying, "Let God be objective then I will believe." And Krishna concedes to his desire. I am not happy with that – because to concede to this desire means to concede that the objective dimension is capable of knowing God. The story says that Krishna then revealed his reality, his vastness; he revealed God. Arjuna started trembling and shaking. He said, "Stop! Enough! I have seen!" He saw Krishna expanding and becoming the whole universe; and in Krishna stars were moving, the sun was rising and the moon and planets and the beginning of the world and the end of the world and all life and all death was there. It was too much; he could not bear it. He said, "Stop!" And then he came to believe.

But this belief does not change the object, this belief does not change the objective dimension. He did not believe because he could not see; now he has seen so he believes – but God remains in the objective world, God remains a thing. I am not happy with Krishna for doing this. It should not be done. It is conceding to a foolish disciple's desire. The disciple needs to be changed from his dimension; he should be made more subjective.

But we remain – we go on changing forms but we remain the same.

I have heard:

The funeral was over. Still sobbing, Goldberg, the new widower, followed his late wife's sister into the waiting limousine. As the big car passed through the cemetery gates the sister was horrified by Goldberg's hand, which was slowly but passionately creeping up her leg. With her body still wracked with sobs of bereavement, she screamed,

"Goldberg, you monster, you fiend, you animal! My sister is not yet cold in her grave. What is the matter with you!"

In a voice shaking with emotion, Goldberg replied, "In my grief do I know what I am doing?"

People remain the same in their grief or in their other moods – they remain the same, they don't change the dimension.

So this is the first thing to understand: you need a shift from the objective to the subjective. Meditate more and more with closed eyes about your emotions, about your thoughts. Look deeper into the inner world, the world that is absolutely private to you. The objective is public; the subjective is private. You cannot invite anybody into your dreams, it is not possible. You cannot say to your friend, "Tonight come into my dream," because the dream is absolutely yours. You cannot even invite your beloved who may be sleeping just on the same bed, who may be sleeping just by your side, you may be sleeping hand in hand. But you dream your dreams and she dreams her dreams. Dreams are private. The subjective is the private; the objective is the public, the objective is the marketplace. Many people can watch one thing, but many people cannot watch one thought; only one person can – the person to whom the thought belongs can watch it.

Remove your consciousness more and more toward the private. The poet lives a private life; the politician lives a public life. Mahatma Gandhi used to say that he didn't have any private life. That means he must have had a very poor life. A private life is a rich life. The politician's life is there to be watched by everybody: on the TV, in the newspapers, in the street, in the crowd. The politician only has a public face. When he goes home he is nobody. He loses all face.

You have to find your private face. The emphasis should be more on the private than on the public. And you should start learning how to love the private – because the private is the door to God. The public is the door to science, but not to religion, not to God. The public is the door toward arithmetic, calculation, but it is not the door to ecstasy, to love. And enjoy things which are very private: music, poetry, painting. Hence the insistence of Zen on calligraphy, painting, poetry, gardening – something that is absolutely private, something that you live from the in toward the out, that rises as a wave in the innermost core of your being and spreads outward.

The public life is just the reverse: something rises outside and fades into you. In a public life the original, the source, is always outside. Your center of being is never within yourself, it is always outside. That's why a politician is always afraid of the outside – because his life depends on the outside. If the people don't vote he will be nobody.

But that doesn't make any difference to a painter or to a poet. Nobody purchased Vincent van Gogh's paintings. During his whole life not a single painting was sold; but that didn't matter, he enjoyed himself. If they sold, good; if they did not sell, good. The real prize was not in their being sold and appreciated, the real prize was in the painter's creation of them. In that very creation he has attained his goal. In the moment of creation he becomes divine. You become God whenever you create.

You have heard it said again and again that God created the world. I tell you one thing more: whenever *you* create something you become a small God in your own right. If God is the creator, then to be creative is the only way to reach him. Then you become a participant, then you are no longer a spectator.

Van Gogh, appreciated or not, lived a tremendously beautiful life in his inner world – very colorful. The real prize is not when a painting is sold and critics appreciate it all over the world – that is just a booby prize. The real prize is when the painter is creating it, when the painter is lost in his painting, when the dancer has dissolved into his dance, when the singer has forgotten who he is and the song throbs. *There* is the real prize, *there* is the real attainment.

In the outside world you depend on others. In the public life, in the political life you depend on others, you are a slave. In the private life you start becoming a master of your own.

Let me insist and emphasize it because I would like all of my sannyasins to be creative in some way. To me, creativity is of tremendous import. An uncreative person is not a religious person at all. I am not saying that you all have to be van Goghs – you cannot. I am not saying you all have to be Leonardo da Vincis or Beethovens or Mozarts; I am not saying you all have to become Wagners and Picassos, Rabindranaths – no, I am not saying that. I am not saying that you have to become a world famous painter or poet or you have to win a Nobel Prize – because if you have that idea, again you fall into politics. The Nobel Prize comes from the outside; it is a booby prize, it is not a real prize. The real prize comes from inside. And I am not saying that you are capable – all are not capable of becoming Picassos. And there is no need either, because too many Picassos would make a very monotonous world. It is good that there is only one Picasso and it is good that he has never been repeated, otherwise it would become boring.

But you all can become creators in your own way. It does not matter whether anybody comes to know about it or not, that is absolutely unimportant. You can do something out of love – then it becomes creative. You can enjoy something while you are doing it – then it becomes creative.

While I am talking to you Astha is cleaning my bathroom and my room. I inquired of her if she would like to drop this work and come to the talk. She said, "Osho, cleaning your bathroom is enough for me." It is a creative act, and she has chosen it out of love. And certainly she is not missing anything. Whether she listens to me or not is not the point. If she loves cleaning the bathroom, if she loves me, it is prayerfulness. You can be here, but you may listen to me or you may not listen to me. She is not here, but she has listened to me. She has understood me. Now the work itself becomes worship. Then it is creative.

I would like to remind all of my sannyasins again and again: be creative. In the past the majority of the religious people proved to be uncreative. That was a calamity, a curse. Saints were simply sitting doing nothing. That is not real religion. When real religion explodes into people's lives, suddenly much creativity explodes also.

When Buddha was here a great creativity exploded. You can find proofs in Ajanta, Ellora. When Tantra was an alive religion a great creativity exploded. You can go to Puri, Kanorak, Khajuraho. When Zen masters were alive they created many really new dimensions – out of small things, but very creative.

The question is, if you are uncreative it simply means that you must have practiced your religion, you must have forced yourself into a certain pattern, and you have got blocked, frozen in that pattern. A religious person is flowing, streaming, riverlike; seeking, exploring, always seeking and exploring the unknown, always dropping the known and going into the unknown, always choosing the unknown for the known, sacrificing the known for the unknown. And always ready. A religious man is a wanderer, a vagabond; into the innermost world he goes on wandering, moving from one place to another. He wants to know all the spaces that are involved in his being.

Be more creative. Dance, and don't bother whether somebody likes your dance or not – that is not the question. If you can get dissolved into it, you are a dancer. Write poetry. There is no need even to show it to anybody. If you enjoy it, write it and burn it. Play on your flute or guitar or sitar. You must see our tabla player, Bodhi. How meditatively he plays on his tabla! That's his meditation. He is growing: going into it, dissolving, melting.

The subjective is the realm of all art and creativity. These are the two ordinary realms of being.

The third, the really religious, is the transcendental. First is the objective: the objective is the world of science; second is the subjective: the subjective is the world of art; and third is the transcendental: that which goes beyond both, is neither objective nor subjective, is neither out nor in. In it both are implied, in it both are involved, but yet it is higher than both, bigger than both, beyond both. The subjective is closer to the transcendental than the objective, but remember, just by being subjective, you don't become religious. You have taken a step toward being religious, a very important step, but just by being subjective, you don't become religious. You can find poets who are not religious, you can find painters who are not religious... Religion is more than art, more than science.

What is this third? First, you start looking into your thoughts. Drop the public world and move into the private: look into your dreams, your thoughts, your desires, your emotions, your moods and the climates that go on changing inside you, year in, year out. Look into it. This is the subjective.

Then the last and the ultimate jump: by and by, by looking into thoughts, start looking into the looker, the witness, the one who is watching the thoughts.

First move from things to thoughts, then from thoughts to the thinker. Things are the world of science, thought is the world of art and the thinker is the world of religion. Just go on moving inward. The first circumference around you is of things, the second of thoughts, and the third, the center, your very being, is nothing but consciousness. It is nothing but a witnessing.

Drop things and go into thoughts; then one day thoughts also have to be dropped and then you are left alone in your purity, then you are left absolutely alone. In that aloneness is godliness, in that aloneness is liberation, *moksha,* in that aloneness is nirvana, in that aloneness for the first time you are in the real.

The objective and subjective are divided; there is a duality, a conflict, a struggle, a division. The person who is objective will miss something – he will miss the subjective. And the person who is subjective will miss something – he will miss the objective. Both will be incomplete. The scientist and the poet both are incomplete. Only the holy man is complete; only the holy man is whole. And because he is whole I call him holy.

By "holy" I don't mean that he is virtuous, by holy I mean that he is whole. Nothing is left, everything is involved. His richness is whole: the subjective and the objective have both dissolved into him. But he is not just the total of subjective and objective, he is more. The objective is without, the subjective is within and the religious is beyond. The beyond comprehends both without and within and yet is beyond.

This vision is what I call spirituality: the vision of the beyond.

A few more things. In the world of the objective, action is very important. One has to be active because only action is relevant in the world of things. If you do something, only then can you have more things; if you do something, only then can you change in the world of objectivity.

In the world of subjectivity there is inaction. Doing is not important, feeling is. That's why poets become lazy. And painters – even great painters and great poets and great singers, they have bouts of activity and then again they relapse into laziness. The subjective is more sleepy, dreamy, lazy; the objective is active, obsessed with action. The objective person always needs to do something or other, he cannot sit alone, he cannot rest. He can fall asleep – but once he is awake he has to do something. The subjective person is inactive. It is very difficult for him to move into action. He enjoys the world of fantasy – and that is available without action. He does not have to go anywhere, he has just to close his eyes and the world of dreams opens.

The religious person is a meeting of opposites: action in inaction, inaction in action. He does things, but he does them in such a way that he never becomes the doer. He remains a vehicle of God, the passage – what the Chinese call *wu-wei,* inaction in action. Even if he is doing, he is not doing it. His doing is very playful; there is no tension in it, no anxiety, no obsession about it. And even when he is inactive he is not dull; even when he is sitting, or lying down and resting, he is full of energy. He is not lethargic, he is radiant with energy. Because both the opposites have come to a meeting and to a higher synthesis in him, he can act as if he is in a non-doing state, and he can remain in a non-doing state, but still you can feel the energy, you can feel a vibe of tremendous activity around his being. Wherever he moves, he brings life to people. Just by his presence dead people become alive; just by his touch dead people are called back to life.

Like Jesus... When Lazarus died, Jesus was called. He went to the grave where Lazarus was kept and he called out, "Lazarus, come out!" And the dead Lazarus came out and said, "I am here. You called me out of death. I am here."

A religious person is active – not because he is a doer, a religious person is active because he has infinite energy available. A religious person is active – not because he has to do something, because he has an obsession to do, not because he cannot relax, but because he is such a pool of energy that he has to overflow; the energy is too much and he cannot contain it.

So while sitting silently... You can see Buddha sitting silently under the *bodhi* tree but you will see energy playing around him, a great aura of energy.

A beautiful story is told about Mahavira – that wherever he moved, for miles around life would become more alive. And he was an inactive man. He would simply stand or sit under a tree, for hours, for days, but for miles life would start throbbing with a new rhythm. It is said that trees would bloom out of season; trees would start growing faster than ever; dead trees would start producing new fresh leaves. Whether it happened or not is not the point, it may be just a story. But it is very indicative, it is very symbolic. Myths are not historic things, myths are very meaningful symbols. They say something.

What does this myth say? It simply says that Mahavira was such a pool of energy, such an overflowing of energy, such an overflowing of God, that wherever he was, life would move faster. A speed would happen to all the existence around him. He would not be doing anything, but things would start happening.

Lao Tzu has said that the greatest religious person never does anything, but millions of things happen through him. He is never a doer, but much happens through him. He simply goes on sitting and yet the impact of his being on the world of affairs is tremendous. Nobody may ever come to know about him – he may be sitting in a cave in the Himalayas so you never know about him – but still your life will be affected by him because he will be vibrating. He will give a new energy, a new pulse to life; he will impart a new pulsation to life. You may not come to know about him, but you may have been benefited by him.

The opposites become complimentaries in a religious being. Day and night meet and dissolve their conflict; man and woman meet in the religious person and dissolve their conflict. A religious person is *ardhanarishwar* – he is half man, half woman. He is both. He is as strong as any man can be and he is as fragile as any woman can be. He is as fragile as a flower and as strong as a sword. He is hard and he is soft and he is both together. He is a miracle, he is a mystery. Because opposites meet he goes beyond logic, his being is paradoxical. He is alive as nobody else is alive and he is dead, deader than the dead who are in the graveyards. He is dead in a way and alive in a way – together, simultaneously; he has known the art of dying and the art of living simultaneously.

In ordinary life with the ordinary mind everything is divided into its opposites, and there is a great attraction for meeting with the opposite: the man seeks the woman, the woman seeks the man – the yin-yang circle. In a religious man all search has stopped – the man has found the woman, the woman has found the man. In his innermost core the energy has come to a point where everything has dissolved into oneness, into non-duality, *advait.* All opposites become complimentaries; all conflicts dissolve and become cooperation. Then you have come home, then there is no need to go anywhere, then there is nothing to be sought, nothing to be desired. This state is the state of godliness. God is a state, God is not an object. And God is not even a person, because God is neither objective nor subjective. God is transcendental.

If you are in the objective I will say, "Seek the subjective – there is the God." If you are in the subjective, I will say, "Now go beyond. There is no God in the subjective. God is beyond." By and by one has to go on eliminating, by and by one has to go on dropping. God is when there is no object and no subject, when there is no thing and no thought, when there is no this world and no that world. When there is no matter and no mind, God is; God is neither matter nor mind. In God, both exist. God is a tremendous paradox, absolutely illogical, beyond logic. You cannot make an image of God in wood or in stone and you cannot make an image of God in concepts and ideas. When you dissolve all images – when you have dissolved all in/out, man/woman, life/death, all dualities – then that which is left is godliness.

Now this story:

One day, after he had gone blind,
Rabbi Bunam visited Rabbi Fishel.
Rabbi Fishel was famous throughout the land
for his miracle cures.
"Entrust yourself to my care," said his host.
"I shall restore your light."
"That is not necessary," answered Bunam,
"I see what I need to see."

The eyes that see only the outside are blind. They are not really eyes yet. They are very primitive, rudimentary. The eyes that see withinward are more real. The rabbi was right. He said, "Now there is no need to restore my eyes, because although I cannot see objects now I don't *want* to see them anymore. And the world that I need to see, I can see. It is good that blindness happened to me because now I am no longer disturbed and distracted by the world of objects."

It has happened many times. Milton became blind – and all his great poetry was born only after he became blind. At first he was very much shocked, naturally. He lost his eyes and there was no way to restore them. He thought his whole life was finished. He was a good poet, already famous. And, of course, a poet thinks, "Without eyes, how can you see the trees and how can you see the moon and how can you see the river and the wild ocean? And without eyes how can you see the color of life? Of course your poetry will become very poor. It will lose color." But Milton was wrong. He was a religious man and he accepted his blindness. He said, "Okay. If God wills it that way, then that has to be so." He accepted it. And by and by he became aware of an infinite new world available: the world of inner thoughts. He became subjective. Now there was no need to see outside so all his energy was available.

Have you seen blind people? On their faces you will always find a certain grace. Even ordinary blind people look very graceful, very silent. They don't have any of the distraction of the outside world.

Scientists say that man lives through the eyes; almost eighty percent of his life is involved with his eyes. Eighty percent! Only twenty percent is distributed to other senses. You live eighty percent of your life through the eyes. That's why when you see a blind man a great compassion arises in your being. You don't feel that much compassion for a dumb or deaf person, no, but for a blind person great compassion arises. You feel, "Poor fellow. Eighty percent of his life is not there."

Eyes are very important. The whole scientific search depends on the eyes. Have you ever heard of any scientist who was blind? It is impossible. A blind person cannot be in objective research – it becomes difficult. But there have been many blind musicians, blind singers; in fact a blind person has tremendous qualities of the ear which a man with eyes cannot have, because eighty percent of his energy is no longer being wasted by the eyes. That energy shifts to his ears. His ears become very, very receptive and sensitive. He starts seeing through his ears. Hold a blind man's hand and you will be surprised. You will find a very alive touch –

a touch you will not find in people who have eyes. Hold the hand of a blind man and you will feel a warmth flowing toward you, because the blind man cannot see you, he can only touch you. His whole energy moves into his touch.

Ordinarily you touch with your eyes. A beautiful woman passes by – you look. You have touched her through the eyes. You touched her whole body – and without offending her or breaking any law. By and by you forget completely what touch is.

Eyes have become monopolists – they have taken many energies from many sources. For example, the nose. Eyes are very close to the nose. The eyes have taken the whole energy from the nose. People don't smell. They have lost their smell power. Their noses are dead. A blind person smells. His smelling capacity is tremendous. When you come close to him he knows your smell; he recognizes you by your smell. He touches you; he knows you by your touch. He hears your sound; he knows you by your sound. His other senses become alive. And he is very graceful, because the eyes create much tension.

When Milton became blind, first he was shocked, but then he accepted – he was a religious man. He prayed to God and he said, "Thy will be done." By and by he was surprised that it was not a curse, it was a blessing. He became aware of infinite colors inside. It was a psychedelic world. Very subtle nuances, very beautiful dreams started opening up for him. And all his great poetry was born when he became blind. He was a good poet but not a great poet, but when he became blind he was no longer a good poet, he became a great poet. Good poetry is just so-so – lukewarm. Maybe you cannot find any fault in it, but that's all. Great poetry has a penetrating energy in it; great poetry is a revolutionary force; it has an impact strong enough to shake the whole world, to change the whole world.

It has happened many times. If, when a certain person has suddenly become blind, he can accept it, that very acceptance gives him a new world. The objective disappears, the subjective opens its door. And the subjective is closer to the transcendental opens its door. And the subjective is closer to the transcendental – that's why all meditators close their eyes.

Have you observed? All women close their eyes when you make love to them; men never close their eyes. They are foolish. The man wants to see the woman when he is making love to her. He would like to have the light on so he can see. And there are many foolish people who have mirrors in their bedroom. Not only would they like to see the woman, they would like to see all the reflections around. And there are a few who have fixed cameras in their room – automatically taking pictures – because if they miss something right now, later on they can see it!

But women are still not that foolish. I don't know about liberation women – maybe they are doing the same thing because they have to compete with everything, whatsoever it is. They may be making love with open eyes – but then they will miss something. Men make love in the objective dimension; women make love in the subjective dimension. Women immediately close their eyes because it is so beautiful inside, what is there to see outside? When you are moving in love energy, melting, flowing, and an orgasm is opening inside you, it is there that reality has to be looked at. The man is just foolish, he is just looking at the body; the woman is more understanding, she is looking at the psyche – a higher standpoint.

But still it is not religious – artistic, aesthetic, but still not religious. When you become religious, then the tantra attitude arises. Then you don't see with open eyes, you don't see with closed eyes, you simply see the seer! You are not worried about the experience, you look at the experiencer, you look at the witness. Then love becomes tantra. Whether it is a man or a woman who is moving into the dimension of tantra, he or she is not interested in what is happening; rather, he or she is more interested in the witness who is watching it all. Who is this witness? And when the energy is exploding in such a natural, spontaneous realm it is better to watch. Just be a watcher on the hill. Forget about your being a man or a woman, forget about your being in the body, forget that you are a mind and just be a witness – and then you have become transcendental. Tantra is transcendental.

And this dimension has to evolve in all your ordinary life situations. Whatsoever you do, you can do in three ways: objectively, that is the scientific way, the Western way; or subjectively, that is the Eastern way; or the religious way, the transcendental way, in which East and West meet and dissolve. The religious way is neither Eastern nor Western. The West is scientific, the East is poetic; the West thinks in terms of history, the East thinks in terms of myths, *puranas*. The West is more concerned about what reality is, the East is more concerned about the fantasy about the reality, the dream about the reality. The West is more concerned with the conscious mind, the East is more concerned with the unconscious mind. But religion is beyond both. Religion is of the super-conscious mind, the transcendental mind – it is neither Eastern nor Western.

Just as man and woman meet, so East and West meet. West is more male, East is more female; West is more will, East is more surrender. But religion is beyond, and both.

"That is not necessary," answered Bunam, *"I see what I need to see."* Certainly a great religious statement – it's enough, more than enough, if you can see the seer. If you can see the seer, if you can be your consciousness, your awareness, that's enough. All is available. You have become a God, nothing else is needed.

Strive for that state of being. If you are coming from the West, struggle for it; if you are coming from the East, surrender for it. If you are coming from the West, will it; if you are coming from the East, be passive, wait for it.

And if you are my sannyasins, who don't belong to the East or to the West, then drop all duality, be non-dual. Then drop all division, then just be individual. If you belong to me then you belong to the transcendental. That is the whole meaning of being initiated by me. I bring you the transcendental, I bring you the ultimate, I bring you that which cannot be seen on the outside, that which cannot be seen on the inside – but you can become that because you are already that.

Enough for today.

10

Beyond East and West

The first question:

Osho,
You seem to be against the demystification of life. In this reference is it right to say that movements in the West like Arica, Zen, Sufism, EST, TM, etc., are the inevitable synthesis between Eastern mysticism and Western science?

The real synthesis will be the disappearance of East and West; it will not be a meeting. In the real synthesis the East will not be there and the West will not be there. That's what yesterday I called the transcendental.

East and West are polarities. If you try to synthesize them, take something of the East and something of the West and make a hotchpotch out of it, it will be a compromise and not a synthesis. It will be mechanical, not organic. You can put things together – that is a mechanical unity – but you cannot put a tree together, you cannot put a human being together. The unity of a tree grows, it comes from its own innermost core and it spreads toward its circumference. It arises in the center. A mechanical unity can be put together from the outside; you can put a car or a clock together, but the clock has no center to it, the car has no center to it, the clock has no soul. That is what we mean when we say the clock has no soul; it means it has no center of its own. It is a unity put together from outside. It works; it is utilitarian.

But a tree, a bird, a human baby – you cannot put them together. They grow. Their unity comes from their innermost core. They have a center.

A compromise is a mechanical unity; a synthesis is an organic growth. So whatsoever is happening right now in the name of EST, TM, Arica, is a sort of mechanical unity. And mechanical unity has its own dangers. The greatest danger is this: the East has developed a great insight into religion and the West has developed a great insight into science. When a Western person starts searching in the East, his attitude is scientific. He can understand only that which is scientific in the East. Try to understand this. And the East has not developed any scientific attitude; Eastern science is very primitive and rudimentary. When a religious person goes to the West from the East, he looks into Western religion, which is very rudimentary, very primitive. And he can understand only the religious language.

So when somebody from the East approaches the West, he approaches the West from the weak point in Western growth. And when somebody comes from the West to the East he approaches the East from the weakest link in its growth.

Now what is happening? East and West are meeting in Arica, EST, TM and other so-called spiritual movements – and just the opposite to what was expected is happening. It is not Eastern religion meeting Western science, it is Eastern science meeting Western religion. It is an ugly affair.

You must have heard:

A French actress told George Bernard Shaw that she would like to get married to him.

Bernard Shaw inquired why.

She said, "The logic is simple. I have a tremendously beautiful body. Look at my face, look at my eyes, my form – it is perfect. And you have a beautiful intellect, the greatest intelligence ever. Our child will be a beauty: your brain and my body."

George Bernard Shaw said, "I am afraid things can go wrong. Our child may have my body and your intellect."

This is what is happening!

He declined the offer to marry. He said, "It is dangerous. There is no certainty about it."

Of course, George Bernard Shaw had a very ugly body – and actresses have never been known to have any intellect. Intelligence is a strange phenomenon to actresses, otherwise why would they be actresses in the first place?

Arica, EST, and TM are just by-products of the marriage between George Bernard Shaw and the actress. Things have gone wrong. This is not a synthesis; this is a compromise, a hotchpotch. And it is very dangerous.

A great synthesis is needed. That synthesis will not come through movements, it will come only through a few people who attain to that synthesis in their souls. It is not a question of reading the Bible and reading the Bhagavad Gita and finding out the similarities and making a synthesis out of it – that would be a mechanical unity. Many people have done that.

Dr. Bhagwandas has written a very scholarly book: *The Essential Unity of All Religions*. The whole thing is silly. Read the Koran, read the Veda, read the Bible, read the Dhammapada, find the similarities – it is very easy to find similarities – but in fact the Koran is beautiful only because of those things which are not in the Gita. The beauty is in its uniqueness. When you find something, as Mahatma Gandhi has done… He read the Koran and found things which were similar to the Gita. He was looking for the Gita in the Koran. It was unjust to the Koran; it was not good manners either because he was imposing some alien element on the Koran. And whatsoever was not similar to the Gita, in tune with the Gita, he would forget about. He would forget that it existed in the Koran. And that which was dropped is the uniqueness of the Koran.

The same can be done by a Christian. He can look into the Gita and find something which satisfies his Christian mind – then he is looking for the Bible in the Gita, but the Gita is beautiful only where it is not at all similar to the Bible. There is its uniqueness. Beauty is in uniqueness; similarities become clichés, similarities become meaningless, similarities are monotonous. The Himalayas are beautiful because they have something unique that is not in the Alps. And the Ganges is beautiful because it has something that is not in the Amazon. Of course both are rivers, and there are a thousand and one similar things, but if you go on looking for similarities you will live in a very boring world. I am not in favor of it.

I will not tell you to look into Eastern scriptures and into Western scriptures and to find some sort of compromise, no. I would like you to go into your innermost being. If you go beyond the object, you have gone beyond the West; if you go beyond the subject, you have gone beyond the East. Then the transcendental arises and *there* is the synthesis. And when it has happened within you, then you can spread it without also. The synthesis has to happen within human beings, not in books, not in dissertations, not in PhD theses. An organic unity is possible only in an organic way.

This is what I am doing here. I am hammering you to make you go beyond the objective and beyond the subjective. I am not telling you to make subjective and objective meet inside you, because that meeting will not be able to bring the higher into existence. You have to go beyond. The humanity of the future has to go beyond East and West; both have been only half, both have been lopsided. I am neither for East nor for West, I am for a total world, a world that is whole.

But it is natural in a way – Arica, EST, TM – in a way

natural. This is because the common humanity, the ordinary human mind, always tries to find cheap methods, shortcuts. People are not really interested in the ultimate truth; they are interested at the most in a convenient, comfortable life. They are not really interested in being alive and being an adventurer, they are really afraid of all adventures. They want to put things together in such a way that things become comfortable and one can live comfortably and one can die comfortably. Comfort seems to be the goal, not truth.

And everybody has his own prejudice. The Christian, the Hindu, the Mohammedan all have their prejudices. They are very deep-rooted. You can talk about love, but that is always superficial.

Let me tell you an anecdote:

The distraught young man was perched on the fortieth floor window ledge of a midtown hotel, threatening to jump. The closest the police could get was the roof of an adjacent building a few feet below. However, all pleas to the man to return to safety were of no avail.

A priest from the nearest parish was summoned and he hastened to the scene.

"Think, my son," he intoned to the would-be suicide in a very loving way. "Think, my son, think of your mother and father who love you."

"Oh, they don't love me," the man replied. "I am jumping."

"No, my son, stop!" cried the priest with great love in his voice. "Think of the woman who loves you."

"Nobody loves me. I am jumping," came the response.

"But think, still think, my boy," the priest implored. "Think of Jesus and Mary and Joseph who love you."

"Jesus, Mary and Joseph?" the man queried. "Who are they?"

At which the point the cleric yelled back, "Jump, you Jew bastard, jump!"

All love disappears immediately. All talk of love is just superficial; all talk of tolerance is intolerant deep down.

People say, "Tolerate each other." What do you mean when you say, "Tolerate each other"? It is already intolerant. The very word *tolerance* is ugly. When you tolerate somebody, do you love him? When Hindus tolerate Mohammedans, do they love them? When Mohammedans tolerate Hindus, do they love them? Can tolerance ever become love? Tolerance may be politics, but it is not religion.

One who wants to know the truth – the truth that is beyond all polarities: man–woman, East–West, good–bad, heaven–hell, summer–winter – one who is interested in knowing, in inquiring into the truth which is beyond all dualities, has to drop all his prejudices. If he still carries his prejudice, that prejudice will color his mind.

To know truth you need not be a Hindu, you need not be a Mohammedan, you need not be a Christian, you need not be a Jew – to know truth you have to drop all this rubbish, you have to be just yourself. You need not be Indian, you need not be American, you need not be English, you need not be Japanese, Chinese. To know truth you have just to be immense, huge, vital, alive, loving, inquiring, meditative, but with no prejudice, with no scripture, with no concepts, with no philosophy.

When you are completely nude of all that has been taught to you, when all the conditionings have dropped, then suddenly there is the highest truth – and that highest truth is a synthesis unto itself; *you* need not synthesize. It is an organic unity. And from that altitude you can laugh at all the nonsense that goes on in the name of religion, in the name of tolerance, in the name of love, in the name of churches and temples and mosques.

The revolution has to happen within you; it has not to be introduced into the world. Because only *you* are alive – society is dead, society is just a name. Only *you* have something of the soul. The synthesis has to happen there. The synthesis does not have to happen in Pune or in New York or in Timbuktu or in

Constantinople, the synthesis is going to happen within you, within me. And each individual has to become a great experiment toward that synthesis. But remember, when that synthesis arises, you will not be able to say whether it is a synthesis between East and West, between Mohammedan and Christian, between Hindu and Jaina. No, you will immediately be able to see it is a transcendence. Synthesis, real synthesis, organic synthesis, is a transcendence; your altitude has changed, you are standing on the highest peak. From there you look.

Whatsoever we look at, whatsoever we see, is not very important. The important thing is where you stand. If you are clinging to the East, whatsoever you see in the West will be a misinterpretation.

Just the other day I was reading a newspaper; someone had written an article against me. The article asked how Americans can understand religion, how Western people can understand religion. They cannot, so my whole effort is wastage. This is the Indian chauvinist mind. The Indian thinks that nobody can understand religion except the Indian. And this is not only so with the Indian, this is so with everybody. Everybody deep down carries this nonsense: "we are the chosen few." This idea is very destructive.

It is not a question of being American or Indian; truth has nothing to do with all these labels. Truth is available to anybody who is ready to drop all these labels. Truth is understood only when you are neither American nor Indian nor Hindu nor Christian. Truth is understood by a consciousness that is no longer clouded by any conditionings, which is no longer clouded by the past. Otherwise we go on seeing in things only that which we can understand.

I was reading a very beautiful anecdote:

The family managed to bring the patriarchal grandfather from Hungary and he came to live with his daughter and her family.

The old man was fascinated by New York and all it had to offer. One day his grandson, Yunkel, took him to the zoo in Central Park.

Most of the animals were familiar to the old man. However they came to the cage where the laughing hyena was confined and the old man became curious.

"Yunkel, in the old country I never heard of an animal that laughed."

Yunkel noticed the keeper standing nearby and approached him.

"My grandfather recently came from Europe. He says they don't have any laughing hyenas there. Could you tell me something about it so that I can in turn tell him?"

The keeper said, "Well, he eats once a day."

Yunkel turned to his grandfather and said in Yiddish, "He eats once a day."

The keeper continued, "He takes a bath once a week."

"He bathes once a week."

The old man listened intently.

The keeper added, "He mates once a year."

"He mates once a year."

The old man shook his head up and down thoughtfully.

"All right. He eats once a day, he bathes once a week, but if he mates only once a year, why is he laughing?"

Now this old man is not so old. His mind is still clinging somewhere to his youthful days. His mind is still sexual. He cannot understand why the hyena is laughing if he mates only once a year.

There are people who cannot understand that happiness is possible in any way other than sex. There are people who cannot understand that there is any bliss beyond sex. There are people who cannot understand that there is any happiness except in food. There are people who cannot understand that there is any happiness except in big houses, big cars, much money, power and prestige. It is impossible to understand beyond your own standpoint – people remain confined within their own standpoints.

That is the real prison. If you want a synthesis you have to drop all the imprisonment, you have to drop out of your cages. They are very subtle cages and you have decorated them for a long time. You may have even started loving them. You may have forgotten completely that they are prisons; you may have started thinking that they are your home. A Hindu thinks Hinduism is his home, he never thinks that it is a barrier. All "isms" are barriers. The Christian thinks that Christianity is the bridge; he never thinks that it is Christianity that is not allowing him to reach to Christ. The church is not the door; it is the wall, the barrier, the Wall of China.

But if you have lived with this wall for too long, for centuries, if the mind has become accustomed to it, you think of it as a protection, as a shelter, as security. And then you look at other people; from your cell in the prison you look outside. Your presence in the cell corrupts your vision.

Come out under the sky and under the stars – and synthesis will take care of itself. You need not synthesize East and West, you are simply to go beyond these standpoints. Move to the transcendental, and there is synthesis.

The second question:

Osho,
I have heard you saying that man is a goal-oriented
process and his destination is the stars. Can you
please open this flower for me for a deep smell?

The flower is open. I suspect your nose is closed.

Your nose has to be opened and you have to reclaim the capacity to smell. You may have lost the sensitivity to smell. You have lived so long in lies that when you come across truth you cannot recognize it. Even truth has to come to you – if truth wants to be recognized – in the garb of a lie. You cannot see it directly. You have learned how to look sideways; you never look directly, your look is never immediate. You are always wavering this way or that and you are always losing the fact.

I am here. This is the flower I am talking about. I am your future. That which is going to happen to you has happened to me. If you cannot smell then don't blame the flower – blow your nose.

But that is difficult for the ego; the ego is always ready to deny, it is never ready to transform itself. The ego can say, "There is no God"; it cannot say, "Maybe it is because I have got so many blocks that I cannot feel God." The ego can deny that there is a flower, but it cannot recognize the fact that it has lost the capacity to smell.

Hence there are so many people who deny God. It is easy to deny God, it is comfortable in fact, because if there is no God you need not bother about your nose, you need not work upon your being. If there is no God then there is no work, then there is no growth, then there is no search – you can be lazy, you can drown yourself in lethargy. If there is no God then there is no guilt.

I am against guilt, the guilt that has been created by the priests, but there is a different type of guilt which is not created by the priest. And that guilt is very meaningful. That guilt arises if you feel there is something more in life and you are not working hard to get to it. Then you feel guilt. Then you feel that somehow you are creating barriers to your own growth, that you are lazy, lethargic, unconscious, asleep; that you don't have any integration; that you cannot move toward your destiny. Then guilt arises. When you feel that you have the possibility and you are not turning it into actuality, then guilt arises. That guilt is totally different.

I am not talking about the guilt that priests have created in humanity: don't eat this otherwise you will feel guilty, don't do that otherwise you will feel guilty. They have condemned millions of things, so if you eat, if you drink, if you do this and that, you are surrounded by guilty feelings. I am not talking about that guilt; that guilt has to be dropped. In fact that guilt helps you to remain where you are. Those guilty feelings don't allow you to know the real guilt inside.

They create so much fuss about small things. You eat in the night and the Jainas create much fuss: you are guilty, you are a sinner. Why have you eaten in the night? Or you have divorced your wife or your husband and the Catholics create a guilty feeling in you; you have done something wrong. It was not wrong to live with the woman and continuously fight, it was not wrong to destroy the woman and destroy yourself, it was not wrong to destroy the children – just between the two of you they were being crushed, their whole life was conditioned in a wrong way. No, that was not bad; but if you get out of that marriage, if you get out of that hell, you feel guilty.

These guilt feelings don't allow you to see the real spiritual guilt, which has nothing to do with any politics, with any priesthood, with any religion or church. This guilt feeling is very natural. When you see that you can do something and you are not doing it, when you see how potential you are but you are not changing that potentiality into actuality, when you see that you are carrying tremendous treasures as seeds which could bloom, and you are not doing anything about it and you are just remaining in misery – then you feel a great responsibility toward yourself. And if you are not fulfilling that responsibility, you feel guilty. This guilt is of tremendous import.

I am here; the flower is here. In Zen they say that the flower does not talk, but I would like to contradict that. I would like to say to you the flower talks too, but one thing is needed: you need the capacity to hear, you need the capacity to smell. The flower has its own language. It may not talk in the language that you understand. Your language is a very local language; the flower speaks the universal language.

I am here; look into me, feel me, try to imbibe my spirit in you, let my flame come closer to you. Any moment there can be the jump – my flame can jump and light your unlit candle.

THE ART OF DYING

Just come close, come close... And when I say come close, I mean be more and more in love. Love is the only closeness there is; love is the only intimacy there is. It is not a question of physical closeness; it is a question of inner intimacy. Be open to me, as I am open to you. Be available to me, as I am available to you. Don't be afraid; you have nothing to lose – except your chains.

The third question:

> Osho,
> Somewhere there is a fear which makes me closed
> and hard and sad and desperate and angry and
> hopeless. It seems to be so subtle that I don't even
> get really in touch with it. How can I see it more
> clearly?

The only problem with sadness, desperateness, anger, hopelessness, anxiety, anguish, misery, is that you want to get rid of them. That's the only barrier.

You will have to live with them. You cannot just escape. They are the very situation in which life has to integrate and grow. They are the challenges of life. Accept them. They are blessings in disguise. If you want to escape from them, if you somehow want to get rid of them, then the problem arises – because if you want to get rid of something, you never look at it directly. And then the thing starts hiding from you because you are condemnatory; then the thing goes on moving deeper into the unconscious, hides in the darkest corner of your being where you cannot find it. It moves into the basement of your being and hides there. And of course the deeper it goes, the more trouble it creates – because then it starts functioning from unknown corners of your being and you are completely helpless.

So the first thing is: never repress. The first thing is: whatsoever is the case is the case. Accept it and let it come – let it come in front of you. In fact just to say "do not repress" is not enough. If you allow me, I would like to say, "Befriend it." You are feeling sad? Befriend it, have compassion for it. Sadness also has a being. Allow it, embrace it, sit with it, hold hands with it. Be friendly. Be in love with it. Sadness is beautiful. Nothing is wrong with it. Who told you that something is wrong in being sad? In fact only sadness gives you depth. Laughter is shallow; happiness is skin-deep. Sadness goes to the very bones, to the marrow. Nothing goes as deep as sadness.

So don't be worried. Remain with it and sadness will take you to your innermost core. You can ride on it and you will be able to know a few new things about your being that you had never known before. Those things can be revealed only in a sad state; they can never be revealed in a happy state. Darkness is also good and darkness is also divine. The day is not only God's, the night is his also. I call this attitude religious.

"Somewhere there is a fear which makes me closed and hard and sad and desperate and angry and hopeless. It seems to be so subtle that I don't even really get in touch with it." It becomes subtle if you want to get rid of it. Then of course it protects itself, it hides in the deepest corners of your being. It becomes so subtle and so garbed that you cannot recognize it. It starts coming under different names. If you are very much against anger then anger will arise under a different name – it may become pride, it may become ego, it may become even a religious pride, it may become even pious. It may hide behind your virtues, it may start hiding behind your character. Then it becomes very subtle because now the label is changed. It is playing somebody else's role, but deep down it remains anger.

Let things be as they are. This is what religious courage is: to allow things as they are.

I am not promising you any rose garden – there are thorns, roses also. But you can reach the roses only when you have passed the thorns. A man who has never been sad cannot really be happy. It is impossible for him to be happy. His happiness will be just a forced gesture – empty, impotent. You can see it on people's faces when they laugh: their laugh is so shallow, it is just painted on their lips. It has no relationship with their heart, it is absolutely unconnected.

It is just like lipstick – the lips look red and rosy, but that redness does not come from the redness of the blood. It is good if lips are red, but the redness should come from aliveness, from your blood cells, from your energy, vitality, youth. Now, you paint your lips – they look red, but it is ugly. Lipstick is ugly. And you will find only ugly women using it. What does a beautiful woman have to do with lipstick? The whole thing seems to be absurd. If your lips are red, vital, alive, what is the point of painting them? You are making them ugly and false.

Your happiness is also like lipstick. You are not happy and you know you are not happy, but you cannot accept the fact because that would be too shattering for your ego. You – and not happy?! How can you accept it? Maybe you are not happy inside, but that is your own problem, you must not express it, you are not to say the truth. For the world you have to keep a face, you have to maintain a personality. So you go on laughing. Watch people's laughter and you will immediately see which laughter comes from the heart. When laughter comes from the heart you can immediately feel a different vibe – an overflowing. That man is really happy. When laughter is just on the lips it is empty. It is just a gesture; nothing is behind it. It is a facade.

The man who cannot laugh deeply is the man who has repressed sadness – he cannot go deep because he is afraid of sadness. Even if he goes deep into his laughter, there is a fear that sadness may surface, may bubble up. He has to be always on guard.

So please, whatsoever the situation is, start allowing it. If you are sad, you are sad. This is what God means for you – at this moment at least he wants you to be sad. So be true – be sad! Live this sadness. And if you can live this sadness, a different quality of happiness will arise in you; it will not be a repression of sadness, it will be beyond sadness.

A person who can be patiently sad will suddenly find that one morning happiness is arising in his heart from some unknown source. That unknown source is existence. You have earned it if you have been truly sad; if you have been truly hopeless, desperate, unhappy, miserable, if you have lived in hell, you have earned heaven. You have paid the cost.

I was reading a joke:

Mr. Goldberg came home from the office unexpectedly and found his wife in bed with Mr. Cohen, the next-door neighbor.

Distraught and angry, he ran next door and confronted Mrs. Cohen.

"Mrs. Cohen!" he cried. "Your husband is in bed with my wife."

"Calm down! Calm down!" Mrs. Cohen said. "Look, don't take it so hard. Sit down, have a cup of tea. Relax."

Mr. Cohen sat quietly and drank his cup of tea. It was then that he noticed a little glint in Mrs. Cohen's eye.

Coyly she suggested, "You want a little revenge?"

And with that they withdrew to the couch and made love. Then they had another cup of tea, then a little more revenge, a little more tea, more revenge; more tea...

Finally Mrs. Cohen looked at Mr. Goldberg and asked, "How about another revenge?"

"I will tell you, Mrs. Cohen," said Mr. Goldberg quietly, "to be truthful, I've got no hard feelings left."

Whatsoever the situation, if you are sad, be sad; if you are in a revengeful mood, take your revenge; if you are jealous, be jealous; if you are angry, be angry. Never avoid the fact. You have to live it, that is part of life's progress, growth, evolution. Those who avoid remain immature. If you want to remain immature then go on avoiding; but remember, you are avoiding life itself. Whatsoever you are avoiding is not the point; the very avoiding is an avoidance of life.

Confront life. Encounter life. Difficult moments will be there, but one day you will see that those difficult moments gave you strength because you encountered them. They were meant to be. Those difficult moments are hard when you are passing through them, but later on you will see they have made you more integrated. Without them you would never have been centered, grounded.

The old religions all over the world have been repressive; the new religion of the future is going to be expressive. And I teach that new religion. Let expression be one of the most fundamental rules of your life. Even if you have to suffer for it, suffer. You will never be a loser. That suffering will make you more and more capable of enjoying life, of rejoicing in life.

The fourth question:

> Osho,
> You are the best whiskey-coke I have ever had. I
> stumble out of your lectures every day, my head
> spinning. Should I give you up as a bad habit?

It is very difficult to give up bad habits. Good habits are very easy to drop.

Who has ever heard of any man or woman capable of giving up a bad habit? And if religion has become your bad habit, or sannyas, you are blessed, you are fortunate. If I am your bad habit then you are fortunate. I would never like to become a good habit to you, no, because a good habit can be dropped very easily!

Let me tell you an anecdote:

St. Peter, concerned about the state of affairs in America, sent his most dependable and conservative disciple, St. Theresa, to look over the situation and give him a personal report. She stopped first in New York and phoned at the end of three days to say that things were even worse than they had feared.

"Let me come home," she begged.

"No," said St. Peter. "Finish the job. Go on to Chicago."

She called him again from Chicago with an even more dismal tale. "It is a mess of corruption," she reported sadly. "Sinners on all sides. I can't take any more of it. Allow me to return to heaven."

"Patience and fortitude," consoled St. Peter. "They tell me Hollywood is worst of all. Have a look around out there and then you can come home."

Two weeks went by, then four weeks went by, then six weeks went by without further word from St. Theresa. St. Peter, beside himself with anxiety, was about to turn the case over to the celestial FBI when the phone finally rang and the operator said,

"One moment, please. Hollywood calling."

And then a sweet voice came over the wire, "Hullo, Peter darling! How divine! This is Terry."

I would not like you to become St. Theresas. Even if you go to Hollywood, Hollywood is not going to corrupt you because I have corrupted you finally, utterly. I am a bad habit. And nobody can make a good habit out of me because good habits are not reliable. At the drop of the hat, good habits disappear. Let religion be your bad habit; let meditation be your bad habit. Yes, it is perfectly good – let me be your whisky-coke.

The fifth question:

Osho,
When I first saw you, I felt I had found protection. Osho will protect. But now I am asking myself, "How is Osho going to protect me from Osho himself?"
Please comment.

That is not your problem. That is my problem. How am I

255

going to protect you from myself? That is my problem. It is none of your business.

One thing I can say... Let me say it through an anecdote:

Edwin's life was over. His wife had left him and taken the children. He had lost his job. The bank had just foreclosed the mortgage on his house. He decided the only thing left for him to do was to jump off a bridge and kill himself. He walked to the Brooklyn Bridge, climbed as high as he could and was just about to jump when he heard a voice down below, screeching.

"Don't jump! I can help you."

He yelled back, "Who are you?"

To which the voice replied, "I am a witch."

Curious, he climbed down and there before him was an ugly old crone. She looked at him and said,

"I am a witch and if you do as I say I will grant you three wishes."

He thought to himself, "Things can't be any worse so what do I have to lose?" So he said, "All right. What do I have to do?"

She said, "Come home with me and spend the night."

He went with her to her hovel and she commanded him to make wild love to her. With great effort he accomplished all her bidding and finally fell asleep in a completely exhausted state. When he woke up there was the ugly old woman standing in front of him.

He said, "Now that I have done your bidding old witch, you must keep your part of the bargain and grant me my three wishes."

The hag looked at him and asked, "How old are you?"

He replied, "Forty-two."

The old woman sighed, "Do you mean to tell me that you still believe in witches?"

Listening to me for so long, do you tell me you still believe in Osho?

My whole effort is to take all the props away from you, all beliefs, Osho included. First I pretend to give you help, because that is the only language you understand. Then by and by I start withdrawing myself. First I take you away from your other desires and help you to become very passionate about nirvana, liberation, truth. And when I see that now all desires have disappeared, there is only one desire left, then I start hammering on that desire, and I say, "Drop it because this is the only barrier."

Nirvana is the last nightmare. You cannot go back because once you have dropped those futile desires, you cannot get back into them. Once you have dropped them, the very charm, the very mystery disappears from them. You cannot really believe how you were carrying them for so long. The whole thing looks so ridiculous you cannot go back.

And I start taking the last desire from you. Once the last desire disappears, you are enlightened. Then you are Osho. My whole effort here is to make you capable of declaring yourself that you are also a master – and not only declaring it, living it too.

The sixth question:

Osho,
When I think about your life on this earth and why you have come, it seems that there must be a risk in your undertaking – and the possibility of failure, that your work cannot be granted, that you also must be able to err, to commit a mistake. It seems that if there is no freedom to err, then there is no freedom at all.
But when I look at you there is no question of mistakes; egolessness is perfect. Please comment.

The first thing: I am not under any obligation to do anything. This is not an undertaking. I am not doing any work actually; it is not work that I am doing. It may be work for you, it is not work for me. I am enjoying the game. It is a play. And in a play it does not matter whether you make mistakes or not. It does not matter.

Mistakes become very, very important when you are serious about a thing. When you are doing it as serious work then mistakes become very important. But I am not doing it seriously at all. It is laughter, it is a dance, it is a play for me. I am enjoying it. And I have no plan, no reverence for it. How can I commit a mistake? You can commit a mistake if you have a plan – then you know where you missed. I carry no plans with me. I have no blueprint. I simply go on doing whatsoever happens in the moment. So whatsoever happens is perfectly right because there is no way to judge it, there is no criterion, there is no touchstone. That's the beauty of it. And that's what freedom is. In serious work you can never be free; in serious work anxiety will always haunt you; in serious work you are always afraid that something can go wrong.

With me nothing can go wrong because there is nothing that is right. If something is right then something can go wrong; if nothing is right then nothing is wrong. That's the meaning of the Eastern concept of *leela* – play. It is a playfulness. While I am here I am enjoying this playfulness, I am enjoying it terribly, enjoying it terrifically.

You ask, "When I think about your life on this earth…" You are thinking in wrong terms. You are thinking in the terms that religions have conditioned your minds to think in. You are thinking as Christians, Hindus, Mohammedans, Jainas do. You have not yet learned my language.

Christians think that Christ came to deliver the whole world from sin – all nonsense! You can see the world is not delivered yet. In fact if the world were completely delivered from sin there would be no work left for Christ. He would go broke. He would go bankrupt. He would have to close the shop. Jainas think that *tirthankaras* come to help humanity. I can understand – you want help, so you project help.

But a *tirthankara* is not going to help you. He is simply enjoying. And if you want to enjoy, you can participate. He simply opens a door to spiritual enjoyment, to spiritual bliss. And he is not worried whether you come or not, he is not worried whether a few people come or millions come. If nobody comes it is as good as if millions come. He is not in search of customers. He is happy; things are going perfectly well for him. If a few people come and dance with him, good. If nobody comes, he dances alone. His dance remains perfect, it is not a work.

Hindus think avatars come when the world is in misery, when the world is in ignorance. When religion disappears from the world then avatars come. All nonsense! Avatars have come many, many times, but the misery has not disappeared, the ignorance has not disappeared.

Religion never becomes an established fact; in fact the moment religion becomes established, it is no longer religion, it becomes a church. Established religion is no longer religion, religion remains only unestablished. Religion is a rebellion. You cannot make anything established out of it; it is intrinsically rebellious. And the play continues.

But I can understand why people have projected their need for help all over the world. This is their hope. They are in misery, that is certain, and they want somebody to help them. Why do you want somebody to help you? – because you don't want to take the responsibility on yourself. First you say that others have made you miserable, now you say that somebody has to take you out of the misery. What are *you* doing? You don't create your misery, you can't drop it.

Do you exist or not? Responsibility is existence, responsibility gives you being. If you go on throwing responsibility on to someone else – it is the Devil who is creating misery and it is God who becomes Christ, becomes Mohammed, becomes Mahavira, and takes you out of the misery – then what are you doing? You seem to be just like a football: on one side is the Devil, on one side is God, and you are being kicked from this side to that. Enough! Simply say, "Enough! I am not going to allow myself to be kicked anymore." Are you a football? Claim responsibility.

I am not here to help you. You may be here to be helped, but I am not. I am just enjoying my thing. I am doing my thing. And you will be benefited more if you drop your idea of help and work and Christ and avatars. You will be helped more if you drop all concepts of help. Simply be with me. Don't bring business into it. Let it be pure play.

"...it seems that there must be a risk in your undertaking..." There is nothing, no risk – because it is not an undertaking. I am not risking anything because there is nothing to risk, there is nothing to lose. All that is, always is. And that which is not, never is. So what is the risk?

If somebody comes and kills me, he kills only my body, which is already dead, has always been dead; it is part of the earth. So, dust unto dust. He cannot kill me. I was before I was born; I will be after death has happened. So what has he done? – nothing serious; nothing of much importance. The person may think he had done a very serious thing: that he has killed me, that he has crucified a Jesus or killed a Socrates. That is his idea. But in me, that which is matter is going to fall into matter and that which is consciousness is going to fall into consciousness, so nobody can kill me. You can shoot at me, but you cannot shoot me. You can cut my head off, but your sword will not touch me. The sword is material and it cannot touch the spiritual.

There is no risk and there is no possibility of failure – because there is no possibility of success either. I cannot succeed so how can I fail? In fact the very terminology of success, failure, benefit, loss, is absurd, irrelevant.

You ask: "...that your work cannot be granted, that you must be able to err, to make a mistake. It seems that if there is no freedom to err then there is no freedom at all." Freedom is so absolute that there is no right and no wrong. Freedom is so absolute that whatsoever you do is right. It is not that you have to do something and sometimes it is right and sometimes it is wrong. Try to understand my standpoint from my grounding, from my centering. Whatsoever you do is perfectly right – not that it fulfills any criterion of what is right. Simply there is *no* criterion of what is right. That's why I can be with Hasids, I can be with Sufis, I can be with *tantrikas,* I can be with yogis. It is very difficult for so-called religious people; if they are with Mahavira, how can they be with Mohammed? Impossible. If one is right then the other is wrong. If they are with Krishna, how can they be with Christ? If one is right, the other is wrong. Their mathematics is clear: only one can be right. To me there is no criterion.

You cannot judge who is right and who is wrong. Mahavira is right because he enjoyed his thing; Buddha is right because he also enjoyed his thing; Mohammed is right because he enjoyed his thing, tremendously. Bliss is right. So whatsoever I am doing I am enjoying it tremendously – and to be blissful is to be right.

Even if I commit mistakes according to you... Maybe sometimes you feel I am committing a mistake. That will be according to you, because you carry some criterion.

I stayed in a Jaina family once. An old man came to see me – ninety years old. And he touched my feet and said,

"You are almost a twenty-fifth *tirtankara.*"

I said, "Wait, don't be in a hurry. Just watch me."

He said, "What do you mean?"

I said, "Simply watch me. Otherwise you will have to take your words back."

He became a little disturbed. It was dusk, the sun was setting, the evening was descending and a woman, my host's wife, came in and said, "Your food is ready."

I said, "Wait."

The old man said, "What? The sun has already gone past the horizon. Are you going to take your food?"

I said, "Yes, I am telling the woman to wait. I will have to take my bath and then I will take my food."

He stood up. He said, "Sorry. I must take my words back. You were right. You can eat at night? You don't know even this much? Then what type of enlightened person are you?"

He has a certain criterion: an enlightened person cannot eat at night. This is the Jaina criterion.

If you go to any person he has criteria and he looks through those windows to see if I fit or if I don't fit. But I am not here to fulfill your expectations. I am always right because I don't carry any criteria. There is no way. You cannot even find contradictions in me, because whatsoever I have said up to this moment is irrelevant. I don't bother a bit about it. Now it is for foolish scholars, it is finished for me! The moment I say something, I enjoy saying it – that's all. More than that is not my concern. The moment I do something I enjoy it infinitely – beyond that it is not my concern.

"But when I look at you there is no question of mistakes; egolessness is perfect." How can egolessness be perfect? The very idea of perfection is the ego; egolessness cannot be perfect. Egolessness simply means an absence of the ego. Can absence be imperfect? Absence cannot be imperfect, so how can absence be perfect? Absence is simply absence. Ego can be imperfect, ego can be perfect, but egolessness cannot be either. There is nobody to be perfect.

Seeing the point that the whole game of ego is absurd, ego disappears. Nothing is left behind. There is a wholeness, but there is no perfection. There is totality, but there is no perfection.

The old religions were all perfection-oriented; my whole teaching is whole-oriented. I say be whole, I don't say be perfect. And the difference is tremendous. When I say be whole, I allow you contradictions. Then be wholly contradictory. When I say be whole, I don't give you a goal, a criterion, an ideal;

I don't want to create any anxiety in you. I simply want you, in this moment, wherever, whatsoever you are doing, and whatsoever you are, to be total in it. If you are sad, be totally sad – you are whole. If you are angry, be totally angry. Go into it totally.

The idea of perfection is absolutely different, diametrically opposite – not even different, opposite. The perfectionists will say, "Never be angry; always be compassionate. Never be sad; always be happy." They choose one polarity against the other. In wholeness we accept both the polarities: the lows and the highs, the ups and the downs. Wholeness is totality. And you have to see the whole nonsense of the ego; otherwise it can come in from the back door. If I say, "Now become *perfectly* egoless," you will have to prove that there exists nobody who is more egoless than you.

Let me tell you an anecdote:

A family with a son about to be bar mitzvahed wanted to celebrate the occasion in a unique way. Money was no object. The caterer suggested many things: flying the party out to Disneyland, renting out the White House, having the affair in a nuclear submarine. All of these ideas were rejected by the family as old hat. It was not until the caterer came up with the idea of having the bar mitzvah on safari in Africa that the family grew excited. Invitations were issued to two hundred guests, two hundred plane tickets were bought and the group set off for Africa.

In Africa the bar mitzvah party was met by two hundred elephants, fifty guides, seven buglers and three hundred native porters who were to carry their food. Each guest mounted his own elephant with the father of the bar mitzvah boy in the rear of the procession.

They were only several miles into the jungle when the whole caravan came to a sudden halt.

From the rear elephant the father cried, "What is going on there?"

And the question was repeated two hundred times till it reached the head guide at the front of the procession. The answer came back up the line.

"We have to stop here for a little while."

"Why?" wailed the distressed father.

"Why?" wailed the two hundred guests as the question proceeded up the line.

And then came the answer.

"There is another bar mitzvah party ahead!"

The whole ego trip is like that. You move in a circle, you can never be in the front – never. Again there will be a bar mitzvah party ahead. Even in the darkest jungles of Africa you cannot do anything that has not been done before, you cannot be anything that has not happened before, you cannot be unique. That's why the ego can never be satisfied. The ego remains imperfect and goes on demanding perfection.

My whole message is to see the truth, to see the hell that ego creates in the name of perfection, uniqueness, and to let it drop. Then there is a tremendous beauty – no ego, no self, just a deep emptiness. And out of deep emptiness is creativity, out of that nothingness arises bliss, *sat-chit-anand*, truth-being-bliss, all arise out of that absolute purity. When the ego is not, you are a virgin. Christ was born out of a virgin; your nothingness is that mother virgin, Mother Mary.

The last question – and the most important one. In fact a question of historic importance:

> Osho,
> Why do you always carry a towel? And why don't you
> drop it now?

The first thing: the towel has been with me for almost twenty-five years. It is a silver jubilee year! And I am very surprised by the question because only last night I decided to drop it.

I am reminded of a story:

A man became very old, he became a hundred years old, and the journalists came to interview him. They asked many questions. One journalist, hesitating a little about whether to ask or not – that must also have been the case with the person who asked this question; he or she must have hesitated many times whether to ask such an absurd question or not – the journalist asked, "Sir, one thing more I want to know. What do you think about women?"

The old man said, "Strange, only this morning I decided not to think about women at all!" A hundred-year-old man, and he decided just that morning! And he said, "Please, don't tempt me again!"

I decided just last night.

But it is good that you have asked. It is a long history how the towel started to be with me, and before I part company with it I had better tell the story to you:

When I started living in Jabalpur, there were so many mosquitoes – don't laugh, because you have nothing in Pune compared with Jabalpur; that's nothing – I had to chase them with the towel the whole day. It was impossible to sit still.

Once a Buddhist monk, a very famous scholar, Bikkshu Jagdish Kashyap, stayed with me. He was my guest.

When he saw the mosquitoes he said, "I used to think that Sarnath was the tops for mosquitoes, but now it seems that Jabalpur has defeated Sarnath."

And he said, "I will tell you a story about Sarnath, concerned with Buddha.

"Buddha came to Sarnath only once. His first sermon was delivered at Sarnath – but he never came again. So down the centuries Buddhists have said he never came again because of the mosquitoes."

I told Bikkshu Jagdish Kashyap that once I left Jabalpur I would not go back again. And I have not been there since I left. I can understand Buddha's difficulty. How could he have managed without a towel? Throughout his life he visited the same towns many times – Shravasti at least thirty times, Rajgrih at least forty times – and he never came back to Sarnath again. There must be some secret in it.

In fact mosquitoes are old enemies of meditators. Whenever you meditate, whether the Devil comes to tempt you or not, the mosquitoes will always come.

For eighteen years I was in Jabalpur. My towel became my constant companion. When I left Jabalpur and came to Mumbai I was thinking of leaving it, but then people started spinning esoteric theories about it. So just to save the theoreticians I continued using it.

Now it is a superstition. The word *superstition* comes from a root which means: something that was useful sometimes, but the circumstances have now changed, it is no longer useful. But it continues. This towel is a superstition and I have continued carrying it just for your sake – because there are theoreticians, esoteric people around who have to have something to base their theories upon.

One woman, one of my beautiful sannyasins from the Phillipines, told me that she had found out the truth about my towel. I asked what it was. She said, "You are a nobody, you live in nothingness, you have to hold something otherwise you will disappear."

I said, "Right! Absolutely right!"

I had just three things: my *lungi,* my robe and my towel. My *lungi* is gone, you can see. Parijat helped me to renounce it. Parijat is my official seamstress – appointed by His Holiness, Osho Shree Shree Shree Oshoji Maharaj! She made the robe so beautifully that the lungi became almost absurd with it. It started looking like a bullock cart by the side of a Cadillac. So out of necessity I had to drop it.

Now here goes my towel. The only thing left is my robe. Please never ask any question about it!

Let me tell an anecdote:

A young Jewish couple was being wed in the usual Jewish tradition surrounded by at least two hundred relatives and friends. The room was in complete hush as the rabbi reached the part of the service which said: With all my worldly goods I thee endow.

The best man turned to the maid of honor and said, "There goes Erwin's bicycle!"

And here goes Osho's towel. It is all that I have. So I must remind you again: never ask any question about my robe.

I will throw the towel. Whosoever it lands upon becomes its proud owner, but nobody must raise their hands or try to catch it. Hmmm? You just be in a meditation, absolutely passive. That is the way godliness also descends. If you try to catch it you cannot be the owner of it.

And if some problem or some dispute arises that two or three persons claim the towel, you can always go to Mulla Nasruddin. It will be difficult to locate him because he is a very subtle and invisible man. But he's the best. If you cannot locate him then you can go to the next best person, Swami Yoga Chinmaya. He will decide the dispute – who the owner is. And if it cannot be decided then you can always divide it.

Remember that you are not to catch it. If you try to catch it, you miss the opportunity. Let it land on you.

Here goes Osho's towel!

Enough for today.

About Osho

Osho's unique contribution to the understanding of who we are defies categorization. Mystic and scientist, a rebellious spirit whose sole interest is to alert humanity to the urgent need to discover a new way of living. To continue as before is to invite threats to our very survival on this unique and beautiful planet.

His essential point is that only by changing ourselves, one individual at a time, can the outcome of all our "selves" – our societies, our cultures, our beliefs, our world – also change. The doorway to that change is meditation.

Osho the scientist has experimented and scrutinized all the approaches of the past and examined their effects on the modern human being and responded to their shortcomings by creating a new starting point for the hyperactive 21st Century mind: OSHO Active Meditations.

Once the agitation of a modern lifetime has started to settle, "activity" can melt into "passivity," a key starting point of real meditation. To support this next step, Osho has transformed the ancient "art of listening" into a subtle contemporary methodology: the OSHO Talks. Here words become music, the listener discovers who is listening, and the awareness moves from what is being heard to the individual doing the listening. Magically, as silence arises, what needs to be heard is understood directly, free from the distraction of a mind that can only interrupt and interfere with this delicate process.

These thousands of talks cover everything from the individual quest for meaning to the most urgent social and political issues facing society today. Osho's books are not written but are transcribed from audio and video recordings of these extemporaneous talks to international audiences. As he puts it, "So remember: whatever I am saying is not just for you...I am talking also for the future generations."

Osho has been described by *The Sunday Times* in London as one of the "1000 Makers of the 20th Century" and by American author Tom Robbins as "the most dangerous man since Jesus Christ." *Sunday Mid-Day* (India) has selected Osho as one of ten people – along with Gandhi, Nehru and Buddha – who have changed the destiny of India.

About his own work Osho has said that he is helping to create the conditions for the birth of a new kind of human being. He often characterizes this new human being as "Zorba the Buddha" – capable both of enjoying the earthy pleasures of a Zorba the Greek and the silent serenity of a Gautama the Buddha.

Running like a thread through all aspects of Osho's talks and meditations is a vision that encompasses both the timeless wisdom of all ages past and the highest potential of today's (and tomorrow's) science and technology.

Osho is known for his revolutionary contribution to the science of inner transformation, with an approach to meditation that acknowledges the accelerated pace of contemporary life. His unique OSHO Active Meditations™ are designed to first release the accumulated stresses of body and mind, so that it is then easier to take an experience of stillness and thought-free relaxation into daily life.

Two autobiographical works by the author are available:
Autobiography of a Spiritually Incorrect Mystic,
St Martins Press, New York (book and eBook)
Glimpses of a Golden Childhood,
OSHO Media International, Pune, India (book and eBook)

OSHO International Meditation Resort

Each year the Meditation Resort welcomes thousands of people from more than 100 countries. The unique campus provides an opportunity for a direct personal experience of a new way of living – with more awareness, relaxation, celebration and creativity. A great variety of around-the-clock and around-the-year program options are available. Doing nothing and just relaxing is one of them!

All of the programs are based on Osho's vision of "Zorba the Buddha" – a qualitatively new kind of human being who is able *both* to participate creatively in everyday life *and* to relax into silence and meditation.

Location
Located 100 miles southeast of Mumbai in the thriving modern city of Pune, India, the OSHO International Meditation Resort is a holiday destination with a difference. The Meditation Resort is spread over 28 acres of spectacular gardens in a beautiful tree-lined residential area.

OSHO Meditations
A full daily schedule of meditations for every type of person includes both traditional and revolutionary methods, and particularly the OSHO Active Meditations™. The daily meditation

program takes place in what must be the world's largest meditation hall, the OSHO Auditorium.

OSHO Multiversity
Individual sessions, courses and workshops cover everything from creative arts to holistic health, personal transformation, relationship and life transition, transforming meditation into a lifestyle for life and work, esoteric sciences, and the "Zen" approach to sports and recreation. The secret of the OSHO Multiversity's success lies in the fact that all its programs are combined with meditation, supporting the understanding that as human beings we are far more than the sum of our parts.

OSHO Basho Spa
The luxurious Basho Spa provides for leisurely open-air swimming surrounded by trees and tropical green. The uniquely styled, spacious Jacuzzi, the saunas, gym, tennis courts...all these are enhanced by their stunningly beautiful setting.

Cuisine
A variety of different eating areas serve delicious Western, Asian and Indian vegetarian food – most of it organically grown especially for the Meditation Resort. Breads and cakes are baked in the resort's own bakery.

Night life
There are many evening events to choose from – dancing being at the top of the list! Other activities include full-moon meditations beneath the stars, variety shows, music performances and meditations for daily life.

Facilities
You can buy all of your basic necessities and toiletries in the Galleria. The Multimedia Gallery sells a large range of OSHO media products. There is also a bank, a travel agency and a

Cyber Café on-campus. For those who enjoy shopping, Pune provides all the options, ranging from traditional and ethnic Indian products to all of the global brand-name stores.

Accommodation
You can choose to stay in the elegant rooms of the OSHO Guesthouse, or for longer stays on campus you can select one of the OSHO Living-In programs. Additionally there is a plentiful variety of nearby hotels and serviced apartments.

www.osho.com/meditationresort
www.osho.com/guesthouse
www.osho.com/livingin

Books by Osho in English Language

Early Discourses and Writings
The Art of Living
Astrology
Breaking All Boundaries
Compassion and Revolution
A Cup of Tea
Dimensions beyond the Known
Earthen Lamps
Falling in Love with Darkness
From Sex to Superconsciousness
The Great Challenge
Hidden Mysteries
I Am the Gate
Life Is a Soap Bubble
Love Letters to Life
New Dimensions of Yoga
The Path of Meditation
The Psychology of the Esoteric
The Search for Peace
Seeds of Wisdom
Silence: The Message of Your Being
Three Steps to Awakening
Work Is Love Made Visible

Meditation
And Now and Here
In Search of the Miraculous

Meditation: The Art of Ecstasy
Meditation: The First and Last Freedom
The Inner Journey
The Perfect Way

Buddha and Buddhist Masters
The Book of Wisdom
The Dhammapada: The Way of the Buddha (Vols 1-12)
The Diamond Sutra
The Discipline of Transcendence (Vols 1-4)
The Heart Sutra

Indian Mystics
Enlightenment: The Only Revolution (Ashtavakra)
Showering without Clouds (Sahajo)
The Last Morning Star (Daya)
The Song of Ecstasy (Adi Shankara)

Baul Mystics
The Beloved (Vols 1 & 2)

Kabir
The Divine Melody
Ecstasy: The Forgotten Language
The Fabric of Life
The Fish in the Sea Is Not Thirsty
The Great Secret
The Guest
The Path of Love
The Revolution

Jesus and Christian Mystics
Come Follow to You (Vols 1-4)
I Say Unto You (Vols 1 & 2)
The Mustard Seed
Theologia Mystica

Jewish Mystics
The Art of Dying
The True Sage

Western Mystics
Guida Spirituale (Desiderata)
The Hidden Harmony (Heraclitus)
Reflections on Kahlil Gibran's The Prophet
The New Alchemy: To Turn You On (Talks on Mabel Collins'
Light on the Path)
Philosophia Perennis (Vols 1 & 2) (The Golden Verses of
Pythagoras)
Zarathustra: A God That Can Dance
Zarathustra: The Laughing Prophet (Talks on Nietzsche's Thus
Spake Zarathustra)
The Voice of Silence (Talks on Mabel Collins' Light on the Path)

Sufism
Just Like That
Journey to the Heart
The Perfect Master (Vols 1 & 2)
The Secret
Sufis: The People of the Path (Vols 1 & 2)
Unio Mystica (Vols 1 & 2)
The Wisdom of the Sands (Vols 1 & 2)

Tantra
Tantra: The Supreme Understanding
The Tantra Experience: The Royal Song of Saraha (same as Tantra
Vision, Vol. 1)
Tantric Transformation: The Royal Song of Saraha (same as Tantra
Vision, Vol. 2)
The Book of Secrets: Vigyan Bhairav Tantra

The Upanishads
Behind a Thousand Names (Nirvana Upanishad)
Finger Pointing to the Moon (Adhyatma Upanishad)

Flight of the Alone to the Alone (Kaivalya Upanishad)
Heartbeat of the Absolute (Ishavasya Upanishad)
I Am That (Isa Upanishad)
The Message beyond Words (Kathopanishad)
Philosophia Ultima (Mandukya Upanishad)
The Supreme Doctrine (Kenopanishad)
That Art Thou (Sarvasar Upanishad, Kaivalya Upanishad,
Adhyatma Upanishad)
The Ultimate Alchemy (Vols 1 & 2) (Atma Pooja Upanishad)
Vedanta: Seven Steps to Samadhi (Akshaya Upanishad)
The Way beyond Any Way (Sarvasar Upanishad)

Tao
The Empty Boat
The Secret of Secrets
Tao: The Golden Gate (Vols 1 & 2)
Tao: The Pathless Path (Vols 1 & 2)
Tao: The Three Treasures (Vols 1-4)
When the Shoe Fits

Yoga
Yoga: The Science of the Soul (Vols 1-10)
The Path of Yoga (Vol.1)
Yoga: The Science of the Soul (Vol.2)
Yoga: The Mystery beyond Mind (Vol.3)
The Alchemy of Yoga (Vol.4)
Yoga: A New Direction (Vol.5)
Essence of Yoga (Vol.6)
Yoga: The Science of Living (Vol.7)
Secrets of Yoga (Vol.8)
Yoga: The Path to Liberation (Vol.9)
Yoga: The Supreme Science (Vol.10)

Zen and Zen Masters
Ah, This!
Ancient Music in the Pines
And the Flowers Showered

Zen: The Quantum Leap from Mind to No-Mind
Zen: The Solitary Bird, Cuckoo of the Forest
Zen: The Special Transmission

Osho: On the Ancient Masters of Zen
Dogen: The Zen Master
Hyakujo: The Everest of Zen – With Basho's haikus
Isan: No Footprints in the Blue Sky
Joshu: The Lion's Roar
Ma Tzu: The Empty Mirror
Nansen: The Point of Departure
Rinzai: Master of the Irrational

Responses to Questions
Be Still and Know
Beyond Enlightenment (Talks in Bombay)
Beyond Psychology (Talks in Uruguay)
Come, Come, Yet Again Come
From Bondage to Freedom
From Darkness to Light
From Death to Deathlessness
From the False to the Truth
From Unconsciousness to Consciousness
The Goose Is Out
The Great Pilgrimage: From Here to Here
The Invitation
Light on the Path (Talks in the Himalayas)
My Way: The Way of the White Clouds
Nowhere to Go but In
The Osho Upanishad (Talks in Bombay)
The Path of the Mystic (Talks in Uruguay)
The Razor's Edge
Sermons in Stones (Talks in Bombay)
Socrates Poisoned Again After 25 Centuries (Talks in Greece)
The Sword and the Lotus (Talks in the Himalayas)
Transmission of the Lamp (Talks in Uruguay)
Walk without Feet, Fly without Wings and Think without Mind

The Wild Geese and the Water
Yaa-Hoo! The Mystic Rose
Zen: Zest, Zip, Zap and Zing

Osho's Vision for the World
The Golden Future
The Hidden Splendor
The New Dawn
The Rebel
The Rebellious Spirit

The Mantra Series
Hari Om Tat Sat
Om Mani Padme Hum
Om Shantih Shantih Shantih
Sat Chit Anand
Satyam Shivam Sundaram

Personal Glimpses
Books I Have Loved
Glimpses of a Golden Childhood
Notes of a Madman

Interviews with the World Press
The Man of Truth: A Majority of One

For any information about OSHO Books, please contact:
OSHO Media International
17 Koregaon Park, Pune – 411001, MS, India
Phone: +91-20-66019999 Fax: +91-20-66019990
E-mail: distribution@osho.net
Website: www.osho.com

For More Information

For a full selection of OSHO multilingual online destinations, see osho.com/allaboutosho

The official and comprehensive website of OSHO International is osho.com

For more OSHO unique content and formats see:
- OSHO Active Meditations: osho.com/meditate
- iOSHO, a bouquet of digital OSHO experiences featuring OSHO Zen Tarot, TV, Library, Horoscope, eGreetings and Radio. Please take a moment to do a one time registration which will allow you a universal login. Registration is free and open to anyone with a valid email address: osho.com/iosho
- The OSHO online shop: osho.com/shop
- Visit the OSHO International Meditation Resort: osho.com/visit
- Contribute in the OSHO Translation Project: oshotalks.com
- Read the OSHO Newsletters: osho.com/NewsLetters
- Watch OSHO on YouTube: youtube.com/user/OSHOInternational
- Follow OSHO on Facebook: facebook.com/osho.international.meditation.resort
- and Twitter: twitter.com/OSHO

Thank you for buying this OSHO book.

JAICO PUBLISHING HOUSE
Elevate Your Life. Transform Your World.

ESTABLISHED IN 1946, Jaico Publishing House is home to world-transforming authors such as Sri Sri Paramahansa Yogananda, Osho, The Dalai Lama, Sri Sri Ravi Shankar, Sadhguru, Robin Sharma, Deepak Chopra, Jack Canfield, Eknath Easwaran, Devdutt Pattanaik, Khushwant Singh, John Maxwell, Brian Tracy and Stephen Hawking.

Our late founder Mr. Jaman Shah first established Jaico as a book distribution company. Sensing that independence was around the corner, he aptly named his company Jaico ('Jai' means victory in Hindi). In order to service the significant demand for affordable books in a developing nation, Mr. Shah initiated Jaico's own publications. Jaico was India's first publisher of paperback books in the English language.

While self-help, religion and philosophy, mind/body/spirit, and business titles form the cornerstone of our non-fiction list, we publish an exciting range of travel, current affairs, biography, and popular science books as well. Our renewed focus on popular fiction is evident in our new titles by a host of fresh young talent from India and abroad. Jaico's recently established Translations Division translates selected English content into nine regional languages.

Jaico's Higher Education Division (HED) is recognized for its student-friendly textbooks in Business Management and Engineering which are in use countrywide.

In addition to being a publisher and distributor of its own titles, Jaico is a major national distributor of books of leading international and Indian publishers. With its headquarters in Mumbai, Jaico has branches and sales offices in Ahmedabad, Bangalore, Bhopal, Bhubaneswar, Chennai, Delhi, Hyderabad, Kolkata and Lucknow.

SINCE 1946